Moreton Morrell Site

£27.95 O
799.
1775
BuL
(D22)

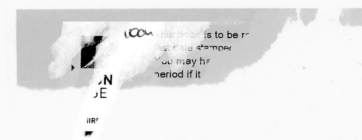

D1339618

00667575

Pike and the Pike Angler

Fred Buller

Pike and the Pike Angler

'. . . that terrible and majestic fish.'
D.M.WRIGHT, in the *Field*

EXCELLENT PRESS
LUDLOW

By the same author
Rigs and Tackle
Pike
Falkus and Buller's Freshwater Fishing
Successful Angling
(*with R. Walker, F. J. Taylor and H. Falkus*)
The Domesday Book of Mammoth Pike
Pike and the Pike Angler
Angling: The Solitary Vice
Dame Juliana: The Angling Treatyse and its Mysteries
(*with Hugh Falkus*)
Great Pike Stories
More Mammoth Pike

*For Richard Walker, Hugh Falkus and
Jan Eggers*

First published in 1971 as *Pike*
Second edition published in 1981 as *Pike and the Pike Angler*
This edition published in 2007 by
Excellent Press
9 Lower Raven Lane
Ludlow
Shropshire
SY8 1BW

© Fred Buller 1971, 1981

A copy of the British Library Cataloguing in Publication Data for
this title is available from the British Library

ISBN 978 1 900318 26 6

Printed and bound in Great Britain by TJ International Ltd

Contents

Foreword to the first edition

Richard Walker

In all my angling career, I have known no one whose enthusiasm for catching and learning about a particular species of fish equals that of Fred Buller for pike.

In their pursuit he has travelled many thousands of miles. Not only has he fished for them in an enormous variety of rivers, lakes, lochs, loughs, ponds, pits and reservoirs; he has also investigated the distribution, behaviour, growth, breeding and physiology of the species exhaustively, as well as studying the history of pike fishing and the authenticity of accounts of captures in the past. Ingenious, resourceful, capable and painstaking, Fred Buller has studied the pike as it has never been studied before, and I was delighted when he consented to write this book, setting out what he has learned for the benefit of other pike-fishing enthusiasts.

But for an unreliable knot, Fred Buller would now hold the world record for *Esox lucius*. This I know, because I saw the immense fish he hooked on Loch Lomond, at a distance of not more than six feet. It frightened me. Hooking it was no matter of luck, nor was its escape due to any lack of ability on Buller's part, for the fish was well under control when the knot failed. The experience proved that much larger pike exist than any that have been caught on rod and line. I am sure that this book of Buller's will make the capture of some of these monsters a great deal more likely.

Preface to the first edition

The incomparable H. T. Sheringham once wrote: 'Of late there has been great activity among the anglers who wield pens. . . . But I have not heard or seen it suggested that anglers are yet weary of reading about their sport.' Sheringham's words have a timeless quality, for do not we moderns find as much enjoyment from reading an angling book as did our forefathers, and is there not still great activity from those who wield pens?

For nearly five centuries, books have given generations of anglers a great deal of enjoyment. Have they done more? I am sure they have. Undoubtedly improved communications, together with refined weapons, were the means by which human animals established themselves as the world's most successful predators. In the same way it was as much from reading and writing, as it was from the practical development of fishing tackle, that man found means of exploring and expanding his dominion over the fishes.

Angling has been described as the 'gentle art' and 'the contemplative man's recreation'; even so, whenever we take up a rod, read an angling book or write about our sport, the reality of our activity, however disguised, is an attempt to find expression for those innate and immutable hunting instincts that yet lie within us.

You may wonder how I came to be yet another among the anglers who wield a pen – contributing as it were to the endless chapter. The answer is quite simple: I was asked by Richard Walker to write a book on the pike, one volume in a library of angling books (each comprehensively descriptive of a single species), of which he was to be the general editor. Immediately comprehending the enormity of the task, my instinctive, exclamatory and inept reply to his invitation was to say, 'You can't be serious', knowing all the time, of course, that he was. But if you, reader, have the same ungrudging respect for him that I have, you will understand the implication of his offer; it was a challenge, and there was no appeal! So, it is he you must thank if my book gives you some pleasure; and it is to him that you must look for redress if it should not. For my part I obtained such a generous response from those whom I contacted for help that the writing of the book became such a great pleasure.

I owe much to many others, including:

Dr W. E. Frost, of the Freshwater Biological Association, who sent a constant flow of handwritten replies to my constant stream of questions.

Mr Alwyne Wheeler, of the British Museum (Natural History) whom I respect as our foremost taxonomist, and thank for the courtesy extended to me during frequent visits to the museum.

Dr E. J. Crossman, of the Royal Ontario Museum, for his generosity in allowing me to reproduce much material from his researches on pike.

Dr Michael Kennedy, of the Inland Fisheries Trust, Dublin, for an illuminating picture of the Irish pike-fishing scene.

Bill Giles, of Norfolk, for his interest and for his invaluable help with details of Norfolk pike fishing.

My old friends, Harry Britton and Jackie Thompson, both now deceased, salmon and sea-trout fishers of Loch Lomond, who would always put down their rods to talk pike with me.

I must thank others, including H. A. Toombs of the British Museum (Natural History); Hugh Falkus, prince of sea-trout fishermen; Miss C. Kipling and the late G. Thompson, MBE, of the Freshwater Biological Association; Miss G. Roche of the National Museum of Ireland; Keen Buss and Jack Miller of the Pennsylvania Fish Commission; F. J. Taylor; P. Butler; C. Loveland; M. West; E. Hunter-Blair; Miss Henniker-Hughan; R. Hancock; A. Cove; D. Pye; P. Moylett; Ken Sutton, who read the proofs; the Irish Tourist Board, which provided the photographs which introduce the three parts of the book; and last but not least of all, my secretary Mrs M. G. Lewin, who interpreted my longhand with much patience.

Note Throughout the book I have tended to use the word loch where I might have used the Irish 'lough' or English 'lake'. To me there is a special significance in the word loch, because I associate it with larger expanses of water, where trout flourish in the company of related forms like salmon, sea-trout, chars and the whitefish family. May I say that I am aware that I might have chosen the word lough for the same reason.

Introduction to the first edition

Most thoughtful and experienced pike anglers over forty have, wittingly or unwittingly, gradually changed their approach to the sport of pike fishing. Methods, devised by a more ancient school of pike fishermen, have been improved by a slow evolutionary force; and now, as a result, there is every hope that we can anticipate a period of great promise, a period that may yet compare with the golden age of pike fishing. This 'golden age' was the last quarter of the nineteenth century when the giant intellects of writers like Francis Francis, Alfred Jardine, John Bickerdyke and Frank Buckland sought to give greater depth and dignity to the sport of hunting the pike with a fishing rod.

Those who can still look forward to their fortieth birthday will have benefited from the common use of all manner of modern tackle improvements in the form of fixed-spool reels, nylon lines and glass rods. But young anglers who know only the fixed-spool and multiplier reels will have missed the satisfaction and reward that came with the eventual mastery of the Nottingham reel – a satisfaction unknown to the apprentice, and barely tasted by the improver. And they will certainly have missed the special dignity assigned to all who could cast directly from the revolving-drum reel, without getting snarled up with over-runs. Also, many will have missed the old-time pleasure of fishing in a strange and fancied spot, for in pre-war days, most riparian owners would gladly give a day's fishing free of charge if it were requested in a proper manner.

The new age which is now upon us is marked by a rebirth of interest in pike fishing, a sport held in high esteem by discerning anglers since the great Dame Juliana first described it, in 1496. Already anglers are starting to comb the forgotten lochs of Britain in search of great specimens, to give substance to the fact that the pike is the largest freshwater fish that swims in our waters. Perhaps, like me, your intensity of feeling for the pike will lure you on a voyage of discovery, as it did Francis Francis, who described with perfection in 1874 the ultimate justification for taking oneself into wild places:

One seems to want to lie down in the heather with a cigar and gaze on it all day without moving; to listen to the waterfall, and to skylark and mavis, curlew and grouse cock, and drink in all sorts of heavenly and earthly sounds and scenes in exquisite and healthy laziness, in perfect abandon to the bliss of complete rest of mind and body; to re-instil into one's faculties some of that essence of nature which is gradually worn away in the daily friction of the world and the insane requirements of society, who race with bankruptcy and paralysis and get beaten on the post – don't take your families to the seaside, don't be cheated by hags and devoured by bugs, and humbugged by conventionality into the belief that you have enjoyed yourself when you know you have been miserable and devoured by ennui; but if women will go there, send 'em and come here yourselves for a season. So shall you have rest for your souls, and fortify yourselves with powers of endurance against the shocks of business and the agonies of Mrs Grundy in the future.

We who go in search of pike today are perhaps the last who will be able to fish waters 'as found'. At present we can still set out in the hopes of taking a bag of fish from a naturally occurring, self-sustaining, indigenous fish population, which natural conditions have provided in naturally forming bodies of water.

But the historical role of 'man the fish gatherer' is nearly over. (Its fate was sealed as the first carp slipped from the monk's hand into the first stew pond.) Tomorrow will be different. Our fisheries will follow the pattern of our farmlands which have to produce an ever-increasing crop to sustain an ever-growing human population. We shall need to introduce more and better fish to sustain an equally fast-growing army of anglers. Soon we may be fishing for exotic fish of whose existence we never dreamed, for these will be the ones best able to take advantage of the environment we provide. The rainbow trout is an example of an introduced exotic fish, and the mirror carp another.

In the future, our fish will be more disease-resistant and more palatable, for these are considerations to which our scientists will pay due attention.

What will happen to our *native* pike? Well, I have provided a possible clue in my chapter on hybrids. Perhaps we shall be fishing for the Amur pike of Russia, a fish with which Dr Crossman tantalizes us in his splendid contribution. He has described them as the strongest of all pikes. Perhaps the Amur pike and other pikes will be subjected to a form of controlled selection, which will produce for our delight some even faster-growing and more sporting varieties of pikes.

Early days

Although deeply fascinated by all fishes, for a long time I have been aware that pike provoke the most powerful response within me. I believe that a response of this nature originates long before youthful imagination is tempered by the sobering realities of experience. My fishing education was of the normal classical type. With the hand-net I caught numerous types of small amphibians, and I must admit to having brought home my full share of expired or expiring sticklebacks. Later, like other boys, I underwent a metamorphosis, to emerge with a Chinese beanpole fishing rod in my right hand.

And like them, I soon learned to interpret the twitchings of a float, so that gudgeon should pay the price for sucking down my lethal number twelve 'Lucky Strike' hook to undrawn gut hidden in a ball of paste.

In time the first roach came and caused a stir – good ones still do! The first small carp impressed as a potential money-spinner; indeed, for a time, the income we obtained from selling carp allowed my friends and I to shade our prices in the horse-dung business. And of course there were many small perch. But that was all. Then one day it happened. . . . A big fellow, he must have been at least 13 judging by his long trousers and cycle clips, had just artistically navigated the pillars (naïvely installed by the Council to prevent cyclists from using this particular thoroughfare), and pulled up with a sideskid. He announced to my friends and me that in his saddlebag there was a pike which he had just caught from Durweston Mill. Did we want to see it?

What a beauty! It needed two hands to hold it properly for it must have weighed nearly 3 lb.

Things were never the same after that.

The next morning we all contrived to be at the scene of that amazing capture. Once arrived, we settled down to eat a second breakfast which was achieved by sacrificing our packed lunches – it would leave the day free for the business of catching pike, or at least that is what we told ourselves. In retrospect, it would be hard to judge whether our decision was inspired by gluttony or by the uncluttered minds of true hunters.

For some hours our concentrated efforts brought no reward, so we relaxed. The pause gave us time to investigate our surroundings (boys always find time to investigate their surroundings), and just round the bend of the river we chanced upon a real pike fisherman fishing for livebait. He was a kindly man who patiently* responded to our questions – for it

* Perhaps patience is, after all, a useful qualification for an angler; leastways it is if he wishes to pass on all that he knows of the sport to youngsters. Otherwise, we know that patience is a burden, for hasn't Richard Walker rightly stated that what a good angler needs is *controlled* impatience?

was our intention to have all the secrets of pike fishing out of him in the instant. Once our brains were surfeited with pike lore we talked of the day's prospects. How exciting they seemed, even if in the event they failed to materialize. I suppose the incident that turned our heads and made us pike anglers for life was when our new-found mentor told us of the existence of a huge pike which lived in the millpool . . . it had broken him many times. After he recounted his exploits with the big one, we must have understood instinctively all that pike fishing has to offer: the essential ingredients of anticipation, drama, anguish and jubilation. We had become pike anglers without having caught a pike.

'Among our fish the pike is king of all,
In water none is more tyrannical.'
JOHIANNES DE MEDIOLANUS,
Regimen Sanaius Salerni (1099)

'It is the Pike in the Pond of Europe that prevents us all
becoming Carp.'
BISMARCK

Introduction to the second edition

Twelve years ago – after handing over the manuscript of the first edition of this book – I took, albeit I suppose somewhat arrogantly, a fresh pad of paper and started to make notes for this edition. I did this because I knew in my heart that any book which attempted to embrace the immense scope implicit in my title might become definitive but, in the event, could only remain fleetingly so while there was always so much more to know about the natural history, the behaviour and the means of catching such a great sporting fish.

To see just how much pike fishing has progressed we need to look back to a period that lasted for over half a century, when most but not all pike fishermen were dull, myopic fellows: dull in the sense that they were content to go on using, almost unchanged, the rigs and tackles devised by the Victorians, and myopic in their near total addiction to livebaiting.

In those days, if you chanced upon a pike fisherman you usually found him sitting behind one or perhaps two short stiff rods. From his Buddha-like silhouette you could imagine him contemplating the random rovings of his float and its attendant pilot, watching to see if they inspired hope or indicated yet again that his bait was caught up. Occasionally those aldermanic indicators – in spite of their arbitrarily suspending the livebait to within a few feet of the surface – would disappear and galvanize the proceedings.

Now a great change has taken place because most pike anglers, if not all, take the trouble to experiment with modern techniques; it is a time when every method is being developed and refined to a remarkable degree.

To mark this change in the development of pike fishing I have enlarged the chapters on the techniques of deadbaiting. The deadbait method, described in the first-ever book on angling – Dame Juliana Berners's 'Treatyse of Fysshynge wyth an Angle', now lately elabor-ated – probably accounts for the capture of more pike (in British waters) than any other.

I have tried in this edition to note any changes in emphasis similar to that underlining the growing popularity and success of dead-baiting and the decline of interest in livebaiting. In addition, I have cut out some of the items, particularly the tackle items, originally discussed and have replaced them with items currently relevant.

For me the most interesting study undertaken for the first edition was the study of fossil pike. The material was already extant, so my task was one of collection and organization. Through my exertions my readers were able to read an essay on the subject without searching among various books and scientific papers for material that never before had been *collected* and published with this end in view.

The most interesting study for this edition has been the research I undertook in the Dordogne area of France and at the British Museum (Natural History) in London. This was done with an eye to present what is known about the pike fishermen who lived during the European Stone Age. I end the chapter on Stone Age pike with this remark: 'The story of pike and troglodyte pike fishermen will undoubtedly be revised in the near future.' The remark, I submit, is apposite with or without the word 'troglodyte'.

In the preparation of this new edition I have been given inestimable help by my secretary Ann London and by Emily Wheeler of Hutchinson. Their objectivity, in spite of their knowing nothing of fishing, made this book much better than it would otherwise have been. I must also thank Edward Wade for allowing me to include his beautiful painting at the front of the book. Those who greatly helped me to prepare my European Big Pike List are mentioned on page 112.

Part One
The Fish

A cursory study of this photograph (courtesy of Seeley, Service & Co. Ltd) tells you why a pike is so-called and why Holder's classic description, 'The pike is a living lance', is so apt. It is also clear why the elegant streamlined shape of a pike inspired the designer of the Mosquito aeroplane to copy its shape when he was designing the fuselage of that very successful hit and run bomber of the second world war. The pike in question, a cased specimen, happened to be on view at Salisbury Hall, near St Albans, while that place was functioning as a wartime aircraft design centre. The Hall had previously been the home of Jennie Churchill, mother of Sir Winston Churchill

1 What's in a name?

Charles H. Cooke once wrote in the *Country Life* magazine *Angling* (now, sadly, defunct) a fine piece about some familiar common names and some less familiar local names for pike. His example inspired me to take a closer look at the best-known ones, *pike* and *luce*.

Historically there seems to be an element of fashion in any contemporary first choice of a name for the species *Esox lucius*. As an example let me quote the great scholar/angler of the nineteenth century, Dr J. J. Manley who, while averring that there are etymological difficulties with the names 'luce', 'pike', 'jack', conceded that 'jack' was the name most in use in 1876. None the less, he said, 'I shall never use the terms "jack" and "pike" indiscriminately.' Nowadays the term 'jack' has ·fallen into desuetude.

The word 'pike' – commonly used in Britain to describe one species, *Esox lucius*, and one genera, the pikes (which include five other freshwater species not present in Britain) – is probably of Norse origin.

Aside from describing this family of long, slender fish with long, slender snouts, 'pike', however it is used, is indicative of something pointed. For example, when we speak of the pike of weaponry we are describing a staff dressed with an iron point, and when we speak of the geographical pike, we are describing a mountain point or peak.

The Saxon word *piik* (meaning sharp-pointed) is certainly in accord with our description as are the French words *pique* (*piquer*) – to prick – and *piquant*, meaning sharp, stinging, biting.

The allusion to the pike of weaponry is made more *piquant* by one writer who described the pike as a 'living lance'.

Cholmondeley-Pennell, in *The Book of the Pike* (1876), noticed that Leland, the eighteenth-century British historian, recorded the taking of a great pike from Ramesmere, Huntingdonshire, in AD 958 during the reign of the Saxon king, Edgar the Peaceable. However, I suspect Leland's original reference was to luce rather than pike; in the same century Aelfric, who wrote the *Colloquy* which contains the earliest surviving treatise on fishing in the English language, uses the word 'luce', rather than 'pike'. 'Luce' is, therefore, also a word of great antiquity.

'Luce' was still current in England as late as the reign of Edward III (1312–77) when Chaucer wrote:

Full many many a fair partrich hadde he in mewe
And many a breme, and many a *Luce* in stew.

'Luce' of course is derived from the pike's Latin name, *lucius*.

Shirley, in his book *The Anglers' Museum*, first published in 1784, vividly imagined that a pike in its first year was called 'a shottrel, the second year a pickrel, the third a pike, the fourth a luce'. How this nomenclature can be reconciled with his statement that people believed a pike lived to be either fifty or a hundred years old is hard to imagine, since in the first case some ninety-six names are wanting, not to mention the difficulty of ascertaining the birth dates of pike aged between one and four.

2 Anatomy of the pike

Figure 1, which shows the internal structure of the pike, along with the photographs in Figures 2–4, depicting the bone structure of the pike's head, probably give as much information on the anatomy of a pike as an angler will ever need to know.

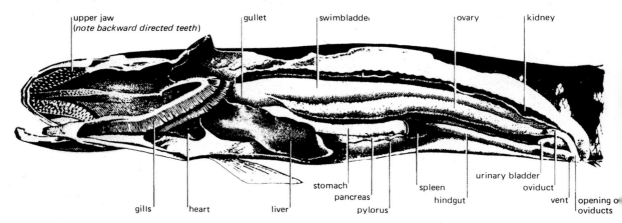

Figure 1 The internal structure of the pike (After Vogt and Hofer, ed. Grote, *Die Susswasserfische Mittel-Europa* (1909), fig. 265)

Figure 2 Bone structure of the pike's head

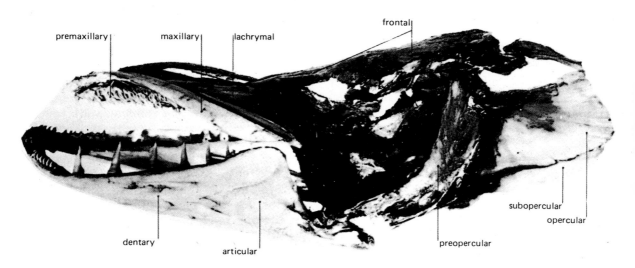

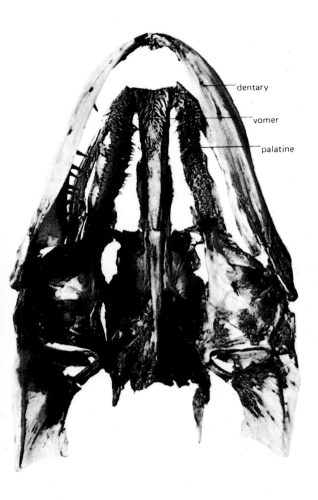

Figure 3 A view of the bone structure of a pike's head from below

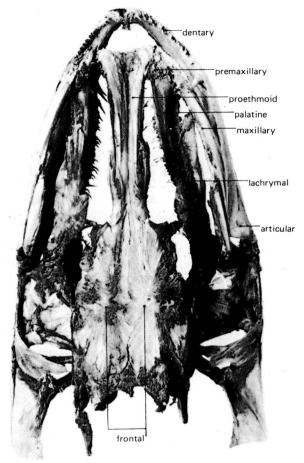

Figure 4 A view of the bone structure of a pike's head from above

3 Fossil pike

In 1968 Alwyne Wheeler, of the fish section of the Zoology Department of the British Museum (Natural History), who has helped me on numerous occasions with inquiries of a different nature, was kind enough to introduce me to H. A. Toombs of the Palaeontology Department. I had come to study the pike fossils referred to by Dr Crossman later in this book (page *270*).

I learned from Mr Toombs that only a few specimens of the fossil *Esox papyraceus* exist; indeed, surprisingly, there are none in the Natural History Museum. *E. papyraceus*, first found in the lignites of Rott, near Bonn in Germany, belonged to the Upper Oligocene, a period which according to the geological time scale occurred some thirty million years ago. There are, on the other hand, some wonderful fossil specimens of *E. lepidotus* to be seen. A photograph of the best of these is shown here.

I am impressed by the fact that the modern pike, *E. lucius*, appears to have changed very little in appearance from the ancient pike, *E.*

A fossil pike – *Esox lepidotus* (By courtesy of British Museum)

lepidotus, although the latter was found in the Upper Miocene deposits (about twenty million years old) at Oeningen in Baden, Germany. It occurred to me that within such a large collection of *E. lepidotus* fossils there might be one with a clear impression of an opercular bone from which I could make an age determination. If this were possible, it would be very pleasing to be able to say, pointing to a particular pike: 'That pike died about twenty million years ago at the age of ten!'

The earliest pike fossils yet found in Britain came from the Cromer Forest beds at West Runton in Norfolk. The beginning of the glaciation in Great Britain occurred about one million years ago. The polar ice at one time reached as far down as the River Thames; but there were warmer periods when the ice retreated. During these interglacial periods, plant and animal life adapted to warmer climates, advanced north again, only to be driven back or destroyed by the next glaciation. Cromer today is a Norfolk coastal town, but when the tides are exceptionally low the fossil stumps of the old Cromer Forest are revealed.

According to the modern carbon dating

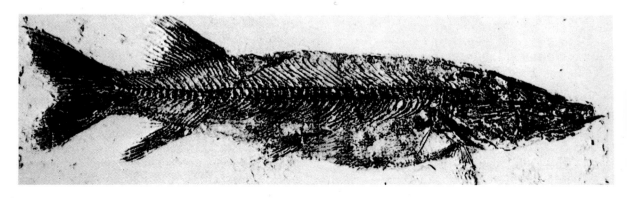

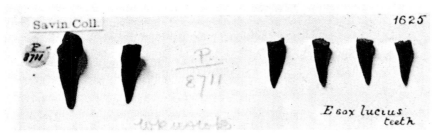

Esox lucius: teeth (By courtesy of British Museum)

Savin Coll.

1625

E sox lucius teeth

Esox lucius: right lower jaw

system, the Cromer Forest flourished during an interglacial period just over half a million years ago. At that time, so much of the ocean waters was tied up in the glaciers that the sea level was lower than at present. This explains why the Cromer beds are now below sea level. Of course, the pike would have lived in lakes or rivers within the forest area. In spite of their antiquity the Cromer fossil pike have been identified as the same species as those we fish for today: *E. lucius*. As Dr Crossman says, it is convincing evidence that pike were not introduced into the United Kingdom by man. Certainly we can dismiss the popular legend which tells of the monks introducing pike to Britain, unless of course we find a fossil monk at West Runton! For the edification of readers unable to make the journey to the Natural History Museum, I took a few photographs of some of the best Runton fossils and reproduce them here.

Hugh Falkus, reading the manuscript of this book, pointed out that I was in error in supposing that evidence of the existence of fossil pike in the United Kingdom is proof that pike are indigenous to this country.

'Could not the pike (*E. lucius*) have been destroyed or driven out by the advancing ice sheet, which in Pleistocene times reached as far south as Essex?' he asked, and, 'If once destroyed – is it not possible that pike were unable to re-establish themselves, until reintroduced by the monks?'

Hugh was right, of course. Evidence of fossil pike at West Runton does not in itself constitute acceptable proof that pike have existed in the United Kingdom *in an unbroken line* since Pleistocene times.

Having conceded the point, I thought that if pike were restricted to a southern European habitat (southern France and southern Spain, etc.), during the ice age, it would seem likely that they re-colonized the United Kingdom through the land–river bridge then in existence.

It occurred to me that if I hoped finally to demolish the theory of pike having been introduced by the monks, it would be necessary to be able to demonstrate that pike flourished during this interval.

I began to search for any recorded instance of the finding of pike remains in the breccia on the sites of prehistoric dwellings. Once again I elicited the help of Alwyne Wheeler of the British Museum. Mr Wheeler was intrigued at the prospect of finding such evidence. Moreover, our conversation reminded him of a paper that he had read many years ago.

Later, Mr Wheeler was able to give me a reference which proves conclusively that pike existed in the United Kingdom, between *post*-Pleistocene and pre-Roman times.

Dr J. G. D. Clark, Professor of Archaeology at Cambridge, published a paper, 'The development of fishing in pre-historic Europe', in the *Journal of Antiquaries* (vol. 28 [1948], pp.

45–85). In his paper, Dr Clark quoted another paper, written by H. Godwin in 1933, 'British maglemose harpoon sites' (*Antiquary*, vol. 7, pp. 36–8), which gives details of items found on a peat site at Skipsea, near North Atwick, on the Yorkshire coast. Here, Godwin recorded that in a 6-inch brown sandy silt layer, were found: '. . . fragments of *Pinus* bark, flint artifacts, stone fruit of (?) *Prunus* and fins of pike (*Esox lucius*)'.

From this evidence, we can reasonably infer that since pike bones were found 'in association' with harpoon heads, our ancestors, who lived during a period starting *c.* 9500 BC, hunted pike, and therefore that pike are an indigenous species to the United Kingdom.

Incidentally, Mr Wheeler tells me that he is in agreement with Dr E. J. Went of Dublin, who has pointed out that pike are not native to Ireland. Mr Wheeler suspects that the only native Irish freshwater fish are sticklebacks, salmonoids, eels and shads. An interesting sidelight relating to the introduction of exotic species before the fourteenth century will be known when Mr Wheeler has had time to sort and identify a collection of fishbone remains, which have been unearthed from the site of an Irish dwelling.

As I re-read the 'fossil pike' chapter of the first edition of this book, during my preparation for this edition, I was suddenly struck by a passage that read: 'The earliest pike fossils yet found in Britain came from the Cromer Forest beds at West Runton in Norfolk.' My authority for this statement was none other than H. A. Toombs of the Palaeontology Department of the British Museum (Natural History). But the cutting that I held in my hand, culled from the 1 March 1862 edition of the *Field*, made me realize that the British Museum might not have been privy to the information that it contained, namely:

At Bedlington Colliery, near Morpeth, a pitman, on Friday last, while labouring in the mine, stuck his pick into the roof of the level, and among the DEBRIS of the fall something curious in the shape of a fossil fish fell. It was picked up and taken home. On being examined by practical men, it was pronounced, from the form of the head, to be one of the ESOCIDAE, or fresh-water pike tribe. It is 14 inches long, and may be seen at any time at Bedlington Colliery, and weighs at least a stone. – Signed: ESOX, jun.

Despite intensive inquiries,* I do not yet know whether the colliery fossil was an example of *Esox lepidotus*, which occurred some twenty million years ago, or *Esox papyraceus*, that preceded it by some ten million years. What I do know is that it could not be a fossil of *Esox lucius* – our so-called oldest recorded British pike fossil laid down during an interglacial period that occurred only some half a million years ago.

Stone Age pike

The Esocids (or pikes) are represented by five species and a sub-species in North America, two species in Asia and only one in Europe.

The finding of fossil remains in the Cromer Forest beds at West Runton in Norfolk is proof that the pike (*Esox lucius*) lived in the rivers and lakes of what is now East Anglia some 500,000 years ago. At about this time, or during the preceding half million years of the Pleistocene era (the great ice age), pike probably spread throughout the temperate zones of Asia, Europe and North America.

In those days the intercontinental spreading of any freshwater species depended on the temporary removal of the salt-water barrier. This occurred during the colder periods of the Pleistocene epoch when land bridges linked Britain, for example, to the European con-

* When I located John Weeks (grandson of the general manager of Bedlington Coal Company in 1862), he told me that some of the 'furniture' at Bedlington was sold off after nationalization and the rest after the colliery closed down.
Miss Sue Turner of Hancock's Museum in Newcastle believes that the fossil may have been that of a pike-like sea-fish, since the period when the coal seams were laid down does not coincide with that associated with *Esox lepidotus* or *Esox papyraceus*.

To understand the time scale during which man has been hunting the pike, perhaps some 400 centuries, we have to remember that the pike featured in this photograph, *Esox tiemani*, flourished some 60 million years before man's first appearance on earth (see pages 30–31)

tinent. That central Europe is the ancient habitat of the pike family is almost certainly confirmed by the finding of much older fossils: *Esox papyraceus* in deposits about thirty million years old, and *Esox lepidotus* in deposits about twenty million years old. Significantly, no fossils have yet been found in the continents of Asia and America (see 'The oldest Esox', pages 30–31).

Although one or more species of the genus *Homo* have inhabited the European continent for the past half million years, there is, as yet, no evidence to show that the men who lived during the Lower Palaeolithic period hunted the pike. It seems likely, however, that they would have done so had they possessed the means, since they depended on hunting for their livelihoods.

The first evidence of a direct association between man and pike is during the last period of the Old Stone Age (Upper Palaeolithic) which started in 36,000 BC and lasted until about 9100 BC (see Figure 5). Perhaps the hunting of pike – and salmon – depended on the development of suitable weapons. There is some evidence for believing that the homonids – by now *Homo sapiens* – who lived during the

25

Geological period	Type of industry		Date BC	Art	Weaponry	The sites where pike were used as a theme by prehistoric artists
Post-Wurm or post-glacial episode	Neolithic			Pottery	Polished stone, axes, the barbed fish hook, the net, the funnel fish trap, perforated harpoon. Dogs first used for hunting? Bone fish-hooks	
	Mesolithic		9,100			
	Azilian		9,500	Geometrical representation		
	Magdalenian VI		10,000	Decorated harpoons with fish as the fundamental theme	Double-sided harpoons	Duruthy pike
Wurm IV or fourth glacial episode	Magdalenian V		11,000	Polychrome paintings with hatching fish/phallus, favourite combined theme for decorating arrow-straighteners	Bone spear-throwers, one-sided harpoons, harpoon prototype	
	Magdalenian IV					
	Magdalenian III		15,000		Bone fish gorges	
	Magdalenian II			Very fine engraving		Cougnac pike Pech Merle pike
	Magdalenian I					
	Magdalenian $\bar{\text{o}}$				Bone and ivory spear-points	
Interglacial episode	Solutrean Final		17,000	Medium engraving	Laurel and willow leaf-shaped flint assegais and arrow-heads made with Solutrean 'retouched' flints	
	Solutrean Upper		17,500			
	Solutrean Middle				Primitive arrowheads with tang	
	Solutrean Lower		19,000			
	Proto-Solutrean					
Wurm III or third glacial episode	Aurignacian V					
	Perigordian VII Proto-Magdalenian		20,000	Simple decorations of pierced staffs or arrow-straighteners	Pierced staffs used for straightening spear-shafts or possibly even arrow-shafts	
	Perigordian VI		21,000			
	Perigordian V		22,000		First bow and arrow?	
	Perigordian IV	Aurignacian IV				
	Perigordian	Aurignacian III		Sculptured ivory	Bone and ivory spearheads	
Interglacial episode	Lower ,,	Aurignacian II	27,000	Deep engraving with continuous lines	First pierced staffs made from reindeer horn	
	Lower ,,	Aurignacian I	29,000			
	Lower ,,	Aurignacian $\bar{\text{o}}$	32,000			

Figure 5 The time scale

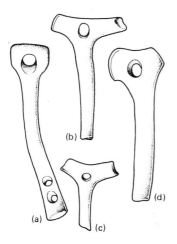

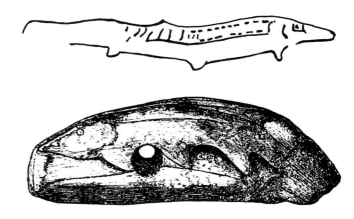

Figure 6 These Aurignacian shaft-straighteners (*b, c* and *d*) – the originals are in the collection by M. Didon – display a close resemblance to the modern shaft-straightener (*a*) described by Dr Boas

Figure 7 A drawing of the Pech Merle pike taken from the original painting of about 18,000 years ago

Figure 8 The Duruthy pike, engraved on a bear's tooth, is about 12,000 years old

Aurignacian period used the bow and arrow. The presence of arrow-straighteners (Figure 6) – similar to those used by modern Eskimos – which were found in cave deposits implies the existence of the arrow itself.

Perhaps it was the harpoon, fashioned from bone, which gave those early hunters the opportunity to come to terms with the pike. The first harpoon prototypes were discovered in a layer of breccia that was deposited during the Magdalenian IV period. The harpoons shown in the photograph were found in deposits belonging to the later Magdalenian VI period. These have retroverted points, and would retain their hold in the fish's flesh.

Barbed harpoons made about 12,000 years ago

Figure 7 shows the pike drawing taken from a polychrome painting which decorates the wall of Pech Merle cave at Cabrerets in France. The pike is part of a large painted panel containing two horses and five drawings of the human hand. As far as we know, this painting represents the earliest surviving example of the use of pike as a subject for prehistoric art.

In Duruthy cave, in the French Pyrenees near Sordes, an engraving of a pike was found on a bear's tooth (Figure 8). This tooth formed part of a necklace. Further north, in an area about 100 miles west of Bordeaux, there is evidence that the famous Perigord cave-dwellers hunted the pike successfully, since pike bones have been found in the hearths of their caves.

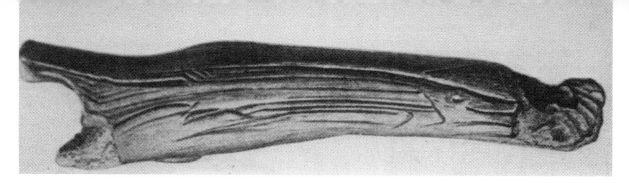

Figure 9 The Cougnac pike engraving (on bone) is about 17,000 years old. The figure, unmistakably that of a pike, was found in the Grotte de Gourdon

The pike engraving on bone (Figure 9) is the work of a Magdalenian hunter. It was found in one of the caves of Cougnac near Gourdon (Haute-Garonne) and is shown in the museum at Les Eyzies. The French village of Les Eyzies lies in the valley of the River Vésère which flows through the heart of the beautiful Dordogne country.

In the surrounding limestone hills of the Dordogne, where water erosion created so many habitable caves, caverns and rock shelters, Stone Age man became conscious of a new and uniquely human dimension of life – artistic creativity. These greatly talented peoples painted, carved and engraved with amazing skill. Some of their best work – in the caves of the Font de Gaume and Lascaux – is thought to have religious or magical significance since these particular caves were not used as living quarters. That a carving of a pike or, for that matter, of any other fish or animal, should act as a talisman to these troglodyte fishermen is not surprising: even some modern anglers believe in the magical qualities of a secret bait!

Among a number of writers, S. Reinach has suggested that because all or most of the engravings portray animals needed for food by hunters and fishermen, they were not drawn for amusement. The aim of the artists was to exercise a magical attraction over the type of animals they drew. William Radcliffe points out that magic is exercised not so much to propitiate some unknown power as to avoid offending it. Instances of fishing taboos are recorded from many parts of the world. J. G. Frazer, writing in the nineteenth century, in *The Golden Bough* observed the fishermen on the north-east coast of Scotland, while at sea, never uttered certain words such as 'minister', 'salmon', 'trout' and 'swine', since it was believed that these words would reduce the catch of fish. That the word 'fush' (or fish), rather than salmon, is still preferred in Scotland seems to endorse Frazer's remarks.

Even today some taboos are observed – on pain of disaster. A Tweed boatman on the Lennel Water was greatly annoyed when the word 'pigs' was used in conversation. The offending anglers were gravely told to substitute the word 'gumphies' should the need arise to mention these creatures of ill-omen; otherwise 'there would be nae fish for anybody'.

Between the Old Stone Age and the New Stone Age (Neolithic), at the close of the glacial epoch about 11,500 years ago, there was a culture known as the Azilian, which takes its name from the cave of Mas d'Azil. It was about this time that man started to penetrate and occupy northern Europe in the wake of the retreating glaciers. This Mesolithic culture, as it is sometimes called, produced more evidence of a relationship between man and pike. On a peat site at Skipsea, near North Atwick on the Yorkshire coast, the bones of pike were found in association with a British Maglemose harpoon site.

The term 'Maglemose' comes from one of the classic living sites of the Azilian peoples. Maglemose is situated near the harbour of Mullerup on the west coast of Zealand in Denmark. At Maglemose the Azilians lived on a great raft of pine trees, anchored about 360 yards off shore. Fortunately, some of their

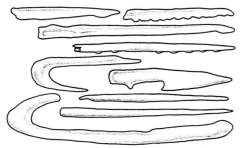

Figure 10 Azilian fish hooks and spearheads in bone and horn, from Obermaier (After Reinecke)

implements dropped overboard and were preserved in the peat until found by archaeologists.

It is interesting to note that the first known fish-hooks (Figure 10) were found in the peat measures underlying Azilian living sites. Radcliffe, in his classic *Fishing from the Earliest Times*, argues that no Palaeolithic hook existed. He refers to the Stone Age implements (Figure 11) as gorges. The Azilians however, were, Stone Age men, and their implements were certainly hooks of a kind. Perhaps, to be precise, they should be termed gorge-hooks. It seems likely that the word 'angle', from which angler is derived, was first used to describe the

Figure 11 Bone gorges (*a* and *b*), and Magdalenian gorges (*c* and *d*) grooved for line attachment, from Santa Cruz, California. Radcliffe suggests that the slight curving in (*c*) may indicate the first step towards the more rounded gorge and, finally, the bent hook

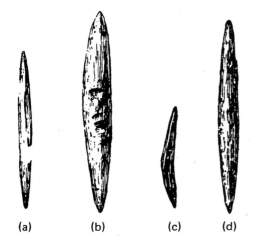

(a)   (b)   (c)   (d)

hook. If so, the Azilian people deserve to be known as the first anglers, since they were the first to fish with the gorge-hook or angle.

Compared with the painfully slow development of weaponry over the 5000 centuries up to the time of the Azilians, the continuous amelioration of the harsh climate during the next few hundred years marked a near explosion in the development of weaponry and ancillary equipment. The Mesolithic hunters not only became the first anglers in history but also the first netsmen, the first boat-anglers and the first to use the funnel-shaped fish traps. At Kunda in Estonia and in Sweden pike remains have been found – still adhering to the spearpoints on which they were originally impaled. The fact that bone remains from eighty individual pike were found at one lake site dwelling in Zealand indicates the importance of pike in the economy of the Mesolithic hunter-fishermen.

Could it be that the pike was the first fish to be caught on the angle? First, the Azilian gorge-hooks were so large and crudely fashioned that, although they might have been used to catch other species known to have been used for food (dace, bream, trout, chub, barbel, carp and eels), their size undoubtedly lessened the chances of success. Second, the pike is probably the easiest fish to catch on a gorge tackle. Third, the pike was the most substantial resident freshwater fish available throughout the season. (Although the salmon was probably the most important food fish, its runs would be seasonal. A noticeable lack of salmon skull bones in the hearth-stuffs indicates that the salmon were caught elsewhere, possibly upstream on the spawning redds, and the heads removed before the fish were brought home to be dried.)

Deposits from the Neolithic lake dwellings have yielded much in the way of fish remains. According to Clark, pike remains predominate. The same writer believes that roach, dace, chub and perch – whose remains were also found – may have been used as livebaits for pike fishing.

From the evidence of the remains of a deep-

29

This harpoon head made from red-deer antler (the best that I've seen) can be viewed in the Stewartry Museum at Kirkcudbright. Kirkcudbright, at the mouth of the River Dee, is known to have been settled by Mesolithic or Middle Stone Age men. From the evidence it seems likely that they hunted seals, gathered shellfish and fished for a living. In 1895 William Pearson, fishing for sparling on the Dee opposite Cumstoun House in Kirkcudbright, dredged up this barbed harpoon. Since the Dee was once a prolific salmon river it is likely that the harpoon was lost in an attempt to spear a salmon. On Mesolithic dwelling sites in Kunda, Estonia and in Sweden, pike remains have been found still adhering to the spearpoints on which they were originally impaled. It is possible that the Mesolithic men of Kirkcudbright once fished for pike in nearby Loch Ken, home of Britain's most celebrated pike, the 72 lb Kenmure monster

water fish, the cod, found together with fish-hooks at a Neolithic settlement at Hemnor, Gotland, it seems likely that fishing lines of some considerable length were a parallel development.

Although there is much that is not known about the Stone Age hunters and fishermen and although there is a great deal that will never be known, new discoveries and new methods of accurately dating deposits will enable scientists to evaluate more effectively the accumulated deposits.

The story of the pike and the troglodyte pike fishermen will undoubtedly be revised in the near future.

The oldest *Esox*

Just as this book was going to the printers I received a note from Dr Peter Forey of the

A close look at the stomach area of this fossil of *Esox tiemani* reveals the backbone of its last victim (also fossilized), swallowed just before the pike's sudden death some 60 million years ago

Department of Palaeontology, British Museum (Natural History). I had consulted him on another matter and was awaiting his reply, when the note arrived, of which the following is an extract.

Dear Mr Buller,   3/4/81
. . . the delay in replying . . . may have been, in retrospect, justified because in this morning's post I received a reprint concerning fossil pikes which records a pike of Eocene age. This is more than twice as old as the hitherto previous record of the antiquity of this group. It also calls into question the current view about the historical biogeography of the pikes.

Best regards,
Peter Forey

The reprint was culled from the *Canadian Journal of Earth Sciences*, pages 307–12, vol. 17, no. 3 (1980), entitled 'Oldest known *Esox* (Pisces: Esocidae), part of a new Paleocene teleost fauna from western Canada'. Its author, Mark V. H. Wilson, works in the Department of Zoology, University of Alberta at Edmonton in Canada.

Briefly the paper, so far as the pikes are concerned, describes a new species named *Esox tiemani* (in honour of B. Tieman, the man who found the original specimens when an access road to an oil well was being cut, and who brought them to the attention of scientists). As a result of this find and subsequent finds many references as to the ancestry and origin of the pikes based on the previously known fossil record are now being questioned. What seems to be beyond doubt is that the basic shape of the pikes and their feeding mechanism have persisted and are largely unchanged during a span of at least 60 million years.

4 The diet of pike

Ever since the first pike fishing story was told, and the first account written, there have been tales of the pike's enormous gluttony. No doubt these tales have conjured a picture in our minds of a fish rapacious in appetite, and ferocious in its pursuit of intestinal satisfaction.

A nineteenth-century writer wrote: 'The pike is a systematic and professional marauder; he respects not his own kith and kin; he prowls up and down, seeking what he may devour, and he has no claim on our consideration, except as a furnisher of sport.' Strong stuff, but the writer was certainly on target with his point about pike eating pike; for in 1955 Dr E. D. Toner, investigating on Lough Mask into the food of Irish pike, reported finding 13 small pike among 323 fish taken from the stomachs of 1790 medium and large pike.

Frank Buckland, in his *Natural History of British Fishes*, records an unusual incident witnessed by a Mr Cramp on Loch Tay in 1870. This gentleman saw two pike struggling and fastened together by the insertion of the head

Another case of the 'Union Jack'. This photograph was published in the *Fishing Gazette* on 17 April 1920. It was sent in by a Mr H. Horwood of Killen, Loch Tay. This brace of pike is not Mr Cramp's brace but it did suffer the same fate. Together the pike weighed 13 lb. It is quite a coincidence that both pairs should have come from Loch Tay. It is even more remarkable to discover that they were – to quote the correspondent – 'found very near the same place'

Pike eating pike. The two pike in this remarkable photograph – which was given to me by Sir Frederick Hoare – were found dead in Staines South Reservoir in April 1972. Each fish weighed just over 6 lb and was about 30 in. long. A pike's mouth contains a large number of backward-facing teeth; thus the attacking fish, whose jaws were extended to their limit, was unable to disgorge its intended prey. As a result both fish died

This photograph (courtesy of Hannes Loderbrauer) depicts an old equation – pike versus pike – with the inevitable result of death to both parties

of one within the jaws of the other. The head of the smaller fish was fixed up to its pectoral fins in the mouth of the larger, and so they were gaffed through both their heads by Mr Cramp's boatman and sent thus (undivided in death) to Mr Frank Buckland, who made a cast of them for his fish museum. The fish together weighed 19 lb; a story of gluttony indeed! But there are many other stories.

Before I move on to discuss the pike's more general culinary enormities it is as well to finish with the pike-eat-pike aspect. It will be seen from the sequence of photographs on the following pages that right from a tender age the pike is absolutely no respecter of persons – unless that person has a bigger mouth (or as big a mouth).

The pike's gastronomic crimes do not end with the eating of its own kind and a hint of what these villainies might be is given in this quotation from an old writer.

Shrouded from observation in his solitary retreat, he follows with his eye the shoals of fish that wander heedlessly along; he marks the water rat swimming to his burrow; the ducklings paddling among the water weeds, the dabchick and the moorhen swimming leisurely on the surface; he selects his victim, and like a tiger springing from the jungle he rushes forth, seldom missing his aim, there is a sudden swirl and splash; circle after circle forms on the surface of the water, and all is still in an instant.

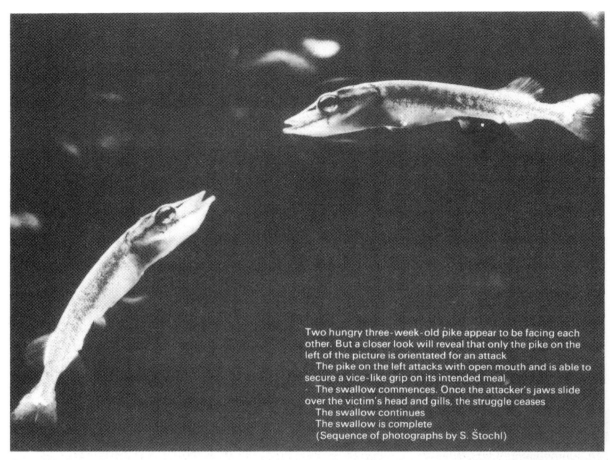

Two hungry three-week-old pike appear to be facing each other. But a closer look will reveal that only the pike on the left of the picture is orientated for an attack

The pike on the left attacks with open mouth and is able to secure a vice-like grip on its intended meal

The swallow commences. Once the attacker's jaws slide over the victim's head and gills, the struggle ceases

The swallow continues

The swallow is complete

(Sequence of photographs by S. Štochl)

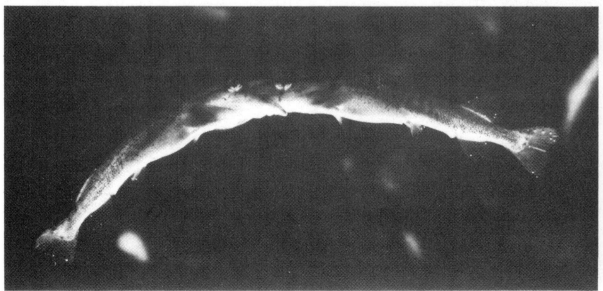

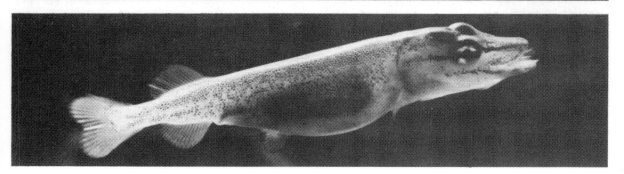

Buckland mentions in his book *British Fishes* the frequency with which rats feature in the pike's diet, and describes an imitation rat plug used by his friend Colonel Martyn with considerable success on Ruislip Reservoir. The following recipe is given for the dressing:

Procure the tip of a tail of a brown calf; make a head with a champagne cork; stick two boot buttons into it for eyes; attach a piece of leather bootlace for a tail; and dress with triangle hooks – they will take it for a swimming water rat, and the chances are they will snap at it, especially on a windy day.

A. Patterson, joining in a general correspondence about pike taking rats and voles published in the Letters to the Editor column of the *Fishing Gazette* (24 January 1920), told of a friend's experience on the Broads:

'Oh,' said he, 'pike after water voles! Why, I've actually, when laying to on the Broads, seen young water voles climb a reed stem to get out of the way of a pike that was after them.' My friend is wholly reliable, and beyond the age and need of saying things that are extravagant.

That pike frequently ate water rats (water voles) and somewhat less frequently, but not infrequently, brown rats, is well documented. In the *Field* (24 October 1974) T. McHugh of Cirencester wrote:

Sir, in my teens back in the twenties I went with a friend to shoot sunning pike in the Avon near Malmesbury, Wiltshire. We shot a pike about 12 lb, only to find there was the head of a rat protruding from its side, drowned presumably in its attempt to gnaw its way out.

The attempts of voles and rats to escape the clutches of a water-borne predator, ending in mutual destruction, are also well documented.

A most fascinating account of the pike's rat-catching proclivities appeared in the *Fishing Gazette* (27 December 1919). The author and his friend, having fished without success on Boxing Day 1917, were chatting to their host's keeper when he said:

'You gentlemen have been here a good few times now; have you ever seen a rat?' We were a bit taken aback and hesitated before replying.

'Well, I don't think so; no, now I come to think, we certainly never have.'

'No, I know you haven't,' said he. 'There ain't none. They gets no chance; the pike sees to that.'

We were sufficiently interested to press the point, and asked if he had ever seen one taken.

'Yes, I have; and if you care to leave your baits in for half an hour and come with me, I'll show you just how and where.'

We willingly concurred, and accompanied him across a part of the park to a small, rather narrow sheet of ornamental water in front of the house, connected with the large lake by a stream. This is quite shallow, having an island in the middle, laid out as a rose garden, with an arbour; access to it is only obtainable by crossing a rustic bridge about three feet wide. In it we could see at least a dozen large pike, put in occasionally from the lake and kept there, safe from capture. The sight made a fisherman long to drop a lively dace within sight of these big fellows, but this was strictly forbidden. Standing on the bridge our mentor pointed to the arbour, and spoke this:

'That is her ladyship's favourite resting place on a hot afternoon, when the roses are out. She was reading there one day some years ago when she heard a slight rustle, and looking up saw a rat run past. Now she has a dread of rats. Next morning I was sent for to go up to the house. My lady comes into the hall and says, "Oh, Jones, I saw a rat on the island yesterday: will you send for the man who kills them and catch it?" Next morning along came the rat-catcher with his ferrets and two terriers. I went and stood on this bridge with my dog. Very soon a rat came out, and was starting to cross, but seeing me and the dog he went back. Then one of the terriers comes for him, and he took to the water. I was for sending Rover in after him, when I saw a sight that made me pause. The rat had swum about a couple of yards from the side, when a pike came slowly up, without any hurry, and with no particular movement of his fins, and opening his mouth wide took the rat in as clean as ever you saw anything, and turned away. There was no disturbance of the water; the whole thing was done as calm and quiet as though I had dreamed it. Well, we found six or seven more in that arbour, and as each was driven to swim for his life, the same thing happened. Not one got more than a few yards from the side before being taken by a pike. I have never seen anything like it before or since, though I've often seen young ducks served the same. I once saw an old one bring a clutch down to the lake from a pollard willow, and while I was looking they were all pulled under.'

This story ended, we turned to walk back to see if our baits had been served as the rats and young ducks. On the way the keeper continued his narrative. He is a keen observer of nature and a thoughtful man. 'This set me wondering,' he said, 'if a rat could be used as bait, and I made up my mind to try. I got a dead rat and threw in close to one of those same big fish. He took no notice. Then I got another some days later, tied him to a long string, and drew him about; but those pike never moved. They wasn't fools. I have heard say as an artificial bait like a rat was tried, but nothing came of it.'

This is a correct recital of what we were told by Jones and may be accepted without doubt as to its veracity. It will answer the editor's enquiry.   J.L.N.

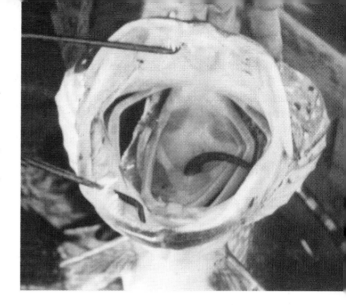

Pike with the tail of a brown rat sticking out of its throat

A full-grown rat is retrieved from the pike

The presence of a rat in a pike's stomach in certain circumstances may be an everyday occurrence, the truth of which I can illustrate with the following account of an experience that I shared with my pike-spinning companion Ken Sutton.

We had elected to spin a lake from a drifting boat – a method that produced us some fifteen pike during the morning session. The last pike caught before lunch fell to my rod; it was a poor-conditioned $14\frac{1}{2}$-pounder which should have weighed well over 20 lb. However, looks were deceptive, for this one fought ferociously, unlike the next fish to fall to my rod in the afternoon session. In spite of its vastly improved physical appearance, this fish came to the net like a lamb. When Sutton gagged open the pike's jaws to unhook the spinner he revealed a thick tail sticking out from the pike's throat (pictured above), which we viewed with mixed feelings of interest and revulsion. A pair of forceps helped to pull out a large brown rat as shown in the photograph.

By the end of the day we had killed five pike out of a total of twenty-seven caught; from this small sample of fish killed we found the remains of two more half-digested brown rats. Naturally we were curious to know why rats should figure in the pike's diet to this extent. Inquiries revealed that the lake was used to

decoy wildfowl in order to ring them for migration studies. To this end, tame ducks were fed near the decoy on a small island to attract their wild counterparts. A large number of brown rats had discovered the duck-feeding routine, and were swimming over to the island for a free supper whenever food was put down. The pike in turn discovered that rats were pleasant to eat and rather easy to catch. In this way a new food chain was established – ending with the pike helping themselves to the swimmers.

The owner of the lake believed that the high loss of ducklings was due to the depredations of the pike, and so he had formally requested that we should kill all pike over 10 lb. With the new-found evidence we wondered whether it might be a better plan to preserve the large pike, for in all probability it was the rats who were killing the ducklings (rats are possibly the most destructive vermin extant where young poultry, pheasants or ducklings are being reared).

Although Buckland gave a dressing for a rat lure (page *36*) I asked Richard Walker to 'tie' me a more modern version and provide a dressing. Here is what he wrote:

Buy a musk-rat pelt, cut it in half, retaining the headed half for the plug. Take a piece of cable-laid (20–30 lb b.s.) steel wire approximately twice the length of the rat's body. Tie and whip No. 1 or No. 2 trebles to each end of the wire. Tie small pieces of squirrel fur round the shanks of the hooks to imitate legs. Fill the body cavity of the pelt with a boat-shaped piece of expanded polystyrene. Bend the wire in the middle to make a front attachment loop and whip sew it to the nose of the fur with terylene

A rat lure

thread. Pull the skin tight over the polystyrene from the back end and sew up. Make a tail from a hairy sliver of seal skin and stitch on. The two flying back trebles can be held up to the rear underside of the plug by means of an elastic thread.

Another good account of the pike's predilection for rats appeared in the *Field* (5 March 1910).

A remarkable instance of the voracity and ferocity of pike occurred the other day at Wretton, near Stoke Ferry, in Norfolk, where some friends of the writer have some shooting. Going to the fen on Saturday last to have a turn at the snipe, which are very numerous, they called at their keeper's cottage on the way, and were shown, hanging up in the game larder, a 13½lb pike with a cock moorfowl firmly fixed crosswise in its jaws and a big bulge in its pouch. Bradenham, the keeper, explained that on the previous day when going his rounds he had a look at an old disused decoy to see whether there were any duck, but the only occupants of the pond were two waterfowl swimming and flirting about. As he stood for a minute watching, there was a sudden rush and swirl; the moorhen was seized from below and quickly dragged under, and the startled cock bird flapped into the rushes. The keeper, of course, at once realised that it was the work of a biggish pike, but he was the more astonished as it was thought that there were no fish of any kind in the pond. Returning some time later, the man thought he would have another look at the scene of the tragedy, and was just in time to see the cockbird launching out again furtively from the shore as if in search of his lost mate. Scarcely had the bird reached deep water when there was another drive and dash, and it was in the grip of the fierce fish. But the keeper was on the alert this time, and, putting up his gun, he let fly just below the bird, and had the satisfaction of seeing the pike 'turn up', still holding fast to its prey. With the aid of an osier wand he brought both ashore. With a lot of flood water about, it is thought that the pike somehow got into the pond from the neighbouring river. From the external appearance of the fish it was thought to have swallowed the first bird, but when opened there were found inside two large rats, one full grown and the other three-quarters grown. In the circumstances it is pretty certain that the moorhen was taken by another pike, and on the assumption that it is still lurking in the pond steps are being taken to ensure its ultimate capture. W. R. H. G.

Lough Neagh. Was it here that the pike consumed five fully fledged moorhens? (Photograph by kind permission of the Northern Ireland Tourist Board)

We can see from his account the keeper believed that the pike which took the first moorhen must have been 'biggish' (I bet he thought it was very big). In the event we find that a pike weighing only 13½ lb (presumably weighed with the rats still in its stomach) was quite capable of dealing with the second moorhen.

The following report in *Angling Times* (23 January 1959) underlines the catholic nature of the pike's diet.

A Christmas dinner

I've just heard of a pike that had a Christmas dinner of its own. The fish in question was taken from Lough Neagh in Co. Derry recently. When opened it was found to contain five fully fledged moorhens. The pike, after cleaning, weighed 28 lb and was exhibited in the local town of Kilrea for a few days – causing quite a stir.

If a pike's judgement of what it can swallow is badly at fault, it will choke. The photograph

(below), which was taken by Mr A. Trimble and first appeared in the *Angler's News* on 1 October 1949, shows a pike that made such a fatal error of judgement. Mr Trimble wrote in more detail to a local Irish newspaper, and Mr J. Leigh of Manchester sent the cutting to the *Fishing Gazette*:

While shooting along the bank of the local canal, Mr Donald O'Neill, Poyntzpass, saw a waterhen which had been swimming on the water suddenly disappear, and a commotion commence below the surface. He discharged a round from his .22 rifle at

The pike that fed on a moorhen. This photograph, taken by Mr A. Trimble, appeared in the *Angler's News* on 1 October 1949

the centre of the disturbance and a 4 lb pike, killed by the shot, bobbed up with the bird, also dead, clamped firmly in its jaws! After photographing the fish, I had the bird removed from its mouth and observed that its head and neck were considerably marked by the pike's teeth. The bullet struck the pike behind the right gill, killing it instantly.

Examination of an adult pike's stomach normally reveals evidence of a fish diet; examination of a larger sample of pike stomachs usually reflects the availability, relative abundance and variety of fish found in the habitat. From time to time, however, more bizarre dietary items are recorded, which include, as we have seen, rats, voles, moorhens and ducklings. In addition, as we shall see from the following series of eyewitness accounts, there is at least one recorded instance of pike eating or attempting to eat a specimen of the following common species: lark, sparrow, swan, pheasant, partridge, sand-martin, teal duck, heron, cat, mole, pig, snake, weasel, fox, rabbit and even man himself.

The finding of curious food items indicates that pike, like most other creatures, are opportunists when it comes to satisfying their hunger. In this connection I like the grim note struck by entomologist Fabre when he wrote, 'The intestine rules the world.'*

In the *Field* of 5 May 1894 a correspondent wrote: 'Once while fishing in a bog a pike took a young moss lark from off a tuft of grass growing on a submerged "water wall", right before my eyes', and in Dr Plott's *History of Staffordshire* the author reported:

At Lord Gower's canal at Trentham, a pike seized the head of a swan as she was feeding under water, and gorged so much of it as killed them both; the servants, perceiving the swan with its head under water for a longer time than usual, took boat, and found both swan and pike dead.

In October 1910 W. Keith Rollo, a much-respected author of angling books, reported an incident of pike behaviour to the editor of the

* Quoted in Geoffrey Bucknall's *Big Pike* (1965).

Fishing Gazette. Part of his letter was published in the 5 November issue:

Dear Sir, Have you ever heard of a pike seizing a shot bird? I was shooting on the banks of the River Forth, near Stirling, on Oct. 24, and shot a pheasant, which fell into the water. It was at once seized by a pike and pulled under. The pike did not let go its hold till the water was thoroughly disturbed by the retriever swimming about. It was still water, about 15 ft. deep.

R. B. Marston, the editor of the magazine, after quoting Rollo, reported two more incidents. In one a partridge was the victim:

The only case of the kind I remember was the famous one of the pointer who was out with his master shooting. The sportsman shot a partridge, which fell out of sight. On getting over the brow of the hill, the sportsman saw his dog pointing at the water of a lake, and then he noticed a big pike near the side. He shot the pike and on opening it found the missing partridge.

In the other incident five young swallows were the victims:

Then there was a story I published nearly thirty years ago about the pike which jumped out of the water five times, and each time snapped a swallow off a bough hanging over the water. I know it was true because I had an illustration showing the pike in the very act.

Marston's recollection of this incident was not accurate. The original account was published in the *Fishing Gazette* in 1883 and it was reprinted on 17 April 1920:

Pike and sand-martins

The curious incident depicted represents a scene from real life, and the following description is by Mr H. Band, who witnessed it. Mr B. was fishing in the Mulde, near Castle Zschepplin. He says:—

'A few paces below me I noticed three young sand-martins perched on a bough which overhung the water. They could hardly fly, and the old ones were fluttering about them. My float lay motionless on the surface. Suddenly there was a tremendous splash in the water directly under the withie bough, which swung up and down. One bird was still on the bough, and another, after fluttering about a little, again settled down on it. I looked on in amazement; the waves, caused by the splash, spread over the river, the surface became smooth and still again, but one bird was missing.

A bite at my line recalled my attention to fishing; but presently there was another splash under the bough, which swayed about again – the other bird was missing, and now only one remained, balancing itself with difficulty on the swinging branch. That the thief was a pike was quite evident. I stuck my rod-butt into the soft bank, and quietly approached the spot, soon finding a convenient place from which to reconnoitre. Steadily I watched for a long time. The final dash of the pike occurred so violently, so suddenly – and this time from the side where I had been sitting – that I could only get an instant's view of what had happened. The third sand-martin was gone. The swaying bough grew still again, and all was over. [From the *Fishing Gazette* of 1883]

We see from this account that Marston's swallows were in fact sand-martins and they numbered three and not five.

In another instance recorded in the *Fishing Gazette* (1887), a pike in a pond at Edmonton captured a sparrow by seizing it with a sudden snap while the bird was perched on the edge of a water-lily.

A note from A. H. Patterson published in the *Fishing Gazette* (1 November 1919) quoted a

The pike and the sand-martins

detail from an interview with an old Broadland gamekeeper named Woolston.

He told pike stories neatly, and without flourishes, scorning to be thought untruthful. He once saw a long sort of fish below the surface, and fishing it up, found it was a pike with another one half-swallowed. A pike once jumped into his boat as he rowed. Why? Because it had overshot its goal – a roach it was it had rushed at. He had . . . seen a small pike with a live snake in its jaws, held by the middle. He once found a pike choked by a perch, and he had taken a weasel out of a pike.

In November 1943 Captain T. G. Wells of Beechville, Co. Armagh, sent the editor of the *Field* an account of a pike taking a heron. His report (published 27 November 1943) went as follows:

On Saturday, October 2nd, fishing in Castledillon Lake, Co. Armagh, I landed an 18 lb pike measuring 3 ft 9½ ins. It was found to have swallowed a heron, not quite fully grown, in which decomposition had hardly set in.

Wild duck are commonly taken by pike on this same lake, and there is a record of a cat being taken in another part of the country, but I have heard of no other case of a heron.

In the *Chronicles of the Houghton Fishing Club* there is an entry on 4 July 1854 noting that 'Mr Warburton killed on a minnow a jack of 2 lb containing an entire mole, recently swallowed.'

Probably the most unlikely food item that has ever been taken from a pike's stomach is a young pig. The story of the finding of this pig was told in the *Field* in 1922:

When I was fishing in the Kennet, near Newbury, on Feb. 19 with a friend, he was fortunate enough to hook a 14 lb 2 oz jack. I was within earshot and hastened to my friend's assistance and managed to gaff the fish for him. According to my general custom, I held a *post-mortem*. It was a well-fed hen fish with long belts of ova well developed. The stomach contained – 'horror of horrors' – a baby Berkshire pig. The head and forelegs were partly digested, but the body and hindlegs were practically intact down to the perfect little hoofs. The fine black hair was also very distinct. The length of the hind legs is about 3½ ins. and the body from 5 ins. to 6 ins.

As the story sounds like a fairy tale, I took the precaution to preserve the whole of the contents of the stomach in 10 per cent. formalin, and today submitted the specimen to a veterinary surgeon, who confirms my view and expresses the opinion that the pig was born (possibly stillborn) and was not foetal. By some means it got into the river and was devoured by the jack. It must have been dead by the time it had drifted down to the jack's haunt. I have not much knowledge of jack and their ways, but the deduction seems to be that big fellows will take dead things. I leave this for the consideration of those with more experience. The fish was caught by my friend with a small spoon.   J.H.C.

The *Angler's News* of 30 November 1918 reported the following 'reversal' of the food chain:

Pig's Diet of Pike

A St Ives (Hunts.) angler the other day left a catch of pike outside an hostelry at Overcote whilst he refreshed the inner man. In his absence the landord's sow came upon the scene and devoured the largest brace, which the angler had intended to present to friends.

There are at least two accounts extant of fateful meetings between the fox and the pike. The first is to be found in *Fuller's Worthies, Lincolnshire* (p. 144):

A cub fox, drinking out of the river Arnus, in Italy, had his head seized on by a mighty pike, so that neither could free themselves, but were ingrappled together. In this contest a young man runs into the water, takes them out both alive, and carried them to the Duke of Florence, whose palace was hard by. The porter would not admit him without a promise of sharing his full half in what the Duke should give him, to which he, hopeless otherwise of entrance, condescended. The Duke, highly affected with the rarity, was about giving him a good reward, which the other refused, desiring his highness would appoint one of his guard to give him a hundred lashes, that so his porter might have fifty, according to his composition. And here my intelligence leaveth me how much farther the jest was followed.

The second recorded incident of pike versus fox took place in Poland in 1723:

It appears that on the occasion of some ponds being

Pike versus fox. In 1723 Ridinger painted this picture of an incident that took place at Pyrbaum in the Countship Waldstein (Poland) between a 15 lb pike and a fox (From E. W. Baillie Grohman, *Sport in Art*, 2nd edn, 1920)

laid dry to get at the fish, the captured 'bag' was carried home in a wooden trough. While being thus conveyed overland by two men, a large pike escaped and three men with torches were sent back when the loss was discovered. They found the lost fish, but in a somewhat peculiar situation! A prowling fox had discovered the pike and, approaching it carelessly the pike had caught his muzzle in his wide maw, retaining him a prisoner.

Going back to the previous century we have a mention, in Dr Crull's *Present State of Muscovy* (1698), of a pike that when opened was found to have an infant child in its stomach.

Ducks and other wildfowl have frequently figured in the pike's diet. Alfred Jardine tells of a visit to Sonning-on-Thames where the land-lord of his hostelry told him of a pike which had swallowed, one by one, twelve from a brood of fifteen half-grown ducks. Jardine was able to witness the demise of yet another of the brood before he set out to catch the pike with a gudgeon-baited paternoster. He duly caught the pike, which weighed 15 lb, and on opening it found the duck inside – 'with the feathers scarcely rumpled'.

Again, Mr M. V. Robinson, according to a note in the *Fishing Gazette* (26 November 1949), caught twenty-two pike up to 30 lb in weight in two days. He was using a Horton Evans Vibro spinner and it is interesting to note that the 30-pounder was attracted by the spoon despite the fact that it had already swallowed two teal ducks, which were found partly digested in its stomach.

Dr Michael Kennedy of the Inland Fisheries Trust, Dublin, advises me that birds occur only very rarely in the stomach contents of Irish pike. He goes on to say that when Irish pike reach 2 lb in weight they are almost exclusively fish-eaters. Dr Frost, writing to me on the same subject, records that rodent remains figured in a Windermere pike's stomach on only one occasion; and a duckling once, from the stomach of a Blenham Tarn pike.

Although it is known that pike regularly make big inroads into the annual brood of young ducks, moorhens and other waterfowl, and although we know that pike will feed on adult waterfowl when it suits them, historically there seems to have been little response from anglers by way of using a bird or an imitation of one as a bait.

It is true that John Murray probably caught his record pike on a trimmer baited with a duck (see page *232*). It is also true that Richard Walker advocated using a stuffed waterhen (moorhen) in *Stillwater Angling* (1953):

The frequency with which pike attack and eat moorhens is well known. Most anglers at one time or another will have seen a moorhen vanish with an anguished cry in the middle of a mighty swirl. Peter Thomas and I once hatched a heroic plot for the catching of a very big bird-eating pike whose whereabouts we knew. The idea was to shoot and skin a moorhen and to sew its preserved hide over an artificial body built mainly of balsa wood, with a lead keel. Artificial green legs were to be arranged, each bearing a substantial treble hook, others being also attached at strategic points. (We decided to try

it out first before including a mechanism with internal pendulum to make the legs kick alternately!) The line was to be attached to the front of the neck, well above water-level, and with the aid of a lead weight on the line, it was thought that a very realistic bobbing motion could be given to the thing.

To use it, one would put it into the water and then, paying out line, walk round the bay in which the pike lived. At a point where angler, 'moorhen' and pike's lair were in line, the 'moorhen' would be worked across. Failing an attack, the angler would return to his starting-point and repeat the process.

This particular floating plug has not yet been constructed, but in the USA attempts to imitate such things as frogs, swimming rats, and the like, have been quite successful. I still incline to the moorhen idea, however, because it will make such a magnificent angling story when the 40-pounder for which it was invented is caught on it.

There is just one account that describes the successful use of a live waterhen as a livebait for pike and although such a practice would not be countenanced today, the account demonstrates that a plug fashioned in imitation of a waterfowl could produce good results. Here is an extract from *The Swan and Her Crew* (*c.* 1860) by G. Christopher Davies:

The next morning as soon as it was light they rowed to the place where the big pike lay. Everything was very still and quiet, and shrouded in a light grey mist, as they pushed their way along a narrow channel to the pool. They had brought with them their strongest rod and their stoutest line, and they carefully tried every knot and fastening of their tackle before commencing to fish. The next most important thing was to bait the water-hen or arm her with hooks properly. This was done by tying a number of hooks lightly to her with thread, and ruffling her feathers so as to conceal them.

'Poor thing,' said Dick, as Frank took up the rod and swung her into the pool.

By keeping a slight pull on the line the bird was induced to turn in the opposite direction, and to swim towards the middle of the pool.

'Another minute or two will show if our plan is successful,' said Frank, 'and if not, the bird shall be let loose.'

'I don't feel much faith in it now,' said Jimmy.

When the bird reached the centre of the pool she dived.

'Oh dear, I did not expect that,' said Frank. 'What shall we do now?'

'She must come up again presently. The pool is twelve feet deep, and she cannot cling to the bottom.'

'I felt her give such a pull just now. She is struggling hard to escape,' said Frank, who was still letting out line. Two or three minutes passed away, and still the bird did not make her appearance.

'Pull in the line a bit, Frank.'

Frank did so, and said, 'She must be clinging to the bottom. I cannot move her,' and he pulled a little harder. 'I say,' he cried, 'I felt such a sharp tug. I do believe the big pike has got hold of her.'

'Nonsense,' said the others.

'But it isn't nonsense,' said Frank, and he held the rod bent so that they could see the top twitching violently. 'It is the pike,' Frank exclaimed excitedly, and he immediately let the line run loose, so that the pike might have room to gorge his prey.

'He must have seized the water-hen as she dived,' said Dick.

'Yes, and won't we give him plenty of time to gorge. I don't want to miss him now we have got such a chance,' said Frank.

And in spite of their impatience they gave the pike half-an-hour to swallow the bird, and then, at the end of that time, there were sundry twitchings of the point of the rod, and the line was taken out by jerks of a foot or two at a time.

'He is moving about,' said Jimmy. 'It is time to strike.'

Frank raised his rod amid a hush of expectation. As the line tightened he struck lightly, and immediately the rod bent double with a mighty rush from the pike as he went straight across the little pool, which was about thirty yards in diameter. After this first rush the pike began to swim slowly about, keeping deep down and never showing himself. Round and round and across the pool he swam, now resting for a few minutes like a log, and from a twitching of the line apparently giving angry shakes of his head. Frank kept a steady, even strain upon him, and as the space was so circumscribed there was no danger of a breakage by any sudden rush. This sort of thing went on for half-an-hour, the line slowly cutting through the still, dark water; and Jimmy and Dick urged Frank to pull harder, and make the fish show himself. But Frank was too wise to give way, and he still kept on in a steady, cautious fashion.

'If we go on much longer we shall be late for Mr Meredith,' said Dick.

'Never mind,' replied Frank, 'he will forgive us on such an occasion as this.'

'Here he comes,' shouted Frank, as he wound in his line.

The pike came rolling up to the surface a few yards from the boat, and they caught sight of him. His proportions were gigantic, and his fierce eyes glared savagely at them. He gave a flounder on the top of the water, then sank down again into the depths.

'What a monster!'

In a few minutes the pike came up again, and this time more on his side, and plainly much exhausted. Three times more did he thus rise and sink again, and each time he seemed more helpless. The fourth time he remained on the surface lying on his side. Dick got hold of the gaff and held it in the water with outstretched arm, while Frank slowly drew the conquered giant towards it. Dick put the gaff under him and sharply drove it into his side, and then Jimmy and he uniting their forces, hauled the pike into the punt, almost upsetting it in their eagerness, and then threw themselves on the fish to prevent it flopping out again. They rowed home in great triumph, and on weighing the pike it was found to be 34½ lbs in weight, and the largest which had been caught in Hickling Broad for many years. The time it took to land it from the time it was struck was fifty-five minutes.

Although in good times pike may have a preference for this fish or that, they are opportunistic enough to eat anything toothsome which they find within their element; so long as the chosen item can be passed through that tunnel of a mouth. When talking of a pike's mouth, it is appropriate to mention that experience has taught a pike to swallow large items head first, since wriggling victims soon give up their struggle when their view is restricted to the inside of his lordship's stomach.

In 1941 I hooked a 6 lb pike at Bryanston on the River Stour. Although it had moved quickly to take my Colorado spoon, I found ugly teeth wounds on both flanks, and the whole skin section starting some few inches behind the gills corroded by digestive juices. The caudal or tail fin was digested away with the ravages of those same juices. No doubt a big pike, tired of trying to contain the struggles of the six-pounder, had disgorged it; a result of attempting to swallow an outsize meal tail first.

When we investigate any preferences for food that a pike may have, we have to consider two aspects: preference for type, and preference for size. As for the type of food, we can lean on the experience of generations of pike fishers whose empirical knowledge has shown what the pike likes best. Some have been convinced that pike refuse to eat tench. All the same, tench have been found in their stomachs on numerous occasions, and we can hazard a guess that the tench concerned did not swim into the pike's mouth by accident!

I have tried tench livebaits without success, but the evidence of Mr Sanders (a taxidermist) is more compelling since he took several tench weighing between 2 lb and 3 lb from three pike weighing between 19 lb and 20 lb. (Mid European anglers frequently use tench as livebaits; some of the pike recorded in the Big Pike List of Europe and North America [pages 114–25] were caught on them.)

Perch are seldom used as livebaits; nevertheless, Edward Spence preferred them to any other and claimed that he had been successful wherever he had tried them. Perhaps the perch is not given a fair trial by most pike anglers; this could well be a mistake, as perch loom large in the diet of most loch pike. Although perch are eaten in great numbers by loch pike, some of us who have seen pike attack a perch can understand their preference for a trout or a roach, as the perch invariably raises his spiky dorsal fin in defence. When this happens the pike is sometimes forced to make several convulsive attempts to dispatch the perch in the direction of his stomach. On these occasions the perch is expelled and re-engulped with a most violent and jerky mouthing operation. The old livebaiter's trick of cutting off the perch's spiny dorsal fin is both barbarous and unnecessary, since the pike will not discover that he has taken a finless wonder until he has grabbed the bait and given the angler his chance.

A more commendable trick is often used by certain Windermere pike anglers who trail a dead perch on late summer evenings. They scrape scales off a dead perch, exposing a whitish patch on the flank. This white patch seems to produce more strikes to the bait. Its success may be due to the similarity of the scraped patch to a natural fungus patch, which in turn may arouse visions of a wounded and easy-to-catch fish, or it may simply serve as a more efficient signal and so increase the range at which the bait can be seen in poor light conditions.

Dace and gudgeon have always been the most popular pike livebaits. I suspect that the convenience of carrying a dozen of these in a livebait can has far outweighed any other consideration, yet we can hardly dismiss the opinion of Jardine who took so many good pike on the dace – which was his favourite bait. Dace and gudgeon are, of course, exceedingly good pike baits, for the pike like them well. The only trouble is that *all* pike, down to those just a foot in length, will attack them, so that one catches many small pike along with the good ones.

My plan is to fish with a livebait which is fairly selective – like a ¾ lb roach or chub. Such a livebait, or deadbait for that matter, will tend to select pike of 6 lb or more, and yet be sufficiently attractive to tempt the really big one if properly presented. To my way of thinking this approach gives a sound win and a place bet at respectable odds. If larger livebaits are used all sorts of problems are created on the equipment side, unless gorge tactics are to replace sporting tactics. However, these problems are discussed in the tackle chapter.

This brings me on to the other aspect of a pike's food preference – namely size. Dr Kennedy tells me that in Loughs Conn and Corrib the pike feed on perch and trout as well as char when the latter come into the shallows to spawn. As the pike grow bigger they tend to select bigger prey, and pike over 20 lb are mainly trout-eaters. Big pike commonly take trout up to 4 lb in weight in the limestone lakes, and in lakes such as Lough Conn the very big pike often take grilse. Dr Kennedy goes on to say that an $8\frac{1}{2}$ lb salmon was found in a 32 lb Lough Conn pike; shades of the 10 lb salmon disgorged by Garvin's record rod-caught Lough Conn pike! Much of the data collected on Irish pike comes by way of a campaign to reduce the density of pike in the Irish limestone loughs in order to improve the quality of the trout fishing. Reference to certain German experimental work on the pike revealed to the Irish scientists that the pike has a 'preference' for food morsels of between 10 and 15 per cent of its own weight and that this may go up to 20 per cent. Occasionally the 'swallow' is as big as 38 per cent.

These figures relate to pike of all sizes, but the percentages are most dramatic when applied to some of the largest pike netted during the period. The three largest weighed 46 lb, 48 lb and $50\frac{1}{2}$ lb. If we apply the 'preference' percentage we find that a $50\frac{1}{2}$ lb pike prefers morsels between 5 and 10 lb; using the 'occasional' swallow percentage we can conclude that a $50\frac{1}{2}$ lb pike could manage a 19 lb dinner. By the same token the 72 lb Kenmure pike could have managed a $28\frac{1}{4}$ lb food item, and probably did sometime in its life, since the River Dee running through Loch Ken is a salmon river that could produce fish of this size.

It would not be unreasonable to conclude that the pike's preferential food swallow, now expressed as a percentage of its own weight, is a built-in instinctive mechanism serving the pike to give it the maximum benefit from its environment. We can express this another way by saying that, where circumstances allow, this instinct would serve the pike with the smallest repair bill for body maintenance and leave the greatest surplus towards body growth.

Working backwards, we can outline conditions which are necessary for the growth of very large pike; and we can deduce that where these conditions are not found, we should hardly expect to find truly monster pike.

If we believe in the existence of 50 lb, 60 lb and 70 lb pike and want to catch them, we are obliged to fish in locations which afford a source of graded food right up to the size of salmon. Furthermore, we are compelled to conclude that a location which enjoys a run of migratory fish throughout the year, together with the counter-run of kelts, is likely to produce bigger fish than a location which enjoys only a summer run of these fish, or no run at all.

I believe that Loch Lomond, Lough Corrib, Lough Conn and Lough Derg are in the top league in terms of these requirements* and I feel sure that some day a fish of 60 lb or 70 lb will confirm my belief. I am also compelled to say that even the wonderful big-pike-producing Broads of Norfolk could hardly produce such mighty fish as these. Nevertheless, since the Broads contain good quantities of graded food-fish up to 5 lb in weight, they should go on producing high-quality pike – perhaps up to a 45 lb ceiling.

From my observations of the pike's diet I have concluded that with the possible exception of the diet of the Wels catfish it must include the widest range of exotic items consumed by any piscivorous freshwater fish in the northern hemisphere.

When this catholic approach to intestine satisfaction is taken into account it comes as no surprise to discover that occasionally pike choke themselves to death. Already in this chapter I have instanced a pike choking on a swan's head and another pike that died while eating a moorhen, and I have also noted pike coming to grief while attempting to swallow a food morsel drawn from a wide range of dietary items.

I found the most frequent cause of choking has been when a pike has attempted to swallow a carp or a salmon that was too large (in relative terms). The Duke of Newcastle's 50 lb pike, No. *28* in my Big Pike List, choked on a 14 lb carp; and, according to Brayley's *History of Surrey*, a $30\frac{1}{2}$ lb pike was shot (in Lower Pond, Busbridge Park, in 1937) when it had rendered itself nearly insensible from its attempt to swallow a 7 lb carp. The bodies of

* Lough Mask also qualifies with trout that grow to salmon size.

And nigh this toppling reed, still as the dead
The great pike lies, the murderous patriarch
Watching the waterpit sheer-shelving dark,
Where through the plash his lithe bright vassals thread.

The rose-finned roach and bluish bream
And staring ruffe steal up the stream
Hard by their glutted tyrant, now
Still as a sunken bough.

He on the sandbank lies,
Sunning himself long hours
With stony gorgon eyes;
Westward the hot sun lowers.

From EDMUND BLUNDEN, *The Pike*

round-sectioned fish like carp and salmon may act as a more efficient plug of a pike's mouth and throat and as such more frequently cause the death of an over-ambitious pike.

I found more evidence of the pike's inability to cope with carp in a copy of the *Field* for 16 June 1890:

Pike Taking Large Carp

The extraordinary voracity of pike is well known; but a fresh instance of it which has just occurred at Sherborne, Dorsetshire, may prove interesting. On the banks of the fine lake in the grounds of Sherborne Castle, the seat of Mr J. K. D. Wingfield Digby, was a few days ago, washed up dead a large male pike, from the mouth of which protruded the tail of a carp. The pike measured 4 ft 2 in long, weighed about 30 lb, while the carp, on which it had shown an unmistakable inclination to dine, was 25 in. in length, and scaled 9 lb. About twenty years ago a pike was found in the lake which had met its death in the same manner.

When a pike chokes to death on a food item we naturally expect the victim to share its fate. This is not always the case. In Simeon's 'Stray Notes' (*Fishing Gazette*, 25 January 1902) we read:

You ask me about the pike who choked himself to death and was survived by his dinner. One day, some years ago, I was fishing from my punt on the Mere, and saw something moving oddly about just beneath the surface of the water a few yards off. I paddled up, and found a carp of about 2 lb weight swimming blindly round and round with a pike on his nose. The pike was dead and limp – several leeches had already fastened upon him – but the carp could not shake or rub him off, the pike's teeth turning inwards and entering deeper the more the carp withdrew. I took them both into the boat, and released the carp. After measuring him and finding him considerably bigger than the pike, I put him into the water again and he swam off with a light heart, but a very sore nose.

Here are a few final dietary notes, the first

This pike was shot in Lower Pond, Busbridge Park, in August 1937 (when partly choked) while it was attempting to swallow a carp of 7 lb. When taken its length was 3 ft 10 in., its girth 2 ft 1 in. and its weight 30½ lb. The pike was set up with the carp still in its throat and the case and contents are still extant. I photographed the pike with the permission of the present owners, the Post Office, which uses Busbridge Park House and grounds as a staff convalescent centre

This picture of a pike's head appeared in the April/June 1940 issue of *Angling*. It was captioned 'Head of a 30 lb pike which was choked when trying to swallow a drowned rabbit'. Unfortunately at the time no other details that could have illuminated this extraordinary incident were published

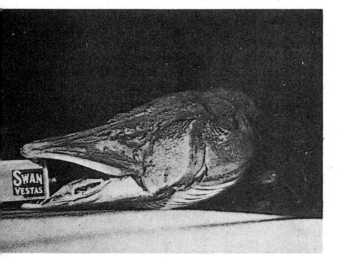

from the *Fishing Gazette* of 25 November 1961:

The Diet of Loughs Conn and Cullen Pike

An autopsy was carried out by the Trust on some of the pike removed from Loughs Conn and Cullen during the season and 64 trout, 15 char, 1 only salmon parr, 146 small pike, 2 crayfish, 6 eels and 9 baby pike were taken from their stomachs!

From the *Field*, 13 April 1901

A pike scaling $20\frac{1}{4}$ lb was caught by a Great Yarmouth angler last week on Ormesby Broad, Norfolk. It was sent to a local taxidermist for preservation, and upon being opened 135 roach were found in its inside.

Speaking of the pike's catholic choice of foodstuffs Dr J. J. Manley asserts that

He would take a pin-cushion stuck full of pins or a young porcupine or full-grown hedgehog, if only presented to him artistically. He may have his predilections for certain good mouthfuls, such as young ducklings, plump puppies just opening their eyes, tender kittens that are not wanted in this world and as a pikist historian relates, for a 'Polish damsel's foot'.... I had the curiosity to open a 14 lb jack I caught at Cranford ... and I found in her the semi-digested remains of a moorhen, two water rats, a bream of about two pounds, innumerable smaller fishes and a variety of other 'foreign substances'. It is on record that the body of a child was once found in the belly of a pike.

Pike Versus Quadrupeds

The Rev. W. B. Daniel in his *Rural Sports* (1801) relates the fierceness of a pike in a report from Gesner:

A famished pike in the Rhone, fixed on the lips of a mule that was drinking, and was drawn out by the beast before it could disengage itself.

And, again in *Rural Sports*, he relates:

In 1798, whilst two gentlemen were angling in a pond near Warnham, in Sussex, a pike, weighing upwards of seven pounds, seized a dog that was lapping the water, and was landed by holding just to the dog, to the astonishment of the fishermen.

The *Fishing Gazette* (6 April 1889) published a story in the same vein:

An Old Pike and Calf Story

(Extract from monthly magazine of date Sept., 1813)

A pike was lately caught in the following curious manner in Windermere Lake. A calf was heard making extraordinary noises near the lake; on going to it a large pike was seen hanging to its nose. The fish had seized the calf while drinking, and the calf had dragged it about fifty yards from the lake. The pike was killed by a blow of a stone, and weighed 45 lb.

The Rev. Daniel had his own calf versus pike story:

Near Youghall, a yearling calf drinking in the river Blackwater, was seized by a pike which was drawn out of the water before quitting its hold; on killing the fish, a water rat and a perch entire were found in its stomach; the pike weighed thirty-five pounds.

Of all the bizarre dietary items known to have been found in a pike's stomach I am persuaded that those discovered inside a 7 lb pike taken from Stoke Newington Reservoir are the *most* curious. The items were recorded by the editor of the *Fishing Gazette* (6 November 1897):

Mr F. Humfrey, of 74, Lower Addiscombe Road, Croydon, called on us last week with a box containing part of the stomach and roe of a 7 lb pike, just as they had been taken out of the fish by Mr A. A. Jackson, fishmonger, of 91, Lower Addiscombe Road, Croydon. Embedded in the stomach were a black glass bottle, 5 in. in length, and about 2 in. in diameter; also an ordinary dinner knife blade, 6 in. long, without a handle. It is evident from the appearance of the stomach and its contents that the bottle and blade must have been there some considerable time, and yet the fish was quite healthy. Mr Jackson sent the extraordinary find to Mr Humfrey, knowing him to be a keen pike angler, and he brought it to us. It seems the fish was taken by a Mr Sydenham Hall, at the Stoke Newington Reservoir of the New River Company, and was given by a lady to Mr Jackson. We give herewith a sketch of the bottle and blade, which caused quite a sensation when exhibited in Messrs. Farlow's window in the Strand.

I can only comment that, although I was previously aware of the pike's predilection for a spoon, I was, until now, unaware of its partiality for a knife!

How much does a pike eat?

Dr L. Johnson's post-graduate research (1966) at the Freshwater Biological Association's laboratory on Windermere, into the food requirements of pike for maintenance and growth, has revealed some interesting facts about the pike's food consumption. In general terms the new evidence conflicts with previous views held by anglers since Cholmondeley-Pennell's time – namely that pike are truly rapacious eaters. Pennell, in 1865, considered that a pike was capable of consuming twice its own weight of fish in the space of a week. This would amount to an annual consumption of some 1040 lb for a pike weighing 10 lb. Johnson proved that a pike's weight could be maintained unchanged for a year, without apparent ill effects, with a food intake weight of approximately its own weight plus 40 per cent. In other words, a 10 lb pike could maintain health without growth with an annual intake of 14 lb of food.

I caught seven pike up to 20½ lb from Loch Lomond using and reusing one shop-bought 6 oz brown trout deadbait. No other deadbait apart from rainbow trout stands up to the strain of casting and to the mouthwork of hungry pike. On waters where trout are a normal item in a pike's diet, no other bait is as attractive to it

It was observed during these experiments that there was a marked increase in the food requirement from May to June, followed by a subsequent decline until the following March. Pike which were offered food in excess of their requirements consumed three and a third times their original weight over the same period. This, liberally interpreted, would mean that a 10 lb pike might consume 35 lb of fish in a year and at the same time show a growth increment. There are, of course, other factors to consider before we can say what pike consume or do not consume in a natural state, since the pike in the experiment were kept in tanks where their activity was strictly limited. Furthermore, the experiments took no account of a consequential loss of weight due to a mature pike's spawning activities (an increase of food intake in these circumstances might be expected). Nevertheless, the growth rate of the tanked pike matched the average growth rate of lake pike. Some caution needs to be exercised before these figures are applied to pike in all age groups, since the pike used in the experiments were young pike (in the age groups 0+ and 1+).

We anglers, interested but without the scientist's need for experimental exactitude, might, in the absence of further evidence, be happy with a figure for a pike's annual food intake as being roughly five times its own starting weight. This would mean that 50 lb of fish would be consumed by a ten-pounder in one year to allow for its growth rate and maintenance.

Interesting facts emerge from the weight-maintenance experiments. Namely, that a pike's food requirement nearly doubles in late spring, reaching a maximum in June, and that although temperature has some significance, it is highly probable that the main factor governing food intake is the relative seasonal incidence of total daylight hours.

It seems that growth closely follows food consumption and reaches a peak in late June – so the angler's best chance for sport should come in that month. My view is that this could well be the case when considering loch fishing, but in waters where weed cover is profuse other complications have to be taken into account. I have a strong feeling that most pike have little difficulty with their ambushing techniques when cover is abundant. In this situation fewer hungry pike would be available to the angler.

Another fact unearthed by pike research shows that the pike compares favourably with plaice and trout in its gross conversion rate capability, that is, its relative efficiency in turning food intake (by weight) into maintenance, and growth (by weight). For pike the figure is 3·41. Trout have previously been demonstrated to give gross conversion rates of 7·1 and plaice 5.

These figures would seem to indicate that in the past the finger has been pointed at the pike quite unfairly. It has been much maligned by generations of writers who have called it greedy, gluttonous, rapacious and ravenous. It was very much maligned by Richard Franck 300 years ago when he wrote: 'He murders all he meets with.' It would now seem that our pike is a most reasonable fellow – the possessor of an intestine which functions with great economy. No need for him to pack his stomach so frequently – like that greedy, gluttonous, rapacious, ravenous fellow, the trout, who murders all he meets with!

5 Enemies of pike

Although seemingly paradoxical, Nature, so that life will continue, has schemed that all living creatures have their quota of natural enemies.

Natural enemies play their part, as do the scourges of drought, disease and starvation, to ensure that a reciprocal counterpoise is re-established in the plant and animal kingdoms after a population explosion of this or that plant or animal has caused a temporary imbalance.

The No. 1 enemy of a small pike is a bigger pike, but the traditional foremost natural enemies of medium and big pike, namely the osprey and the otter, have declined (in numbers) to such an extent that it can be said that in Britain a big pike has only one enemy left – man.

Luckily there are some recorded accounts of battles, which took place in other European countries, between ospreys and pike (when the former took on a pike that proved too heavy to lift) which will serve to remind us of the risk that a British pike once took when it indulged in its favourite summer pastime – lying still, sunning itself below the surface.

This following report, under the heading of 'Pike kills eagle', was published in the *Fishing Gazette* (30 March 1935).

A marauding eagle was observed hovering over Gerich Lake, in East Prussia, by a local shipowner, Adolf Tetzlaff.

Suddenly the eagle made a swoop down to the water and reappeared bearing a huge pike in its talons. There ensued a terrible struggle a few feet above the water. The eagle was trying to rise, but the weight and struggling of the pike prevented this. The struggle lasted for some minutes until the eagle touched the water. The pike, now in his element, drew the eagle under the water, where the struggle seemed to continue. The shipowner had a boat lowered and went to the spot. The pike had drawn the eagle down into deep water and drowned it, but the eagle had not released the pike. After a long time the bodies of eagle and pike were found floating on the surface. Both were dead.

The most dramatic accounts of battles between pike and osprey were published in Mr Lloyd's *Scandinavian Adventures* (1854). In it Mr Lloyd stated that it was not unusual to find both pike and osprey dead when the latter had picked on a big pike that it was unable to bear aloft. A battle to the death was the usual consequence because of the bird's inability to extract its crooked talons from the pike's back.

What is even more remarkable is Mr Lloyd's recording of several instances of battles which resulted in the pike surviving with a drowned osprey still attached to its back.

One of Mr Lloyd's informants, a Mr Ekstrom, found a live pike of nearly 20 lb in weight with the skeleton of an osprey still attached. Another, a Dr Willman, gave him an account of a pike taken from Lake Wettern in East Gothland, again with the skeleton of an eagle attached. This pike had survived for some time; indeed the bones of the osprey had accumulated so much algae that it gave them a greenish hue. Local fishermen who saw this skeleton above water 'believed it to be a harbinger of misfortune' and always 'made for the shore as quickly as possible'.

Yet a third informant recounted an even more remarkable story:

Fishing one day in a large lake in Fryksdal in Wermeland, when they had proceeded a considerable distance from the shore, the fisherman suddenly pulled the boat right round, and in evident alarm commenced rowing with all his might towards the shore. One of the party asked the man what he meant by this strange conduct? 'The *Sjo-troll*, or water-sprite, is here again', replied he, at the same time pointing with his finger far to seaward. Everyone in the boat then saw in the distance something greatly resembling the horns of an elk, or a reindeer, progressing rapidly on the surface of the water. 'Row towards it', exclaimed Lekander; 'the deuce take me if I don't give the *Sjo-troll* a shot; I am not afraid of it'. It was with difficulty, however, that Modin (the fisherman) could be prevailed upon once more to alter the course of the boat, and to make for the apparition. . . . When they neared the object sufficiently, Lekander, who was standing gun in hand, in the bow of the boat, fired, and fortunately with deadly effect. On taking possession of the prize, it was found to be a huge pike, to whose back the skeleton of an eagle was attached. The fish, or rather the bones of the bird, had been seen by numbers for several years together, and universally went under the above designation of *Sjo-troll'*.

Pike fighting

Fights between pike may take place more often than we suspect, and at least one person has witnessed a match between two big pike which excited him more than the prospect of seeing any Beckett–Carpentier fight.

On 2 December 1919, L. W. Lowen of Hadley Wood Herts., wrote:

I had a most interesting and exciting experience the other day whilst fishing, and if you can find space to publish this letter, I am sure some of your readers will be interested.

I was fishing a private lake in Norfolk and noticed a great splashing and commotion in some shallow water near by. I quietly rowed my boat to the scene and was able to get quite close without being observed. The water being bright and shallow, I had a perfect view of what was going on.

A large pike, which, judging by the size of his head and length of body, must have been well over 20 lb, was fighting furiously with a smaller fish, which I estimate was at least 10 lb in weight. The larger fish had evidently taken the smaller fish diagonally across the back in the ordinary way with the intent of swallowing it, but in the struggle the grip of its jaws had evidently slipped (for I could see flesh of the smaller fish was torn from the middle of its body down to near its tail), and when I arrived the larger pike had its jaws firmly implanted across the back of the smaller fish, near its tail. The smaller fish in the course of the fight had somehow managed to turn and had its jaws across the larger pike's belly, below its anal fins. In this position they were rolling and splashing in the shallow water for at least two minutes under my close observation. The smaller pike was drawing a lot of blood from the belly of the larger fish, but the larger fish did not seem to be drawing any from the other's tail. Nevertheless, it appeared to me as though the smaller fish was nearly 'beat'. His gills were standing out with all the red showing, but he held on grimly. Eventually the larger pike evidently saw me and struggled off into deeper water, but for nearly an hour I saw spasmodic splashes on the surface of the water as though they were still at it, but I could not get another close view.

I have been wondering which of the fish will have succumbed first. Maybe they both fell prey to an otter, of which I understand there are some large specimens in that particular water. Anyhow, they both had their jaws so full and so firmly embedded in each other's flesh that I should think it improbable that either of them could have let go. I told the bailiff of what I had seen, and asked him to keep a look-out for any dead pike floating on the surface. If he finds them, I will let you know their state. The bailiff told me that he had seen a duck piloting her brood of ducklings across the lake, and had seen one after the other of the ducklings disappear. This, of course, is well known to happen, as also pike fights, but I think I was more interested in and excited over this fight between two large pike, of which I had such an excellent view, than I should be in all the Beckett–Carpentier fights in the world. I do not suppose I shall have such an experience again in my lifetime.

6 Big waters, big fish

Over the years, writers have noticed a somewhat tenuous connection between large specimens of carnivorous fish such as trout and pike, and the size of the waters which produce them. More precisely, they have noted that the really big fish have been taken from large Scottish and Irish lochs, or more occasionally from the grander English waters. No satisfactory explanation for this phenomenon is ever offered, but it does occur to me that one obvious factor has been generally overlooked – namely, stability of environment. Certainly, if pike are to grow to an impressive size they require to live out their lives, perhaps twenty years or more, in a situation constantly favourable to them. In these great expanses of water which have probably existed since the ice age, the early formative waves of action and reaction between the plant and animal populations have become faint ripples, leaving the economy of the watery kingdom as near stabilized as it can be, notwithstanding human interference.

The impression we get the first time we fish these waters is that conditions have not changed much for thousands of years. This is not strictly true, as most lochs are gradually changing from oligotrophic lochs into eutrophic ones,* but nevertheless change in them is gradual.

Windermere, which is not a particularly rich environment, has been the subject of considerable study and if pike in other, richer,

lochs behave like Windermere pike (especially the pike in those lochs which have populations of whitefish or char), they must enjoy another important advantage. This is best understood by referring to Windermere pike. These pike rarely venture into deep water and virtually confine themselves to the margins of the lake up to the 30-foot contour.

The Windermere pike crop the whole lake by feeding off other lake fish when the latter for various purposes repair to the shallows (for feeding and spawning). Dr L. Johnson, commenting on Dr Frost's pike researches on Windermere, puts it thus: 'The whole of the lake is apparently helping to support the pike population without the pike having to forage beyond the shallows.' In fact, prior to pike-netting operations on Windermere, the pike may have consumed 63 per cent of the total lake production.

This reserve larder is surely an important factor when we consider stability. Here we have a natural example of what modern society creates artificially – a reserve larder to iron out seasonal fluctuations of food supplies. Do we not see the effect of the lack of adequate food reserves on the human race in other parts of the world, and witness the form this deficiency takes in terms of shortened lives and underdeveloped bodies?

Unlike his river cousin, the loch pike, once grown large, lives out his life in a safer environment since there is little chance of

* These terms are used by biologists (as part of a system devised by Naumann in 1919) to classify lakes by reference to the relative richness in their dissolved nutrient salts. Typical highland deep loch, lough and lake waters are usually poor in dissolved nutrient salts and as a consequence are relatively unproductive of contained life. Such waters are said to be oligotrophic in character. In contrast, typical lowland shallow lakes, receiving drainage from agricultural land, or drainage from streams flowing over limestone rock or sewage from human habitation, are usually rich in dissolved nutrient salts, and are consequently relatively rich in contained life. These waters are said to be eutrophic in character.

discovery by his only serious enemy – man. Safer, too, from the great inundations of storm and flood, which do not blight his appetite or hide his prey as they do at times in the flooded river.

Josef Schrank's pike: weight 44¼lb, length 50½in., girth 25¼in. This very fine-looking pike was caught in the Ostersee (Bavaria) in 1974 on a spoon (By courtesy of *Blinker* magazine)

7 Age of pike and growth

We anglers do not have the means of describing or evaluating pike in terms of absolute size or ultimate age. Our task is made no easier when we realize that the vast majority of pike live out their lives without revealing themselves to us.

In the past these difficulties have led to wild speculations, and given rise to grossly exaggerated stories like the one which described the 19 ft, 267-year-old Mannheim pike. Coming down a bit, Pennant referred to a 'ninety-year-old pike', while Sir Francis Bacon said: 'Forty years is more likely to be a maximum.' In 1920 Mr Tate Regan, with scientific bent, read the scales of a 40 lb Lough Conn pike and put its age at twenty-five years.

Spence stated: 'In Russian commercial pike fisheries male pike of five years are rarely recorded while hen fish often attain the age of twelve years or more.' Naturalist Frank Buckland, given a 35½ lb pike from a Windsor

The Windsor Park Lake pike was in fact taken out of Rapley Lake in Bagshot Park. The cased specimen, a fine example of Buckland and Rolfe's work, is now in the possession of the Piscatorial Society. It adorns the members' room at their fishing lodge on the upper Avon

Park lake, was able to assess its age accurately, for the pike in question was one of eight put in the lake some twelve years before at a starting weight of 1½ lb. Buckland described this fourteen-year-old fish as : 'This magnificent pike – I never saw one in more perfect condition – weighed 35½ lb, the length was 3 ft 10½ in. and the girth 2 ft.'

This reminds me of a fish I saw at Blandford which was taken during the close season of 1941 from Spettisbury on the Stour; it weighed 31½ lb and I am obliged to use similar superlatives to describe it. It was deep bodied, magnificently proportioned and to my eye exceedingly pretty.

Bill Giles, who makes a study of scale reading, told me that the oldest pike within his experience was about eighteen years old. He cautiously added the comment, 'By that age their scales are becoming very difficult to read.' In some of the pike which he caught, tagged, released, and re-caught in successive years, Bill found growth rate inconsistent. Several were found to be losing weight; these were generally old fish which were past their prime. Other fish

put on weight quickly: one 16¾ lb pike weighed 21½ lb just a year later, which indicated a growth increment of 4¾ lb.

Apparently the traumatic experience of being hooked and released causes a considerable shedding of a pike's body weight. As evidence of this, Arthur Smith of Norwich caught a 28 lb pike which weighed only 26 lb when re-caught a week later. Presumably it was taking its first meal after getting over the shock. If this meal was not its first then the loss of weight must have been even more dramatic. Bill believes that a pike's digestive system works at a quicker rate than most of us realize. Another indication of the weight-loss phenomenon was again demonstrated by Giles in a letter to me.

This winter, one Thursday, I caught two well-conditioned twenty pounders which I put in a small pool (about a foot deep) near the broad, as I wanted to show them to Reg. Sandys on the Saturday. Never again! the poor things were as thin as rakes. I could hardly believe it. Also they had been attacked by a heron which flew away as we approached on the Saturday morning. They swam all right when we put them back in the broad, but we will recognise them again from the number of stab wounds on their backs.

The growth rate of Irish pike in the great limestone loughs is amazingly fast. Dr Kennedy gave me details of some incidental determinations: on Lough Mask a female pike reached a weight of 41 lb in eight years plus; while another from Lough Cloon reached 36 lb in the same period. The four heaviest pike caught during the period of netting weighed 45, 46, 48 and 50½ lb respectively. These fish were heavy with spawn and Dr Kennedy made the point that Mona's length–weight scale does not hold good for Irish pike of more than about 20 lb in weight (see page 62). As a matter of interest, Richard Walker pointed out to me some years ago that in his opinion Mona's scale was of no use in determining the weight of heavy pike.

The growth rate of Windermere pike is less dramatic, and the heaviest pike taken since netting operations began in 1944 weighed 35 lb.

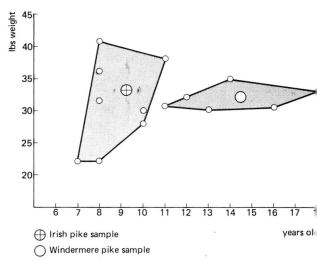

Figure 12 Age of pike and growth: Irish and Windermere pike compared

This particular pike was fourteen years old whereas the oldest pike recorded from Windermere was an eighteen-year-old female weighing 33¼lb (see Figure 12).

There is an obvious environmental difference between the relatively warm, rich, Irish limestone loughs and the colder, less rich, Windermere. One would naturally expect richer feeding in the Irish loughs, and the milder climate would probably prolong the period of high-level feeding activity; nevertheless, one is struck by the relative youth of the big Irish pike. In fact, if we look at the six largest pike taken from Windermere, we find these fish have a mean weight of 32 lb and a mean age of fourteen years; and when we compare these with a random sample of eight Irish pike of a mean weight of 30¾ lb we find that the latter have a mean age of eight and three-quarter years. In a sample of several tons of Irish pike up to an individual weight of 48 lb we find an eight-year-old fish weighing 41 lb; are we to assume that this pike and other fast-growing Irish pike are unable to enjoy the same lifespan as the older Windermere pike? If so we must conclude that Irish pike die off for some unknown reason; or else we must assume that older Irish pike have so far escaped the nets.

While we can believe that a significant

number of large pike may have escaped the nets, including perhaps a record Irish pike, we would be hard put to believe that *all* the elderly pike have so far escaped. If we find it difficult to accept either explanation in the absence of proof, then I think we must look elsewhere for an explanation.

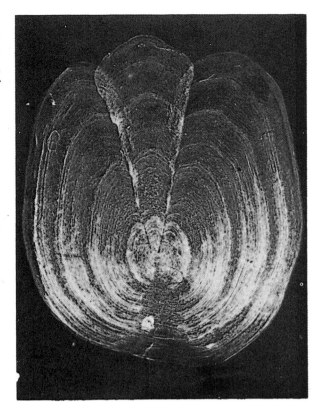

The scale of a five-year-old pike. Although opercular bones are preferred to scales for determining the age of pike, this photograph reveals the annuli or growth checks with remarkable clarity. Scales such as this one are used by the FreshwaterBiological Association biologists to determine the age and growth of pike which have been captured, released and recaptured. It is not possible to determine age from opercular bones if pike are to be released

Josef Schrädler's pike: weight 45¼lb, length 53½in., from Germany. In August 1979 *Blinker*, the West German angling magazine, published the photograph below of a pike which, in spite of being held by a very big German, still looks very big indeed. The caption read: 'Josef Schrädler and his son took the pike of 45¼lb from a net when fishing Schliersee (Bavaria). This is the heaviest ever taken from the lake, beating the previous record – a fish of 35 lb 10 oz taken by Hans Heckenberger. The lake has produced many large pike this season.'

Roy Smyth, a County Down pike angler, with a 21¼ lb pike caught on a plug in 1974

Can it be that the recognized method of age determination (scale and opercular-bone reading) is accurate in so far as it records the true age of a pike during the period of linear growth; but takes no account of a further period of life without linear growth? In human beings, linear growth continues for a time and thereafter ceases, regardless of subsequent changes in weight. We know that growing fish produce a series of rings or circuli on their scales and opercular bones. During periods of fast summer growth these rings are well spaced; but during periods of slow winter growth these rings are close together, and form what is known as a growth check. Counting these checks or annuli is the basis of scale reading and we know that the system has been revised and refined by Dr Frost and Miss Kipling with opercular bones, since pike have been caught, tagged, released and re-caught after known periods of liberty. In cases where the growth increment is small the fish approaches its maximum linear dimension over a longer period of time and as a consequence the steady growth increments are recorded on its scales and opercular bones. Nevertheless, if linear growth stops as a fish approaches the maximum linear dimensional expectation for its species after a relatively short period of fast growth, then no more circuli will be laid down on the scales and opercular bones. If no more circuli are laid down then the last phase of life will not be recorded.

I am encouraged in this theory after a discussion with Walker, who caught the record British carp at Redmire in 1952. This fish weighed 44 lb at the time of capture and its scale reading indicated an age of fifteen years. The oldest fish ever taken from the same water was classified as a sixteen-year-old. Nevertheless, Walker's fish has survived a further sixteen years at the London Zoo and is still alive.* This fish now weighs a lot less than it did when it was caught. In the circumstances we can hardly expect the scales or opercular bones of Walker's fish to record the non-growing phase of its life. We expect the readings to indicate an age of fifteen but we know the fish to be at least thirty-one years old!

Reading the age and growth of pike from opercular bones

Until Dr Frost and Miss C. Kipling of the Freshwater Biological Association used opercular bones (gill-cover bones) to determine the age and growth of Windermere pike (1959), other scientists and naturalists had relied on scale reading. Frost and Kipling were able to demonstrate that for pike, the reading of age and growth from opercular bones was a more reliable method, just as Le Cren was able to do for perch in 1947.

Altogether, from 1945 some 7000 opercular bones were collected and their data analysed. Control data for age and growth determination were obtained from a sample of 500 or more tagged fish which were re-caught after various known periods of liberty.

A simple outline of the method used for bone reading follows. The left opercular bone is removed with a scalpel (Figure 13), put in hot water, and the skin cleaned off with a cloth. After some months of storage (which improves the reading quality) the bones are viewed by reflected light on a dark background under a low-power binocular microscope.

The annuli or growth checks viewed under a microscope appear as a series of 'bands' which

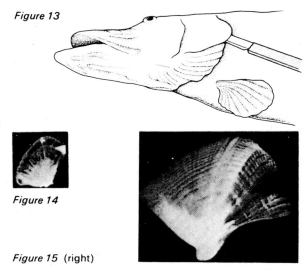

Figure 13

Figure 14

Figure 15 (right)

stand out because they have a different degree of whiteness from the rest of the bone. Each annulus represents a gradual line of discontinuity between summer and winter growth, and is probably formed on the operculum in early May. As most pike in Windermere hatch in April and a few in early May it has been found convenient to take 1 May as the pike's birthday.

Now in, say, November, we would expect a one-and-a-half-year-old pike to display on its operculum one annulus indicating a growth check during the previous May when it was one year old, and also some evidence of further growth representing the fast-growing period which immediately followed. If we refer to Figure 14 we see that this is indeed the case with a one-and-a-half-year-old, aquarium-reared pike. Similarly we can see in Figure 15 the evidence of fourteen growth checks on the operculum of another pike. In fact this particular bone came from a fifteen-year-old pike,

---

* This was written in 1968. In 1971 when the carp died at the age of thirty-four, through the good offices of Alwyne Wheeler I was able to collect the fish (which by now weighed only 27 lb) after an autopsy had been carried out, and have it set up.

In the event my theory – that a fish can live for a period of time without growth (linear) and without recording this non-growing phase of life on its scales and bones – was proved to have substance when a reading of an opercular bone, taken from Walker's carp, showed no indication of the last nineteen years of

its life. However, it must be remembered that the carp in question had been living in an unnatural environment, with limited space and fairly constant water temperature, incidence of light and food availability. Until further research has been made it would be unwise to apply this finding to fish living in natural conditions. It is, however, permissible to say that *in certain circumstances a fish can live for a period of time without growing* (the term growing implies linear growth) *and without recording this non-growing phase of life on its scales and bones.*

which indicates that one annulus is missing or obscured.

The phenomenon of one or two missing annuli is caused by a growth of orange-brown glutinous tissue on the operculum near the point of attachment of the bone to the skull, and affects almost all opercula taken from pike over seven years old.

One of the methods used to obtain corrected ages for bones with obscured annuli is the graphic method known as the Ford–Walford plot. This method is based on the assumption that the yearly increments added to length decrease in magnitude by geometric progression.

Where measurements from the bone are required for back calculation of age or growth, the operculum is placed in a dish of xylol and put on the stage of a projector so that its concave side faces the light source. The image is then projected with a 5·3 magnification down on to a sheet of white paper. A narrow strip of cardboard is laid on the long axis of the image at right angles to a line joining DC (see Figure 16) and the positions of the annuli marked off on the cardboard with a pencil. As growth of the opercular bone and the fish are isometrical (of equal measure), direct proportion can be used to determine growth from the measurements marked on the cardboard.

I would imagine that very few of us who fish for pike would have the sophisticated equipment necessary for 'do it yourself' opercular-

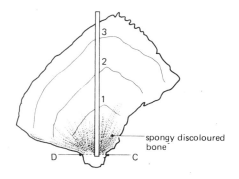

Figure 16

bone reading. Even so, if we have the occasion to kill a pike for any reason, we can prepare an opercular bone in the way described and take a reading with the naked eye, and we would be pretty accurate in our calculations if we counted the annuli and remembered to add one to any number over six.

During the 1970s Dr John Casselman, who was working at the time for Dr E. J. Crossman at the University of Toronto, developed a technique for determining a pike's age by 'reading' its cleithrum bone. He demonstrated that the cleithrum – the flat bony hanger lying immediately behind the gill cover – can be read with greater confidence, and that a pike's length and growth record throughout its life could be accurately calculated from a simple formula of measurement and multiplication.

Below This cased pike, now in the possession of tackle dealer Arthur Cove, weighs 42½ lb, is 45 in. long and was shot at Deene Park Lake

Right I caught this very long (47½ in.) 32 lb pike in the flooded River Aille in October 1977. It had a girth of 23½ in. and its head measured 12¼ in. long. In my researches I have found that a sample of six pike, each weighing 35 lb, whose lengths varied from 45 in. to 50 in., had a mean length of 47.4 in. The River Aille empties its waters into Lough Mask and it is likely that mine was a Mask pike

Mona's scale and length–weight projections

One of the curiosities of the traditional British approach to pike fishing is that the pundits (and by definition this includes nearly every pike fisherman), love to refer to a scale that predicts the weight of a pike from its length.

Rabid roachers, demon dace anglers and fanatical fly fishermen all manage to conduct their affairs without reference to a length–weight scale but, unique among the fishing fraternity, pike anglers, perhaps better comprehending the capacity of a fellow angler to tell a lie, like to have this handy guide to test the veracity of his claim.

There have been many scales, but W. Fletcher's scale, better known as Mona's scale, is justly the most famous (see Figure 17). (Fletcher was the correspondent 'Mona' of the *Fishing Gazette*. He lived close by the River Shannon at Athlone during the late Victorian period, but at the end of his life he resided at Islay.) Mona's scale is based on the supposition that a pike of 40 inches weighs 20 lb. Since its first publication early in the century Mona's scale has featured in innumerable angling books. It has, moreover, been accepted by the majority of authorities as the basis for evaluating the authenticity of big pike reports. I use the word *accepted* advisedly because it had certainly not been rejected by anyone until P. J. Bonfield wrote in *Angling*, 'By now this hoary and fanciful scale should be described as an historical curiosity in angling books of reference. . . .'

In the past many writers, however, have been at pains to point out that a 'condition factor' has to be taken into account when using the scale, since the scale relates to pike that are in good condition, and to be fair it must be stated that other writers, even without the benefit of scientific data, have noted the possible limitations of the scale when applied to pike that are either carrying a heavy load of spawn – or none.

From scientific observation of the size of the pike's preferred food morsel (pages *45–6*) we know the probable extent of the pike's day-to-day weight variation, and that weight is likely to vary by some 15 per cent after the pike has fed but, exceptionally, that it can vary by more than twice this amount. We also know that the length–weight relationship must vary from month to month since there is a build-up of weight in the ovaries, which eventually results in a 20 per cent loss of weight at spawning time.

In the first edition, *Pike* (1971), I asked:

Are we to go on giving credence to the accuracy of Mona's scale even when we have allowed for the incidence of the special factors mentioned? I hope not – for a close perusal of the evidence, past and present, indicates that the scale is positively inaccurate for pike weighing more than 20 lb.

Ireland's best-known 'fish scientist', Dr Michael Kennedy, referring to data collected by the Inland Fisheries Trust, wrote to me in these terms: 'But it is worth noting that Mona's length–weight scale does not hold good for Irish pike of more than about 20 lb in weight. The really big ones are very deep and thick, and are quite different in shape from the smaller pike.' However, he did make a small concession when he wrote: 'The male pike have a length–weight relationship that agrees pretty

(in.)	(lb)	(in.)	(lb)	(in.)	(lb)
20	2·500	34	12·232	48	34·585
21	2·894	35	13·281	49	36·774
22	3·327	36	14·580	50	39·062
23	3·802	37	15·829	51	41·453
24	4·300	38	17·147	52	43·940
25	4·882	39	18·537	53	46·524
26	5·492	40	20·000	54	49·207
27	6·150	41	21·537	55	51·992
28	6·860	42	23·152	56	54·880
29	7·621	43	24·845	57	57·872
30	8·437	44	26·020	58	60·972
31	9·309	45	28·476	59	64·180
32	10·240	46	30·457	60	67·500
33	11·238	47	32·444		

Figure 17 Mona's scale

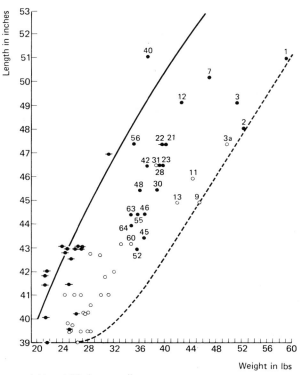

Figure 18 The relationship between weight and (fork)
length of pike in Great Britain (From *Pike*, 1971)

expect to find the plottings of each individual fish coincident with, or close to, the line representing the scale. But what do we find? We find fifty-seven plottings on one side of the line, indicating pike which were heavier than expected, given their lengths; and only seven plottings on the other side of the line, indicating pike which were lighter than their expected weight.

It is interesting to record that two of the three plottings (nos. 9 and 11) that indicate a considerable inaccuracy in Mona's scale were of fish noted to be heavy with spawn, and the third (no. 13) might have been heavy with spawn since it was shot on the spawning shallows. A fourth pike included in my list (no. 48) was also noted to be heavy with spawn. That it was probably measured to the tip of the tail instead of to the fork of the tail, thus giving an excess length measurement of some 2 in., is a likely reason for this fish not providing yet another example of extreme inaccuracy of the scale. The other three pike were measured correctly.

Most of what has appeared by way of argument and deduction in this chapter so far appeared in the first edition, where I followed the scientific discipline of recording pike lengths with a measurement from the tip of a pike's snout to the fork of its tail. This system must be followed when applying Mona's scale, according to Norman Weatherall, who has said in his book *Pike Fishing* (1961): 'Mona's pike scale is based on what pike, in average condition, should weigh, the supposition being that a 40 inch pike weighs 20 lb. *Length is measured from end of snout to fork of tail.*'

However, in my later book, *The Domesday Book of Mammoth Pike* (1979), I changed my tactics and gave my reasons:

Whenever I was able to discover the length measurement of any pike that qualified (by weight) for an entry in this book [*The Domesday Book*], I was faced with a problem of how to record it. I knew that anglers invariably measure their pike from tip of nose to tip of tail (extreme length) – after all the length of a thing *is* its length, surely – whereas scientists, for reasons known only to themselves, measure pike as they do all fish, i.e. to the fork. In

well with Mona's scale.' But since Dr Kennedy wrote in the same letter, 'The largest male pike we have examined was 14 lb, but we have not got many over 10 lb', we can see from his findings that so far as big Irish pike are concerned Mona's scale is pretty useless.

Now what of English pike? If we refer to Figure 18 we can see that the series of plots (marked 'O'), relating to a number of large pike netted from Windermere, is not coincident with the line representing Mona's scale. Figure 19 (page *64*) also gives the plottings of all the big pike from my first Big Pike List whose lengths, as well as weights, were known.

If Mona's scale were an accurate vehicle for forecasting weight from length, we should not

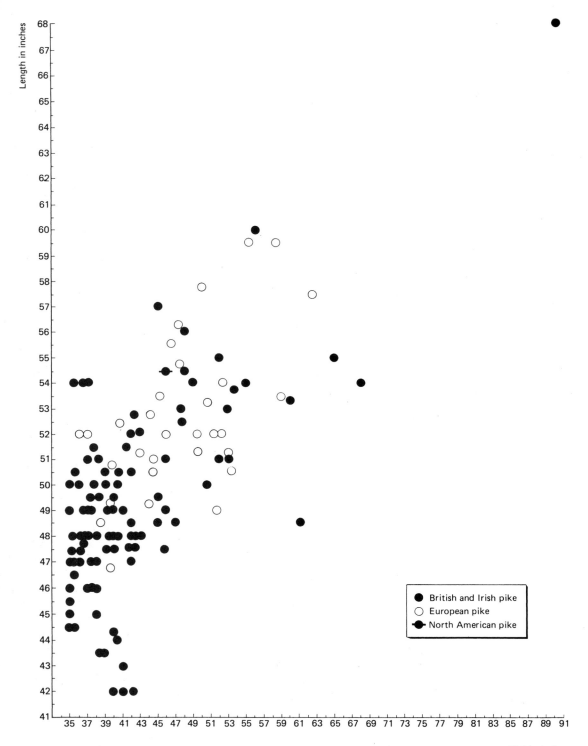

Figure 19 The relationship between weight and (extreme)
length of 125 large pike

my book *Pike* (1971), with the aid of Dr Winifred Frost's formula[1] I attempted to rationalize the measurements by converting anglers' 'extreme' lengths, where they existed, to scientists' 'fork' lengths. After due consideration, I have now reversed this plan, so that all lengths quoted in this book are anglers' lengths, i.e. 'extreme' lengths. I am quite sure it makes better sense to follow empirical rather than new-fangled methods of measuring fish.

As a consequence of my change of plan for *The Domesday Book* which I have now adhered to, I have been able to draw a new graph (Figure 19). This new graph, however, relates to pike that weigh 35 lb or more.

After studying the new graph it occurred to me that if Mona's scale was applied to a pike's 'extreme' length measurement rather than to what has appeared to be a mandatory 'fork' length measurement it would be a much more useful and accurate scale.

When this thought struck me I began to search for the authority for the general belief that Mona's scale refers to 'fork' lengths. I found that among angling journalists and angling editors the belief is universal; or at least it is universally believed by those who consider the matter at all.

Apart from Weatherall's statement, that I have already alluded to, there is the authority of O. M. Reed ('Omar') who, during the 1950s, regularly drew up the annual Big Pike List for the *Fishing Gazette*. For example, in the *Fishing Gazette* of 25 October 1958 he wrote: 'This 26-pounder was a short thick-set fish as its photograph showed, 38 in. long to the *fork* of the tail and 20 in. girth (Mona's Scale 17.147 lb).'

Notwithstanding this and other supporting evidence I attempted to find the original press publication of Mona's scale to see if it were in agreement. In the event I found a letter from him published in the *Fishing Gazette* (28 September 1918) which gave the scale together with the following note.

Mona's Scale of Weight for Length of Pike

Our old contributor 'Mona' sends me the following interesting new scale. I hope anglers will paste it in their tackle-book to test it by their takes of pike:

September 10, 1918.

'Dear Mr Marston, Enclosed I am sending you my scale of weight for length of pike. By it you will see that Mr Graham's 39 in. pike should weigh 18½ lb. However, I find that pike vary very much, and you will often get a 39 in. fish which weighs much heavier. I hope you are having some sport while out of London. My health is very indifferent, and I have not been able to wet a line for a long time. Kind regards.

Yours faithfully, MONA.

From this it is plain to see that Mona merely referred to length without further qualification, so that so far as we can tell his intention may have been to specify 'extreme' lengths rather than 'fork' lengths.

My own considered view, albeit rather late in the day, is that Mona (who by the time his scale was published was quite old) probably never lived to comment on any false interpretation of his scale, and that other people, mindful perhaps of Edward Sturdy's previously published scales for salmon and trout, which required these fish to be 'measured from end of snout to the end of middle rays of tail fin', inferred perhaps in error that Mona's scale was similarly qualified.

Mona calculated his scale for pike ranging from 20 in. to 60 in. In order to relate my data, which consists of two fish that have a recorded length greater than 60 in. I have used Mona's formula (kindly calculated for me by Richard Walker)[2] to work out projected weights for pike measuring between 61 in. and 68 in.:

(in.)	(lb)	(in.)	(lb)
61	70·93	66	89·84
62	74·47	67	93·98
63	78·13	68	98·26
64	81·92	69	102·65
65	85·82		

[1] To convert extreme length to fork length, divide by 1.055. To convert from fork length to extreme length, multiply by 1.055.

[2] Weight $= \dfrac{\text{length}^3}{3200}$

Left A Lough Mask pike netted in March 1957 by Ireland's Inland Fisheries Trust: weight 46 lb, length 47½ in. Holding the fish is Dr Michael Kennedy, one of the Trust's scientists. This picture enables one to imagine the magnificent proportions of a pike some 21½ in. longer. Dr Kennedy wrote about the latter in a note published in *Angling* (May 1956): 'The largest pike of which a fairly reliable record is available would appear to be the dead specimen found in the Shannon at Meelick in 1926, with the remains of a 15 lb salmon in its throat (see the *Field*, 7 April 1927). This specimen was not weighed but was 69 in. long and in life would, therefore, have weighed over 90 lb.' Now that we have projected Mona's scale to deal with a pike that measures as long as the Meelick pike (page 65) we can assume that it probably weighed, at sometime in its life, over 100 lb!

Below Pike fishing on Lough Conn, Ireland. This fine period photograph taken in 1882 gives a vivid picture of the Irish pike-fishing scene of a hundred years ago. Little has changed. Notice the Shannon clinker-built boat; even today this boat is still the first choice of discerning Lough fishermen. The Nottingham reels are still preferred by knowledgeable anglers for 'trolling' both here and in North America. Even the long built-cane salmon fly-rods depicted are the favourites of the Scots and Irish lough trollers – they will still buy every one that comes on the market, if reasonably priced, although it is unlikely that their intention is to fish for pike

Richard Walker's improved scale

One grey November afternoon, sitting as I frequently do at table 41 in the British Museum Newspaper Library at Colindale, I came across a fascinating letter in a very old copy of the *Fishing Gazette*.

The writer gave this formula for calculating the probable weight of a pike from its length:

$$\text{Weight} = \frac{\text{length} + \frac{1}{3} \times \text{girth}^2}{1000}$$

(Notice that length means the length from nose to tip of tail and that measurements are expressed in inches and pounds.)

I sent a copy of the formula to Richard Walker, knowing that he wouldn't be able to stop playing with it until it was either rejected or improved. The last-mentioned alternative proved correct, for in his reply he wrote:

When I applied this fomula to quite large numbers of pike, trout, salmon, barbel, carp and chub, it became apparent that, while the formula gave incorrect results, they were consistently in error and all that was needed was a modification of the divisor; the principle of the formula was right. By altering the divisor and simplifying the formula, we get:

$$\text{Weight} = \frac{\text{length} \times \text{girth}^2}{806}$$

Walker tested this formula on a number of fish known to have been accurately measured and weighed. He found it to be astonishingly accurate with the 'round-bodied' species already named, but to give optimistic figures for oval-bodied species such as roach, rudd and bream. After the formula was applied to certain pike in my Big Pike List, I began to suspect some of the ones with incredibly large girth measurements, but, in defence of those empirical statistics, I am bound to plead that extreme girth measurements, of necessity, change round- into oval-bodied fish, and thereby, defeat the formula – or perhaps in another sense prove it.

8 Spawning and fecundity

William Senior ('Red Spinner'), writing in 1900, gave what was perhaps the first reliable account of the pike's spawning behaviour. He obtained his information from a trained observer – a trout-farm manager – who had studied the activities of pike in a series of lakes prior to turning the latter into trout preserves. The observer, Mr Armistead, wrote thus:

When ready to spawn the female pike, often accompanied by two or three males, would run into the weeds in shallow bays, or up ditches and into bog holes. Here they may be seen and approached if the sun be shining brightly. The eggs are of a light yellow colour, and do not, as I have been told, adhere to each other, but they separate in the water like trout eggs. The weed they seemed to choose for depositing eggs was almost invariably *Ranunculus aquaticus*.

Senior obtained more information from another fish breeder, Mr Thomas Ford of Caistor, who demonstrated the practicability of rearing pike from eggs and milt stripped from parent fish. According to Mr Ford the fertilized eggs become 'eyed' ova after about twelve to fourteen days and hatch out within a period of from twenty to twenty-four days after fertilization. As you will see, Alfred Jardine, writing some 100 years ago, accurately described the pike's spawning location when he wrote: 'Pike deposit their eggs on submerged rushes, sedges, and sub-aqueous weeds in shallow bays and ditches.'

Frost and Kipling (1967) noted that Windermere pike spawn along the relatively sheltered parts of the shoreline and in small bays. Usually the chosen ground is silted and sandy rather than stony, and is within the 12-foot depth contour, where there are submerged single or mixed strands of *Elodea* (Canadian pond weed), *Myriophyllum* (water milfoil), *Nitella* (stone wort), or *Litorella* (shore weed). The evidence of other workers indicates that availability of material determines the pike's choice of vegetation. For example, in a lake in Minnesota, pike spawn on the dead stems of sedges and rushes.

On Windermere the male pike arrive on the breeding ground first, and sometimes stay for a month, although the mean length of stay is fourteen days, whereas the females usually stay for about ten days. It would appear that Windermere pike return repeatedly to the same spawning ground; one tagged pike, first caught in 1959, was recaptured on the same ground in 1960, 1962, 1963 and 1964.

When re-caught during the non-breeding season, pike, originally caught on the breeding grounds, give some evidence of not having moved very far from the general region which contains the spawning site. This evidence is not conclusive, however, since Frost and Kipling were unable to keep track of pike movements between their appearance on the breeding ground to spawn and their recapture later on the same ground. One pike which had spawned in April was recovered in July at a distance of five miles from the spawning site.

The old writers believed that temperature affected the timing of the pike's spawning activities, which they generally noted to be during the months of March and April. Pennell, writing in 1889, said:

The pike spawns about March and April according to the climate, forwardness of the Spring and other local circumstances – the young females of three and four years old taking the lead and the dowagers following, and during this period the male may often be observed following the female about from

Pike mating (Photos: Fabricius and Gustafson)

place to place, and attending to her with much apparent solicitude.

Confirmation of the time of the pike's spawning season comes from several scientists working in the northern hemisphere. Frost and Kipling note that Windermere pike are usually on the spawning grounds by the second week in March, although the peak of their spawning activity is not reached until the second half of April. They found that when spawning occurs the water temperature was usually 6 °C and over.

Water temperature is critical in determining the rate at which the eggs develop. Swift (1965) conducted an interesting experiment at the Freshwater Biological Association on the effect of temperature on mortality and rate of development of the eggs of the pike. He found that the average number of days required to hatch the eggs varied with the temperature, as indicated in the table:

26·4 days to hatch in water kept at 6 °C (43 °F)
16·8 days to hatch in water kept at 8 °C (46 °F)
12·0 days to hatch in water kept at 10 °C (50 °F)
 9·0 days to hatch in water kept at 12 °C (54 °F)
 5·8 days to hatch in water kept at 14 °C (57 °F)
 5·1 days to hatch in water kept at 16 °C (61 °F)
 5·0 days to hatch in water kept at 18 °C (65 °F)
 5·0 days to hatch in water kept at 20 °C (68 °F)

Other writers on pike have frequently quoted evidence of the pike's fecundity by referring to the number of eggs found in specific fish. Buckland, for instance, recorded that a 28 lb pike had 292,320 eggs in it. Frost and Kipling demonstrated that the number of eggs laid down by a pike of any one size varied widely. For example, a pike of 3 lb may lay 28,500–41,700 eggs; a pike of 10 lb, 85,000–122,000 eggs, and a pike of 15 lb, 186,000–226,000 eggs.

These workers found that the weight of the female gonads (ovaries), expressed as a percentage of the total body weight, increases from about 2 per cent in August to about 7 per cent in October; 10 per cent in November; 12½ per cent in December; 14 per cent in January; 15 per cent in February; and finally, when fully ripe, up to 18–20 per cent. In male pike the maximum weight of the testes forms only 2·4 per cent of the total body weight. Spence reasoned that pike found in first-class order during the early season are specimens of a certain, or uncertain, number of fish which do not spawn every season. From the evidence this is unacceptable since (with one exception) Frost and Kipling have always found pike in possession of properly developing gonads; but, as a pike's scales do not erode at spawning time and therefore no spawning mark is left as in salmon scales, no corroborative evidence is available.

From work done by Munro in Scotland (1957), Healy in Ireland (1956), and Frost and Kipling in Windermere, it would appear that most pike spawn for the first time in their second or third year, and from the evidence so far obtained it is concluded that size rather than age determines when a pike will first spawn.

Of the details of the drama enacted each season on the spawning beds we had scant knowledge until Fabricius and Gustafson (1956) used aquarium tanks (24 ft × 28 ft × 14–18 in. deep) to observe the pike's spawning behaviour. They observed that a male pike approached the female by rubbing his nose gently against her head and flanks. If the female was still 'unripe' she was likely to repulse the male with a convulsive jerky head movement. (This behaviour shows a striking similarity to the mouthing movements displayed by a pike about to swallow a large fish, and the scientists say this is probably a 'displacement activity' which has become ritualized in the course of evolution.) On being accepted by a ripe female, the male took up a position parallel to her, and the two moved forward side by side, or more exactly eye to eye. This behaviour ensured that the milt emitted by the shorter male was released in front of the eggs to whirl among them in the jet currents caused by the movements of both fish. The spawning of the pike consisted of a series of mating acts every twenty-four seconds fol-

A 'right and left' at mallard followed by a high teal; and then on the rod a brace of pike together weighing nearly 50 lb – the work of one afternoon. Needless to say, such afternoons are rare, even in the west of Ireland!

lowed by rest periods of a minute or so, extending sometimes up to a period of forty minutes. A portion of milt and a portion of eggs were released when the male flicked its abdomen violently against the side of the female.

The whole operation was completed in one hour forty minutes by one couple and in five hours forty minutes by another. It was usual to find two or three males attending one female where the former delivered their mating thrusts in turn from both sides of the female.

Fabricius and Gustafson were able to show that the spawning of the pike was stimulated by a rise in the water temperature, and by increased light value. They found no evidence of 'territorial' behaviour, and all the males in attendance were able to take part in the spawning operation unless the tanks used in the experiment were small. When a small tank was used, one male became dominant and prevented the others from joining in the spawning operations.

Jardine was able to turn the fact of courtship to his advantage. Once he had caught the female, he deemed that it was true justice to catch the male. (I wonder how he always managed to catch the female first?)

Jardine made one of his rare flights of fancy when he claimed that most female pike of 16–18 lb are attended by male pike weighing 12 lb or so. As we know, male pike of this weight are comparatively rare. Perhaps we should be generous to Jardine and assume that the 12 lb pike which he so frequently caught in the company of bigger pike were other female pike – wrongly identified as male consorts.

Talking of flights of fancy, William Senior used the same expression to dismiss the story that female pike turn around after the spawning act to devour their male attendants. I am not able to say whether they are likely to do this on the instant, but I am quite certain that a dowager pike will hardly be influenced by sentiment once she has done with spawning and the demands of the intestine are with her once more. Nor is she likely to mete out different treatment to her younger sisters, as

witness this account from O'Gorman's *Practice of Angling* (the incident occurred at Dromore):

A large pike which had been hooked and was nearly exhausted, was suddenly seized and carried to the bottom. Every effort was made for nearly half an hour to bring this second fish to shore, but to no purpose; at length, however, by making a noise with the oars and pulling hard on the line, the angler succeeded in disengaging the first fish hooked, but on getting it to the surface it was torn as if by a large dog, though really doubtless by another pike; and as the weight of the fish thus ill-treated was 17 lb, the size of its retainer may be imagined.

Fabricius and Gustafson noticed another interesting aspect of pike behaviour. They found that a male pike was able to follow the scent trail left by a ripe female pike, even though she had been previously removed from a tank to which the male pike had been introduced.

Yarrell in his introduction to volume 1 of *British Fishes* (1836) describes how a 'Mr Jesse once caught a female pike during the spawning season, and nothing could drive the male away from the spot at which the female disappeared. . . .' Yarrell inferred that this behaviour demonstrated '. . . considerable attachment between parent fish'.

Whether Yarrell's inference is valid I am not qualified to say, but we can see from Gustafson's work that Jesse's male pike demonstrated its ability to follow a scent trail.

Why is the male pike smaller than the female?

So far as I am aware no writer or scientist has attempted to account for the fact that male pike (unlike the males of most other indigenous species) are unable to match the growth rate and ultimate size of the female.

After reading detailed reports of the spawning behaviour of pike (Fabricius and Gustafson 1956), it occurred to me that it might be possible to establish a reasoned theory for the phenomenon. Fabricius and Gustafson re-

This old print, *c.* 1805, shows livebaiting for pike with float-tackle

vealed that when a female pike accepts the approach of a male pike both move forward together and the spawning act is achieved while the fish are in motion. During the act the male pike's position in relation to the female is achieved through an eye-to-eye orientation. Now, we know that water displaced by a fish moving forward causes a current to flow in the opposite direction. This being the case, immediately after ejaculation the induced current sweeps the milt cloud 'through' the heavier falling eggs. Should an attendant male pike happen to be longer in body than its mate – so that the vent is to the rear of the female vent when he is moving forward with her eye to eye – then presumably the milt cloud would be released to the rear of the falling eggs, in which case the current would tend to separate the gonad products still further and so frustrate fertilization. When this circumstance obtains, spawning acts would tend to be unsuccessful. As a result, shorter-bodied male pike are likely to become the more successful parents.

If this is a true assessment of the reality of spawning then a process of natural selection would always be operating in favour of smaller male pike. The latter by definition would include a relatively high proportion of the younger element of the male population, which might be a separate factor favouring the overall success of the species.

Large male pike

From time to time reports are circulated announcing the capture of very big male pike. These reports are accepted by the public without question simply because the angler concerned is a respected and skilful pike fisherman. From my own experience most of these 'identifications' are made from mere visual inspection, and are at times mistakenly 'confirmed' when a white fluid thought to be milt is expressed from the vent. Only in rare instances are the pike opened, and when this is done the fatty tissues or 'curds' within the body cavity are usually wrongly identified as male gonads or testes.

In earlier days, when for research purposes my everyday routine found me as a member of a party netting pike out of England's largest lake, we found no positive means of distinguishing male pike from female pike by external features. It is true that towards the late autumn and particularly in the spring the females became bulky with spawn, and as a result we were usually able to distinguish them from their leaner brothers. It should be remembered that if a male pike is swollen with the remains of a recently captured large meal, then shape in itself becomes an unreliable means of identification.

It is probably true to say that there is more of a young pristine look about fast-growing 7 lb to 10 lb female pike, in comparison with the more grizzled and bedraggled look of male pike of the same weight, but this method of identification is not infallible. Normally, if the pike in question weighs 10 lb or more, the likelihood of it being a male pike is about 100 to 1 against, and if the pike in question weighs over 15 lb then the odds against it being a male are astronomical. I think the fact that the three largest males taken from a sample of some 7000 Windermere pike up to 35 lb weighed $11\frac{3}{4}$, $12\frac{1}{4}$ and $12\frac{1}{2}$ lb respectively, gives a fair indication of the validity of my estimate. It is reinforced by details obtained from Dr Kennedy of the Inland Fisheries Trust. From a sample of several tons of Irish pike up to 48 lb, he found the biggest male to be a fourteen-pounder. In Dr Kennedy's own words: 'The largest male pike weighed 14 lb, but we have not had many over 10 lb.'

To give some indication of how easy it is to find that a mistake has been made in determining the sex of a pike I refer readers to the photograph below of a 26½ lb pike caught in March 1968. This fish, sent to me for positive identification, was previously judged to be a male pike by one of the very best and most experienced pike anglers in the country. In the event, the fish proved to be a female as I had expected, but I nevertheless regard it as an unusual specimen for it possessed an undeveloped or diseased ovary on its left side (pike normally have two ovaries or two testes). The right ovary apparently compensated for the space left in the body cavity by growing to twice the normal size, in fact it measured 5½ in. in depth, which is an extraordinary measurement for this organ. The rest of the organs within the body cavity (viscera) were removed from the fish so that the ovaries could be seen

A 26½ lb female pike with one overdeveloped ovary and one undeveloped or diseased ovary, and the remains of a 1½ lb bream taken from its stomach

more clearly. The fish remains found in the stomach were those of a bream of approximately 1½ lb.

I took an opercular bone from the pike and obtained a reading from it – through the kindness of Dr Frost. Although it was not a good bone for reading purposes, the following information was obtained. The fish was eleven years old and measured 40 in. long from nose to fork, and by back calculation the following age/length figures were obtained:

1	2	3	4	5	6	7	8	9	10	11	*years*
10	19	24	31	33	34·5	36	38	39	39·5	40	*inches*

I feel that this information might be useful to Norfolk anglers as it will give them a rough guide to the age of various female pike by means of measurement.

Bucknall, in his book *Big Pike*, refers to a 32 lb male pike caught at Symonds Yat, and another of 29 lb caught near Maidstone. I am bound to suggest that one or other, or both, were females possessing completely diseased or undeveloped ovaries, because I do not know the proven existence of such a large male pike. Undeveloped ovaries look much the same as male testes. Incidentally, I learn from Dr Frost that at least one hermaphrodite pike has been positively identified.

Great care has to be taken not to identify white excreta as milt. Once again this is an easy mistake to make, for it is quite common for

pike excreta to be whitish in appearance. I cannot speak with authority on this matter but I suspect that parts of the bony remains of fish, once the flesh has been completely digested away by the stomach juices, pass through the pike's alimentary canal and are voided in the form of a milky white excrement.

What did the ancients have to say about large male pike? Jardine said: 'I never saw a really handsome male of heavy weight but once and that was a grand specimen of 28 lb which came from Lord Normanton's fishery on the Hampshire Avon.' It seems a pity that Jardine blotted his copy book for just one pike – which somebody else caught and probably identified. Spence, in his admirable book *The Pike Fisher*, looked to John Cooper & Son, the famous taxidermists, for advice on this matter. The Coopers proclaimed that in three generations the biggest male pike to pass through their hands weighed 12 lb.

The largest male pike to come my way will live in memory, but not for its great size. This 10 lb pike fought like a big 'un, and each time it came up to the surface gave the impression that it had come up to assess the tactical situation before rejoining battle. It took some time to subdue – perhaps ten minutes after taking my plug. The line (6 lb BS) was, of course, too light, but in those days (1952) I had not realized that pike which broke the line stood little chance of survival with a plug firmly fixed in their jaws.

Artificially propagating pike

We in Britain, as far as appreciation of the pike goes, have hardly passed through the barbarian stage, since many of us (though not hesitating to describe ourselves as sportsmen) would kick or jump on a pike just as if it were a dangerous snake. Elsewhere in this book we see evidence of the more enlightened views held in America, which, far from treating pike as vermin, actually creates legislation for the pike's protection. We know that in Russia pike are farmed for food production, and that elsewhere in Europe they are treated as a

The Oberegg pike: weight 55¼ lb, length 59½ in. This monster pike was found dead in Gunzstausee near Oberegg (Bavaria) in June 1975. Its body slimness is indicative of its decline prior to death, but its great length indicates a probable weight of some 66 lb during its prime, perhaps even topping 70 lb before spawning the previous April (By courtesy of *Blinker* magazine)

75

valuable crop. If this more enlightened view is supportable, and I for one have no hesitation in saying that it is, it is possible that ultimately we shall see the development of a similar trend in our own country. In this connection it is a pity that our general attitude to fisheries is almost entirely domestic and inward looking; for if we looked outward to other countries for new fishery management techniques we should be able to take advantage of much development work already undertaken.

For details of the American scene, I am indebted to Leroy Sorenson, Keen Buss and Arthur Bradford, who have worked on the artificial propagation of the members of the pike family. In the USA, hatchery propagation of pike dates as far back as 1890, and was done chiefly with muskellunge, which is the doyen of all the American pikes. Nevertheless, serious development of artificial means of propagating the Esocids was delayed until the early 1950s. At first, hatchability of the incubating eggs gave varied results: sometimes it was as low as 6 per cent and other times it was as high as 95 per cent. The research workers noticed that poor hatchability was encountered on the fringe of, or outside, the original natural range of the northern pike and muskellunge, and it was hypothesized that low hatchability was due to bad propagation techniques and/or the limitations relating to the inherent range of the two species. (Some state fishery departments, such as North Dakota, strip large numbers of pike and distribute up to 40 million eggs annually.) Because of the varied results obtained, scientists set out to improve the efficiency of artificial propagation. Their detailed findings would be out of place in this book; but not, I think, an outline of the more interesting points.

In order to remove the damaging silt found in natural sources of water, they installed a 300-gallon filter tank fitted with 4 in. inlet and outlet pipes. This provided the hatcheries with 3000 gallons of water per hour. To prevent damage, knotless nylon nets were used to trap the brood pike. Prior to stripping, each parent fish was anaesthetized with a tranquillizing agent (methyl pentynol). This way few eggs

were broken as the workers were able to work with relaxed fish; moreover, the tranquillizing agent had no detrimental effect on the fish. In time, to improve on the crude method of hand stripping the hen fish, a stripping instrument was developed which works on the same principle as the apparatus used by doctors to test blood pressure.

Because the male pike produces a small yield of milt (approximately 0·2 to 0·3 cubic centimetre) and because of the risk of contaminating the precious sperm with urine or mucus if the parent fish was stripped in the normal fashion, a technique was developed to drain off the urine, before the sperm was collected with a hypodermic needle. The milt thus obtained could be stored in a test-tube for five days if kept in a refrigerator (above freezing). Nevertheless, it was the normal practice to use the sperm fresh at the rate of five to ten drops to 8 oz of pike eggs.

The best rates of fertility (82 per cent) were obtained when the eggs and sperm were gently mixed together for three minutes before water was added, and for a further three minutes after it was added. The eggs were then washed in changes of water and allowed to stand without disturbance for a period of one to four hours. Serious disturbance of the eggs before the eyed-ova stage was reached caused considerable losses. Seventeen minute daily doses of formaldehyde, introduced into the water by way of a constant-flow syphon at a concentration of 1 part to 600, prevented fungus forming on the dead eggs. The brood fish were found to obtain benefit when the same formaldehyde solution was drained into their tanks as it cleared up fungus and infection caused by handling, and prevented new infection forming.

The most successful rearing of hatched fry was done in tanks 20 in. × 20 in. × 10 ft where the fry (1500 per tank) could be fed on graded food and dosed with the fungus-inhibiting daily formaldehyde treatment. After a short period the muskellunge fingerlings were weaned on to graded minnow fry, of which they ate ten per day. The muskellunge them-

A winter fishing party at Gogama, Ontario (By courtesy of Canadian Pacific Railway)

selves were graded at regular intervals to inhibit cannibalism.

It was observed that pike fingerlings would still kill minnows even when their appetites were satisfied, whereas muskellunge fingerlings stopped once this point was reached. If the muskellunge were ever kept short of food they soon resorted to cannibalism.

Four men working at the Union City Hatchery were able to produce in a typical year some 53,000 muskellunge fingerlings for ship-ment, together with 270,000 muskellunge fry. In addition, and in the same period, they produced some 8000 pike fingerlings and 615,000 pike fry.

These then are the latest findings from a comparatively new series of experiments. It takes but little imagination to realize that practical fish-farming developments of this sort will one day be as important to fishery owners as scientific farming developments are to agricultural farmers today. How else can we make room for the anglers joining our ranks, with the advent of ever-increasing leisure time?

9 Pug-nosed pike

When I worked on pike netting for the Freshwater Biological Association, I noticed a significant number of deformed pike, including a few whose scales were laid spiral fashion instead of in the more usual manner of overlapping horizontal lines. Perhaps the most common deformity (or should it be called the most common variation?) I noticed was pug-noses on pike.

As early as 1863, Pennell, in his *The Angler-Naturalist*, described the same deformity in trout. In 1877 Joseph Green of Kingsland caught a 1½ lb jack on Pennell's Spinning Flight (after it had missed the bait three times); it was found to have the pug-nose characteristic. The pike was kept alive in a pond and the water level was lowered so that an artist, Percy Highley, could make a drawing (see below).

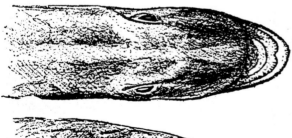

When the pond water was lowered to reveal the pike from which the original of this drawing was made, 'it was found that during the term of its incarceration it had polished off about four dozen roach and dace, a shoal of minnows, with one goldfish as a bon-bouche to top up with. . . .' (extract from the *Fishing Gazette*, 1897)

In 1937 there was another picture of a pug-nosed pike (*Fishing Gazette*, 4 December) with the following letter:

Dear Sir, We think the enclosed photo may be of interest to you. It is, as you will see, of a pug-nosed pike, which was caught on Sunday last by Mr Hodge, and was taken from a lake near Reading. This was a female fish and weighed 9 lb 3 oz. The length from the end of the tail to the tip of the upper jaw was 36 in. and to the lower jaw 37½ in. The fish, as you will see, is in somewhat poor condition, although it fought quite well and when we opened it up the flesh was quite white and very firm, and, we understand, was quite good eating.

In addition to this deformity, one eye was also not normal, for instead of the usual blue-black centre surrounded by a gold ring, in this case the gold part extended almost to the centre, and the blue-black portion was represented by a very small pear-shaped slit. The eye was, however, quite bright and had no sign of any kind of film over it such as one usually associates with a blind eye.

We are enclosing a few scales and shall be glad if you can obtain a reading of same, which we shall look forward to seeing in your paper.
    Yours faithfully,
    Perry & Cox,
    19 King's Road,
    Reading.

The editor responded:

We are pleased to give an illustration of this pike in which the deformity – commonly described as 'pug-nosed' – is very marked. For its length this fish was in very poor condition and should have weighed over 15 lb. We make out the age to be fourteen years.

In January 1980 *Angler's Mail* published yet another photograph of a pug-nosed pike – this time a 21-pounder – caught on a small trailed perch in an Irish lough. Through the good

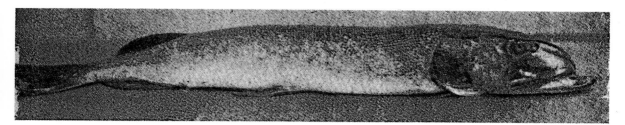

The pug-nosed pike from the *Fishing Gazette*, 4 December 1937

offices of Gerry Hughes of *Angler's Mail* I contacted Roy Smyth, a member of the Pikers' Club, who supplied the original photograph and who very kindly sent me a whole batch of photographs of pug-nosed pike, including the one shown here.

Members of the Pikers' Club have had many dozens of fish displaying the same facial characteristic and most of them were caught in one lake in County Leitrim.

The Pikers, incidentally, are going full-out in a campaign to re-educate their own country-men and continental pike fishermen in the serious matter of pike conservation.

They have a particularly big job on their hands, as the authorities north and south, in order to develop tourism – the lifeblood of their economies – encourage foreign visitors to fish Irish waters even during the period when pike are spawning.

Given time pike fishermen will see where their best interests lie. Let us hope that they will agree to return the vast majority of the pike they catch unharmed; limit themselves to *using* no more than two rods; observe a close season faithfully not only in their own countries but other countries as well.

Roy Smyth's pug-nosed pike

10 Hybrids of the pike family

In North America, hybrids between the various species of Esocids occur naturally, although none have been recorded from the two Eurasian forms, namely pike, *Esox lucius*, and amur pike, *E. reicherti* (this is not surprising since there is no overlap in their respective ranges). The first recording of a natural Esocid hybrid was made in 1918 (Embody) although hybrids in other families of fishes were recorded as early as 1887 (Day). So far in North America, six naturally occurring Esocid hybrids have been identified.

I have the kind permission of E. J. Crossman of the Royal Ontario Museum as well as that of Keen Buss and Jack Miller of the Pennsylvania Fish Commission to describe some of the interesting details of hybridization which have emerged from their combined researches. It was at one time believed that the naturally occurring hybrids were created by the accidental mixing of the gonad products of the different species within the spawning area; it would now appear that this is not the case, and that natural hybrids have resulted from the actual mating of the male of one species with the female of another. In Pennsylvania five members of the pike family namely muskellunge, pike, chain pickerel, redfin pickerel and grass pickerel were used as parent species to make twenty reciprocal crosses. Figure 20 summarizes the hatching results.

The low level of interspecific sterility surprised the biologists; in fact total sterility does not seem to exist, as one or other of the reciprocals was successful in each cross. (This means that if the male of one species was crossed unsuccessfully with the female of another, then the male of the latter species crossed successfully with the female of the former.) It was hypothesized that the various species had not been isolated long enough in time for interspecific sterility to become established. Hubbs noted that more hybrids occurred in a temperate habitat and claimed that this was due to a relatively short period of stabilization since glaciation (the Esocids inhabit temperate fresh waters).

The most interesting hybrid from the

Right: Mrs Dolores Opp Lapp with the record tiger musky of 50 lb 4 oz which she caught in Lac Dieux desert, Wisconsin, in June 1951 (By courtesy of Larry Ramsell)

Figure 20 Hatching results of pike crosses

(+ + + + Excellent hatch; + + + Fair to good hatch; + + Poor hatch; + Very poor hatch; — Unsuccessful cross; * Eggs hatch but all fry die)

| Female of | Result when crossed with male of | | | | |
	Chain pickerel	Grass pickerel	Redfin pickerel	Muskellunge	Northern pike
Chain pickerel	+ + + +	+ + + +	+ + + +	+ + +	+ + +
Grass pickerel	+ + + +	+ + + +	+ + + +	+ + + +	+ + + +
Redfin pickerel	+ + + +	+ + + +	+ + + +	+ + +	+ *
Muskellunge	+ +	+ + + + *	+ +	+ + + +	+ + + +
Northern pike	—	+	—	+ + + +	+ + + +

(1) Muskellunge (*Esox masquinongy*) from eastern Ontario, approximately 43 in. and 26 lb; (2) Redfin pickerel (*E. americanus americanus*), adult; (3) Natural hybrid tiger muskellunge (pike × muskellunge) from Little Vermillion Lake, Ontario; (4) Pike (*E. lucius*); (5) Artificial hybrid (hatchery-reared) pike (male) × chain pickerel, 12 in. long; (6) Chain pickerel (*E. niger*) from Quebec, 14 in. long, 1 lb; (7) Silver pike, spotless mutant of *E. lucius*; (8) Amur pike *E. reicherti*; (9) Grass pickerel (*E. a. vermiculatus*) from Jones Creek, Leeds Co., Ontario

angler's point of view is the one obtained from muskellunge and pike. As early as 1938 the greater vitality and lower egg mortality of this hybrid was known; apparently fish hatchery workers in Minnesota used a male pike to fertilize eggs from a muskellunge when no male muskellunge was available. Later it was noticed that the muskellunge/pike hybrid had a faster growth rate than the pure-bred muskellunge; in four months the former grew to 11–12 in., while the pure-breds grew to 7–8 in. It was further noted that the hybrid was hardier than the parent species.

The North Americans have adopted the name true tiger muskellunge to describe the cross, but this nomenclature is rather confusing, for in certain areas – notably Minnesota and Wisconsin – the pure-bred muskellunge exhibits a barred pattern which had led to the local use of the name tiger musky. Nevertheless, confusion could be eliminated if the name tiger musky was reserved for the hybrid muskellunge/pike. Certainly, the name aptly describes the hybrid; it also provides an acceptable and easily recognizable name for a fish which is otherwise unnamed by scientists (hybrids are not given scientific names).

When we read of the superior sporting qualities of pure-bred muskellunge, most of us who already view the pike with relish would jump with joy at the prospect of having the former introduced into our own waters. It might be argued that introducing them into our own waters could be a dangerous proposition. Against this, however, North American experience demonstrates that where pike are introduced into musky waters the pike generally take over, so we should hardly expect a reversal of this phenomenon if muskies were introduced into British waters; even so, in these matters we are usually served best by adopting a wait-and-see policy – at least until such time as it takes to fully establish the facts.

Tiger muskies, however, could be introduced in waters where pike are absent, without any risk of a population explosion, since hybrid couples are unable to reproduce themselves. By introducing them we would be able to mark the

effect on a local fish population created by a limited number of major predators. It is my contention that an experiment of this kind would enable us to maintain more control than we could expect to have with the introduction of pike, so often advocated by well-meaning anglers who wish to thin out populations of stunted fish (usually roach, rudd, bream or perch), because unless we plant only very large pike we have no means at our disposal of ensuring that we avoid planting fish of both sexes. When pike are introduced for this purpose they are likely to multiply and then we are left with a situation that could well be irreversible.

If tiger muskies were introduced into established pike territories it would be interesting to see if the hybrids followed the behaviour patterns of muskellunge (for example, muskellunge spawn later in the year), or followed the behaviour patterns of pike. If they responded to pike behaviour patterns it is quite possible that female hybrids would pair up with male pike and produce viable eggs since this particular back cross has been obtained by artificial means, whereas the back cross between a male hybrid and female pike is not viable.

It is easy to see one possible outcome which would affect the angler if female tiger muskies did mate with male pike – we would have the same problem of identification when dealing with record claims for pike as we already have with roach/bream hybrids, etc.

Although accounts of the sporting qualities of this hybrid vary, it is generally agreed that they fight harder than pike. If tiger muskies fight better than our own native loch pike then they must be truly great fighters. When we realize that a pure-bred muskellunge is capable of growing to a weight in excess of 100 lb, and when we couple this realization with the known faster growth rate of the tiger musky, we are entitled to visualize the birth of a great sporting fish. Such a fish, in spite of our present limited knowledge, could one day make good the loss of the Atlantic salmon. (The prospect of the extinction of the Atlantic salmon has already been hinted at by researchers.)

11 Notes on the pike (Esox lucius) in North America

Most British pike anglers are content to contemplate pike within the boundaries of the British Isles, although the same species, *Esox lucius*, is widespread in parts of Europe, Asia and North America. The Americans have been at pains to explore the environment and the natural history of their pike and as a consequence are able to tell us much of interest about them. I am indebted to Keen Buss, a noted American Fisheries biologist, for all the details included in this chapter on American pike.

In America the belief that the piscivorous (fish-eating) habits of the Northern pike (our pike *E. lucius*) were detrimental to other fishes has persisted down the years. Indeed, in 1875 the pike was described by the Fish Commissioners of Michigan as the 'Devil fish'.

As a result, a policy of extermination was prescribed and practised, and it was not until 1917 that William Kendall published the first favourable report for the species. He wrote: 'It is also beginning to be recognised that there are still places for them (pike) in both the human and the natural economy . . . there have been waters in which some pike and other fishes have lived in reciprocal counterpoise from time immemorial, notwithstanding the condemned characteristic voracity of the pike.' As time went on pike began to assume in the minds of men their rightful place in the ecology of fishing lakes. By 1930 the State of Michigan placed a legal limit of 14 in. on these fish and allowed a daily limit of five. They were also protected during the spawning seasons in all lakes and in some streams. By 1956 seventeen out of twenty-two states considered Northern pike to be important predators.

Buss tells us that out of a total of 250 references and personal communications, many of the latest reports refer to the im-portance of pike populations in maintaining good lake fishing. States from Montana, Nebraska, North Dakota, and east through the Northern pike range to Ohio and Pennsylvania are attempting to improve these populations through artificial propagation, restrictions, preservation of spawning areas, and research.

Space prevents one from summarizing the findings of American researches but I think the reader will be interested in the following series of somewhat unconnected titbits.

A few adult spawners die each year on the spawning grounds. In Michigan, at least 7 per cent of the breeders died in the spawning area. A number of spawners apparently jumped out on the bank, some died from injuries suffered in spawning and some were eaten by larger pike and other predators.

When it is hatched, the Northern pike fry does not resemble the adult. It is yellowish grey and measures 0·3 to 0·4 in. in length. With the exception of the pectorals, the fins are not yet formed. The fry at the time of hatching has no functional mouth; but as the fry develops, the mouth migrates from a ventral to a terminal position. During this period the fry lives off the yolk sac.

The greatest mortality factor is predation on fry. Two predators which account for large numbers of fry are the *Dytiscus* and *Notonecta* beetles. It has been observed in Sweden that a *Dytiscus* larva would kill about five pike in two days and would attack pike fingerlings up to 3·7 in. long.

When cannibalism occurs, it depends on the variation in the size of the pike, population density, and the available food. The food of the young cannibal is usually less than 80 per cent of the cannibal's length. The presence of a plentiful food supply acts as a buffer against cannibalism. The losses of eggs due to egg

A musky caught at French River, Ontario. Since it is the lady who holds the rod, it would seem that she is the captor of this fine-looking musky that probably weighs over 20 lb. The ladies' record pike in Britain is probably held by Mrs Howes who caught, according to the *Fishing Gazette* of 12 March 1949, a 30 lb pike at Altringham Pond, Norfolk, on 1 March 1922

predators were estimated to be 98 per cent and by the time the fry had reached 0·8 in. the total mortality was 99·4 per cent.

Pike exercise a qualitative choice in their dietary items as well as a quantitative choice (see Chapter 4), since in a European aquarium experiment it was found that pike preferred roach to sticklebacks. As a general rule,

however, the pike's food preference is for the most abundant food item.

In Minnesota, a stomach pump was developed to wash out the stomach and collect the contents in a specimen bottle. Apparently this procedure causes no harm to the fish. It would be a most useful item for the less squeamish British pike angler to have in his kit.

Males rarely exceed 24 in. in length. The largest male reported in Saskatchewan was $30\frac{1}{2}$ in. long, weighed 6 lb, and was ten years old. The largest pike from the American continent was taken in Lake Tschotagama in the St John's drainage system in 1890. It was reputed to weigh 49 lb.

This giant muskellunge, 7 ft 4 in. long, weighed 110 lb. It is probably the largest specimen of any member of the pike family of which a photograph exists. It was taken by an unknown angler on rod and line in Intermediate Lake, Antrim County, Michigan in 1919 (By courtesy of Cord Communications Corporation, New York)

The North American rod-caught record pike weighed 46 lb 2 oz and was 52½ in. long. It was caught from Sacandaga Reservoir, New York, in 1940.

In Michigan, river spawners were found to be more restless and far ranging, while pike which spawned in marshes along the shore were more sedentary in nature. Larger pike were also found to move more than the smaller pike. One pike tagged one year, was caught the following year forty-nine miles from the point of tagging. Another pike travelled ten miles in twenty-two hours at an average speed of about half a mile per hour.

In summer, lake pike are usually found in, or close to, weed-beds in about 4 ft of water; but in the autumn they may move to precipitous stormy shores. In winter they may return to the summer habitat, but larger pike seem to move into deeper water.

The species of fish which are utilized for food influence the habitat of pike and the depth at which pike are found.

This statement is, I think, the most profound in all Buss's collected data since it will help the angler to understand that pike fishing in locations strange to him may be quite different from what he is used to. In Windermere, pike nets are set in water up to only 30 ft deep, as experience shows that nets set deeper than 30 ft rarely catch pike, whereas in Wisconsin pike can be taken in gill nets in water up to 50 ft deep. Pike caught in deep water were following shoals of fish (cisco) in order to feed on them; these pike were never under 3 lb in weight. In Canada pike have been occasionally taken in nets from Lake Nipigon from depths in excess of 100 ft. Most pike, however, are taken from water of less than 15 ft deep.

Pike are more active during certain periods of the day. One study found that they were most active between 8 and 11 a.m. and again between 2 and 4 p.m. There seemed to be a definite rest period between 11.30 a.m. and 1 p.m. These periods of activity probably vary with the seasons and latitude. In the north, where days are longer, the peak of activity may be between 5 and 6 p.m. The catch of anglers is influenced by these periods of activity. Almost all pike returning from their spawning runs have empty stomachs and it is at this time that large catches can be made.

Fish taken early in the morning tend to have empty stomachs due to the previous night's digestion. This is why early morning is considered to be one of the better fishing periods.

The number of canine teeth on the pike's lower jaw is constant throughout life, averaging about sixteen per jaw. Although the canines are subject to loss throughout life, they are constantly replaced by accessory teeth developed in each section of the gum.

Buss enthusiastically quotes Jordan's classic statement which describes voracious pike as 'mere machines for the assimilation of other organisms'.

Part Two

Great Pike

A life-size portrait of the Lough Derg pike, with relics
(Barrie Cooke)

12 The largest pike

The largest pike (*Esox lucius*) ever recorded, to which we can give any credence even though we cannot list it as a rod-caught fish, was a pike weighing 114 lb. On 21 November 1925 the *Fishing Gazette* published in 'Notes from Ireland' an abbreviated story of a huge pike that was stranded on the Washing Bay in Lough Neagh during the Crimean War of 1854–5.

The writer of the note got the story from a Lough Neagh fisherman who was prepared to take an oath on the veracity of his statement about the fish. He said, 'Time and again I heard him tell the story, and he never varied a word: "It was the wayte [weight] of two fifty sixes, and an empty male [meal] bag," roughly 114 lb.'

The world's biggest rod-caught pike

What is known about the capture of the huge 90½ lb pike by John Naughton and Patrick Sheehy in Lough Derg on Friday, 9 May 1862, has been described in *The Domesday Book of*

This fine old picture of the Washing Bay on Lough Neagh is by kind permission of the Northern Ireland Tourist Board

Mammoth Pike. Since that book's publication in 1979, there has been an interesting development.

In late August 1980, when I arrived at my fishing cottage in Co. Mayo, I found a letter from the Irish artist Barrie Cooke. Here is an extract from the letter:

I had thought of writing to you months ago. Because for the last two years I have been working on a painting about the legendary (?) Lough Derg pike. I thought it might interest you. In fact, your splendid Big Pike book was published about midway in the process and gave me a most valuable impetus. Your very credible documentation added to my own belief at just the right time. Anyway, the painting is to be exhibited for the first time at the Exhibition of Living Art in the Douglas Hyde Gallery, Trinity College, Dublin, starting on the 13th August. I hope you'll get a chance to see it. It is titled, *Portrait of the Lough Derg Pike – Life Size with Relics*.

With best wishes, Barrie Cooke.

On my way back to England I saw the painting and subsequently obtained permission from Barrie Cooke to reproduce the coloured original in black and white. Looking at the painting was a stimulating experience,

because the pike was life-size. It gave one the unique chance of seeing a 90-pounder in almost real life.

The largest pike of modern times?

In December 1979 I heard from Richard Lütticken, the editor of *Blinker*, a West German angling magazine, that a new record pike had been caught in Switzerland.

Like so many other big pike this one is also controversial – and no wonder.

It was caught by Jürg Nötzli of Zurich on 15 June 1979, from a pond or small lake – Reuss-Weiher – on a plug bait (or 'wobbler' as the West Europeans prefer to call it), but it was not reported by its captor until November 1979.

It weighed, according to the notice, 62½ lb and it was 57½ in. long.

I wrote to Mr H. J. Dietiker, the editor of the Swiss angling newspaper *Petri-Heil* which first published the story of this monster pike. He very kindly sent me the original report dated December 1979. The report is a long one, and so I have picked out the salient points for my readers.

The editor of *Petri-Heil* admitted that at first he was doubtful, but on checking and re-checking the pieces of information he was satisfied that a new European and probable World-Record-Rod-Caught-pike had been landed.

The bait used was a gold coloured Rapala plug fished on 20 lb BS Platil line in conjunction with an Abu rod and an Abu Cardinal 55 reel. Jürg Nötzli waited four months before announcing details of his catch – not because, as he averred, he had anything to hide – but simply because he wanted to protect his fishing and not be swamped by other anglers. Eventually he was persuaded by Daniel Cuonz, a tackle dealer in Zurich, to tell his story. When he did he was supported by two witnesses, Ludwig Zimmermann and Karl Thalmann.

Jürg Nötzli unfolded his account thus:

He was fishing with natural baits on two float-tackle outfits, idly passing the time

The 62½ lb Swiss pike

betting with himself, in his imagination, that his red float would go down before his yellow float, when suddenly he became aware of the presence of a large predatory fish: a swarm of small fish sprayed out into the air as a dark shadow cut through their middle.

Neither bait was touched, so Jürg broke down one of the float rigs and fitted up a spinning bait tied to a steel trace and cast it to the likely lie. There was no response, so he took off the spoon and put on a large plug and cast towards some reeds where he thought the pike now lay.

After his third cast, and when he had made only two turns of the handle, the rod dipped without recovery and the reel stopped dead, causing his companion to remark that he must be hooked into a sunken log or tree.

Before he could reply, 'all hell let loose' as a long black body shot out of the water and momentarily seemed to hang in the air. As it jumped the fish by chance faced him, and as it stretched open its jaws to their ultimate frightening extent in an attempt to blow out the plug Jürg could see the bait was hooked into, and outlined against, the deep red of its gills. Seconds later the pike fell back into the water.

Jürg, even though he had had experience of fighting many big pike, could only think of one thing – to stop the pike going into the reeds in what was a very restricted playing area. As fish and man pulled in different directions, his friend Charlie, and other passers-by attracted to the scene, offered him advice. During his inquisition he had no fear of his line breaking, but he worried about the strength of his steel trace; and even though the pike twice came close enough to have been netted or gaffed, it played for a full forty minutes before his friend managed to beach it on the field bankside.

With knees trembling and hands shaking he could hardly believe that he had actually landed such a huge fish, indeed, ever since, in those quieter reflective moments when he has relived the battle, his pulse has quickened and he has sweated uncontrollably.

After weighing, measuring and photographing the catch the pike was disposed of in the usual mid-European style, namely, its head was cut off to be preserved as a trophy and the body was cooked and eaten. Fish scientist Dr Bel inspected the head and affirmed that the pike was $12\frac{3}{4}$ years old and commented that he would have liked to have had the opportunity to have studied the fish while it was alive and that a museum should have had the chance to preserve the whole fish.

After the public announcement of the catch and while suspicion and criticism of the handling of the whole affair was mounting, the editor of *Petri-Heil* conducted an experiment and found that a reasonably strong man could hold up a $62\frac{1}{2}$ lb weight with two fingers as Nötzli did in the picture.

Quite naturally all sorts of people wanted to look at the scene of the pike's capture. They were to be disappointed because the pond or small lake outside Berne hardly existed any longer due to a much-lowered water level. Indeed, it was practically dry by now and its population of fish had already been removed by fishery officials. Just the same, witnesses were willing to swear that the water level was normal during the previous June when the pike had been caught.

Amazingly, in one respect this big pike story differs from all previous pike stories. The fortunate angler Jürg Nötzli, since his capture of the $62\frac{1}{2}$-pounder, had caught two more monsters, weighing 40 lb and 42 lb respectively, which he had kept alive in a pond so that any doubters could see for themselves.

Jürg Nötzli's trophy

These pike were duly witnessed by the editorial staff of *Petri-Heil* (the fish were caught by Nötzli in the Türlersee), who hoped to publish details of their capture in the next issue.

The following issue of *Petri-Heil* (February 1980) published a letter from Louis Irion, an official responsible for adjudicating competition entries. The letter was entitled 'Mitchell Fish of the Month', a prize, incidentally, which Nötzli's pike had won. Irion raised the following points:

1 He wanted confirmation of the details of the emptying of the pond or lake by the fisheries officer of the Swiss canton responsible for the area.
2 He wanted to see the negative that produced the print of the pike that graced the front page of *Petri-Heil*.
3 He wanted to see and test the set of scales used for the weighing of the fish.
4 He wanted confirmation of the pike's head *diameter*, stated to be 55 cm, which if it were correct would make the head too big to put in an average-sized bucket of 38 cm diameter.
5 How could he, he asked, as an adjudicator, not be curious when a claimant who, having achieved recognition for a 62½-pounder, now wanted him to believe that he had since caught two more pike, by fair means, weighing 40 lb and another weighing over 42 lb?

In the same issue Jürg Nötzli responded by first reoffering the Mitchell prize to be added to the prizes in the next boys' fishing competition. He then answered Irion point by point:

1 Louis Irion would have to contact the canton fisheries officer directly for his answer.
2 The negative of the photograph (although taken by an amateur photographer) was available for inspection.
3 If Louis Irion contacted him by telephone he would arrange for him to see the scales and share a bottle of wine in the very restaurant where the pike was weighed, prepared, cooked and eaten.
4 He never said that 55 cm was the diameter of the pike's head – only the circumference.*
5 As for the genuineness of the other two pike, the editor of *Petri-Heil* as well as other witnesses had seen them with their own eyes.

Nötzli concluded with these words:

Fishing is my hobby and I don't want my catches to be in any doubt and for this reason I have given details of how and where I made these last catches. I don't want to be involved in any controversy and the nice letters I have received from many fishermen far outweigh the critical ones.

* The editor of *Petri-Heil* admitted that this was the newspaper's mistake.

13 The Big Pike List

William Senior, sometime editor of the *Field*, declared: 'The pike is a most convenient fish for the exercise of imagination.' Nobody who has been close to angling for any length of time would argue with that statement. A splendid example is provided by the 'Emperor's Pike', the biggest pike in literature. Old writers tell us that it was taken from a lake near Mannheim in Württemberg in 1497. Gesner, writing in 1558, put the weight at 350 lb and the length at 19 ft.

A reasonable man would think these measurements quite enough to ensure fame, but no, our Mannheim pike possessed a copper ring attached to its gill, with an inscription indicating that it had been planted in the lake by Emperor Frederick II in the year 1230 – 267 years before. The fish's skeleton was preserved in Mannheim Cathedral and the story greatly impressed early writers, until it was proved fraudulent by a naturalist who found that the pike's backbone had 'acquired' a considerable number of extra vertebrae.

Keen Buss gave the story a new twist when he wrote: 'According to the normal length-weight ratios found in "modern" pike, a nineteen foot pike would weigh about 3,000 pounds.' The photograph of the Mannheim pike is by courtesy of the Natural History Museum, and is taken from a painting in their possession.

For my own part, while I am on the one hand thoroughly entertained by the imaginative stories which adorn pike-angling literature, I am nevertheless more positively fascinated by those accounts that have the ring of truth about them – and more still by those few that have the enduring stamp of authority as well.

For the purposes of this book, however, I shall forgo the temptation of recording the highly improbable and trim my list to the possible, which includes over 100 pike weighing 40 lb or more. It may come as a surprise to some to note the despair that Senior felt in 1900, when compelled to write: 'I myself and John Bickerdyke once strove diligently to obtain facts, and our conclusion was that there was no evidence, which could be considered beyond dispute of any pike of modern times that exceeded the weight of 40 lb.' Senior was obliged to print a footnote to his comment when the bodies of two pike (Nos. 84 and 211 on my list) were delivered to the *Fishing Gazette*, which printed the details in May 1900.

It is my intention now and in the future to collect, and correct by way of research, reports on all pike which would seem to qualify for my Big Pike List in the hope that pike anglers as yet unborn can be weaned on a more reliable list of the big ones.

In order to put this project into effect I would be pleased to receive any communication from readers who can give any information on fish in, or missing from, my list. Please write to:

'Hollytree'
Wood Lane
South Heath
Great Missenden
Buckinghamshire

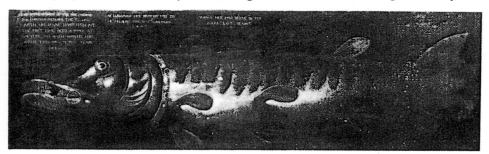

The Big Pike List

No.	Weight lb	oz	Length (in.)	Girth (in.)	Location	Country	Captor
1	96				Broadwood Lake, Killaloe	Ireland	Unknown
2	92				River Shannon	Ireland	Unknown
3	92				River Shannon	Ireland	
4	90	08	68		Lough Derg	Ireland	John Naughton
5	90?		69		River Shannon	Ireland	
6	78				Lake in County Clare	Ireland	Mr O'Flanagan
7	72				Loch Ken	Scotland	John Murray
8	70?				Endrick River	Scotland	Unknown
9	68		54	36	Llangorse Lake	Wales	Owen Owen
10	65				Lough Derg	Ireland	Howill Considine
11	65		55		Lower Lough Erne	Ireland	Fred Johnston
12	64				Lough Derg	Ireland	Jonnie Kane
13	63				Lough Conn	Ireland	
14	61		48½	31¾	River Bann	Ireland	J. Dempsey
15	61				Derries Lough	Ireland	J. Boylan
16	60		53¼		Dowdeswell Reservoir	England	
17	56				Lough Erne	Ireland	Mr Rotherham
18	56		60		Drum Lough	Ireland	William Vogan
19	55		54	28	Lough Gur	Ireland	James Landrigan
20	53	11	53¾	29½	Lough Sheelin	Ireland	Patrick Kenny
21	53				'Tomgraney Lake'	Ireland	Constable Quinn
22	53				Lough Mask	Ireland	Pat Summerville
23	53		53	27	Lough Key	Ireland	P. J. O'Connor
24	53		51	36	Lough Conn	Ireland	John Garvin
25	52		55		Whittlesea Mere	England	Unknown
26	52		51	33	Lough Macnean	Ireland	Thomas Kenny
27	50	08	50		Lough Mask	Ireland	Inland Fisheries Trust
28	50				Duke of Newcastle's lake	England	Unknown
29	49	14	54		Loch Alva	Scotland	Colonel Thornton
30	49				Lough Derg	Ireland	Unknown
31	48				Furnace Pond	England	Unknown
32	48				Lough Corrib	Ireland	Edward McDonagh
33	48				River Camlin	Ireland	J. Delmer
34	48		52½	25	Lough Corrib	Ireland	G. O'Sullivan

Date	Method	Source	Visual evidence
		Belton, *The Angler in Ireland* (1834)	
1822	lifted out	W. H. Maxwell, *Wild Sports of the West* (1832)	
1839		F. Day, *Fishes of Great Britain and Ireland* (1889), vol. 2, p. 145	
May 1862	trailing	*Limerick Chronicle*, 15 May 1862	
Dec. 1926	found dead	*Field*, 7 April 1927	
Aug. *c.* 1830	rod and line	W. Thompson, *The Natural History of Ireland* (1849–56)	
1774	livebaiting	The Rev. W. B. Daniel, *Rural Sports* (1801)	skull preserved
c. 1934	marooned	F. Buller: interview 1967	skull preserved
Nov. 1846	spinning	Col. P. Swills: letter to Lord Inverurie, 1897	cased
1849	unknown	*Field*, 20 January 1877	
April 1880	trailing	*Field*, 14 June 1890, p. 881	head preserved
c. 1856	pitchforked	F. T. Minchin: letter to Lord Inverurie, 1897	
1875	livebaiting	*Fishing Gazette*, 12 May 1900, p. 357	head preserved
March 1894	stunned	*Fishing Gazette*, 19 May 1900, p. 378	
1948	shot	*Impartial Reporter*, 19 August 1948; *Fishing Gazette*, 9 October 1948	
1896	found dead	*Magazine of Sports and Pastimes*, vol. 66 (1896)	cased
c. 1885	trimmer	*Fishing Gazette*, 13 October 1888	
April 1894	lifted out	*Field*, 16 June 1894, p. 874	
Aug. 1909	otter board	*Fishing Gazette*, 25 September 1909	
Aug. 1901	shot	*Field*, 7 and 21 September 1901	
summer 1881	rod and line	*Field*, vol. 97 (1901), p. 125	
May 1898	trailing	*Fishing Gazette*, 28 May 1898	
April 1900	trailing	*Fishing Gazette*, 5 May 1900	
July 1920	trailing	*Fishing Gazette*, 14 September 1929	photo of skull
1851	stranded	R. B. Marston in *Fishing Gazette*, 4 January 1907	drawing
Aug. 1898	spinning	*Fishing Gazette*, 30 July 1898	
March 1966	netted	Dr M. Kennedy: conversation with F.B.	
Oct. 1823	choked	H. Cholmondeley Pennell, *The Book of Pike* (1865)	
June 1784	livebaiting	The Rev. W. B. Daniel, *Rural Sports* (1801)	engraving
c. 1838	unknown	W. Thompson, *The Natural History of Ireland* (1849–56)	
1830	stranded	*Fishing Gazette*, 23 August 1919	
1905	gaffed	*Field*, 6 May 1905, p. 745	head preserved
1910	unknown	*Record of Sports, 1911*, p. 18	
1961	nightlining	Author's visit with G. O'Sullivan, 1970	cased

No.	Weight lb	oz	Length (in.)	Girth (in.)	Location	Country	Captor
35	48		56		Lough Mask	Ireland	Inland Fisheries Trust
36	47	11	53		Loch Lomond	Scotland	Tommy Morgan
37	47		48½	26	Summer Castle lake	England	Unknown
38	47				Lough Sheelin	Ireland	Unknown
39	46		51		Chillington Pool	England	C. F. Giffard
40	46		47½		Lough Mask	Ireland	Inland Fisheries Trust
41	45	08	49	22½	Lough Conn	Ireland	Bernard Browne
42	45				Windermere	England	Unknown
43	45				Loch Leven	Scotland	Unknown
44	45		57		Lough Lene (Westmeath)	Ireland	P. Cruise
45	45		49½	26	Lough Conn	Ireland	Inland Fisheries Trust
46	45				Lough Corrib	Ireland	Peter Lydon
47	44				Lough Carra	Ireland	John Walsh
48	44				Lough Gur	Ireland	P. Higgins
49	43	08			Lough Corrib	Ireland	Danny Goldrick
50	43				River Moy	Ireland	Mr Barrett
51	43				Lowfield Lake	Ireland	J. J. Doyle
52	43		48	26	Lough Erne	Ireland	Mrs McManus
53	43		52		Lough Conn	Ireland	C. Driscoll
54	43				Ballyshannon Reservoir	Ireland	Inland Fisheries Trust
55	42	08	47½		Deene Park Lake	England	Gamekeeper
56	42	08			Lough Mask	Ireland	W. Carney
57	42	08	48	25	Martnaham Loch	Scotland	Angus Macpherson
58	42	08	52¾		Lough Corrib	Ireland	Inland Fisheries Trust
59	42	05			Loughrea	Ireland	Patsy Burrell
60	42		42	33	Munden Hall, Fleet	England	Unknown
61	42				Whittlesea Mere	England	Unknown
62	42				Lough Macnean	Ireland	Mr Farry
63	42				River Nore	Ireland	Mr Despard's herdsman
64	42		47	25	Wroxham Broad	England	John Nudd
65	42				Lough Corrib	Ireland	Unknown
66	42		48½	25½	Lough Arrow	Ireland	John Bourne
67	42		48	30	Lough Derg	Ireland	John Monaghan
68	42				Lough Corrib	Ireland	G. Lyons

Date	Method	Source	Visual evidence
March 1958	netted	Dr M. Kennedy: Inland Fisheries Trust records	photo
July 1945	livebaiting	*Angling*, July 1951, p. 385	photo
June 1799	stranded	The Rev. W. B. Daniel, *Rural Sports* (1801)	head preserved
1896	unknown	*Fishing Gazette*, 13 February 1897, p. 121	
June 1822	unknown	*Annals of Sporting and Fancy Gazette*, June 1822	
March 1957	netted	Dr M. Kennedy: Inland Fisheries Trust records	cased
April 1917	trailing	Letter in F.B.'s possession, 1 May 1917; *Angler's News*, 15 June 1918	
1813	dragged out	*Fishing Gazette*	
c. 1880	unknown	*Fishing Gazette*, 25 August 1883	
1956	unknown	Colin Graham: letter to F.B., 1974	
Spring 1957	netted	Dr M. Kennedy: Inland Fisheries Trust records	cased
1965	longlining	*Angling Times*, 28 May 1965	photo
June 1938	trailing	*Fishing Gazette*, 9 July 1938, p. 69	
1945	spinning	*Angling*, April/June 1946, p. 797	
March 1973	netted	Irish Tourist Board: March 1973 news-sheet	photo
1876	unknown	*Field*, 22 January 1876	
1910	rod and line	*Fishing Gazette*, 9 July 1910	
March 1926	lifted out	*Fishing Gazette*, 12 June 1926	cased
March 1954	trailing	Head of fish given to F.B.	head cased
Feb. 1959	netted	O. M. Reed's papers	
c. 1760	shot	Arthur Cove: conversation with F.B., 1969	cased
July 1932	rod and line	*Where to Fish 1937/38*	
1964	livebaiting	Letter from captor, January 1980	photo
March 1978	netted	Hugh Gough: letter to F.B., 1978	photo
March 1960	netted	Secretary, Loughrea Angling Association, 1973	photo
c. 1790	killed by freezing	The Rev. W. B. Daniel, *Rural Sports* (1801)	head preserved
c. 1850	unknown	J. Wentworth Day: conversation with F.B., 1968	cased
c. 1885	unknown	*Fishing Gazette*, 7 February 1885	
c. 1899	unknown	Hi Regan, *How and Where to Fish in Ireland* (1902)	
1901	livebaiting	*Angling Times*, 12 June 1959	cased
1905	unknown	*Field*, 6 May 1905, p. 745	head preserved
May 1908	hand-netted	*Fishing Gazette*, 10 December 1910	cased
March 1909	netted	*Field*, 24 April 1909	
March 1918	trailing	J. F. Hampton, *Hampton on Pike Fishing* (1947)	

No.	Weight lb	oz	Length (in.)	Girth (in.)	Location	Country	Captor
69	42				Ballyvarey River	Ireland	J. Devaney
70	42				Loughrea	Ireland	M. Coyne
71	42		47½	26½	Lough Conn	Ireland	John Garvin
72	42		52		Lough Ree	Ireland	Peter Egan
73	42		50½	24	River Barrow	Ireland	Mervyn Watkins
74	42				Upper Lough Erne	Ireland	W. Gilroy
75	41	12			Lough Nacrilly	Ireland	Robert Cardwell
76	41	08			Lough Rodgers	Ireland	P. J. Mannion
77	41	08	51½	25½	Lough Sheelin	Ireland	Joe Allen
78	41	08			Lough Ree	Ireland	Jack McNally
79	41		49		Lough Conn	Ireland	Patrick Cawley
80	41		43		Lough Muckno	Ireland	Patrick Hand
81	41		42		Lough Corrib	Ireland	Thomas Courtenay
82	41				Lough Ennell	Ireland	Paddy O'Toole
83	41				Lough Mask	Ireland	Inland Fisheries Trust
84	40	08	50	27½	Lough Arrow	Ireland	Mr Ballintine
85	40	06	44	25	Private lake, Litton Hill	England	Michael Hopwood
86	40	04	48	22	Lough Mask	Ireland	William Burke
87	40	04	49½		Loch Ken	Scotland	Kurt Vogel
88	40	01	47½	26	Horsey Mere	England	Peter Hancock
89	40		42	24	Totteridge Pond	England	Unknown
90	40		49	25	Upton House, Edgehill	England	Col. P. Fitzgerald
91	40				River Don	England	John Young
92	40				Lough Derg	Ireland	'The Olive'
93	40				Unknown	Ireland	Unknown
94	40		44¼		Suffolk	England	R. S. Fennings
95	40				Cosstessey (Norwich)	England	
96	40				Carrick on Shannon	Ireland	William Shanney
97	40		48	28	Lough Derg	Ireland	John Cannon
98	40		49½	26	Lough Conn	Ireland	Unknown
99	40				Lough Erne	Ireland	J. H. Thompson
100	40				Lough Conn	Ireland	Mr Clarke
101	40				Lough Ervey	Ireland	Mr Lynch
102	40				Lough Ennell	Ireland	Paddy Dolan

Date	Method	Source	Visual evidence
April 1936	unknown	*Angler's News*, 5 June 1937, p. 547	
Aug. 1936	rod and line	J. F. Hampton, *Hampton on Pike Fishing* (1947)	
March 1944	trailing	*Field*, 15 July 1944, p. 68	
1955	rod and line	*Angling Times*, 20 May 1955	
March 1964	spinning	Irish Specimen Fish Committee, 24 April 1964	
March 1969	spinning	*Angling Times*, 21 May 1970	photo
	livebaiting	*Angling Times*, 26 April 1963	
June 1922	rod and line	*Where to Fish 1926*, p. 35	
Oct. 1946	trailing	*Irish Angling Magazine*, vol. 1, no. 5	cased
Sept. 1951	rod and line	*Field and Stream in Ireland*, March 1956, p. 18	
March 1938	spinning	*Fishing Gazette*, 20 August 1938, p. 245	
June 1945	rod and line	Hugh Gough: letter to F.B., 1976	cased
June 1956	rod and line	*Fishing Gazette*, June 23 1956	
June 1962	spinning	Hugh Gough: letter to F.B., 1977	photo
March 1963	netted	Dr M. Kennedy: Inland Fisheries Trust records	
May 1900	handline	*Fishing Gazette*, 19 May 1900, p. 378	
Nov. 1979	livebaiting	*Angler's Mail*, 21 November 1979	
April 1958	netted	Irish Radio News, 3 April 1958; *Fishing Gazette*, 12 April 1958	
March 1972	spinning	*Galloway News*, 24 March 1972	
Feb. 1967	deadbaiting	*Angling Times*, 10 February 1967	photo
July 1797	unknown	The Rev. W. B. Daniel, *Rural Sports* (1801)	
Summer 1865	grounded	B. Vesey Fitzgerald: letter to F.B., 1969	cased
1866	rod and line	*Doncaster, Nottingham & Lincolnshire Gazette*, 6 April 1866	
1877	rod and line	*Field*, 28 April 1877	cased
May c. 1888	unknown	*Field*, 14 June 1890	cased
c. 1892	unknown	Dr H. Thirlaway, Piscatorial Society, 1971	cased
	unknown	*Fishing Gazette*, 18 September 1897	
c. 1896	rod and line	*Field*, vol. 97 (1901), p. 125	
April 1909	rod and line	*Field*, 24 April 1909	cased
c. 1920	unknown	Flyfishers' Club: library vol. (1884–1934), p. 35	cased
1922	livebaiting	*Where to Fish 1926*, p. 35	
June 1936	rod and line	*Angler's News*, 5 June 1937, p. 547	
June 1938	rod and line	*Angler's News*, 3 June 1939, p. 264	
1956	rod and line	*Angling Times*, 17 February 1956	

No.	Weight		Length (in.)	Girth (in.)	Location	Country	Captor
	lb	oz					
103	40		48		Lough Fitty	Scotland	Teofil Romanczyk
104	39	14	48		Lough Erne	Ireland	Unknown
105	39	12			Lough Gur	Ireland	James McMahon
106	39	08			Lough Conn	Ireland	T. J. Clarke
107	39	08			Lough Mask	Ireland	Inland Fisheries Trust
108	39	07	49	25	Dorset Stour	England	G. F. Parrott
109	39	03			Westmere	England	Great Ouse Board
110	39				Loch Ken	Scotland	Station Porter
111	39		50½		Lough Derg	Ireland	Shamus Hogan
112	39		50		Lough Mask	Ireland	Sir Patrick Manson
113	39		50	25	Lough Mask	Ireland	P. F. Millar
114	39		43½		Lough Gur	Ireland	Patrick Higgins
115	39				Lough Mask	Ireland	Paddy Walsh
116	39				Lough Mask	Ireland	John Sutton
117	39				Lough Mask	Ireland	Inland Fisheries Trust
118	39		47½	27½	Knipton Reservoir	England	Clive Loveland
119	38	12	49	20	Lough Ennell	Ireland	Mick Leonard
120	38	08	43½	27 (?)	Lough Derg (?)	Ireland	Thomas Moore
121	38	08			Lough Mask	Ireland	P. Connor
122	38	08			Hatchett's Lake	England	Unknown
123	38	08	51		Lough Ennell	Ireland	Michael O'Malley
124	38	08			Lough Ramor	Ireland	W. Oulton
125	38	04	47½		Clea Lough	Ireland	Dan McCrea
126	38	04			Abberton Reservoir	England	P. Emmings
127	38	02	46	26	Lower Lough Carrib	Ireland	Brendan Hardiman
128	38				Bethels Pond nr Rise	England	Unknown
129	38				River Wye	England	Mr Tilly
130	38				Lough Nafooey	Ireland	W. B. Gavin
131	38				Denton Reservoir	England	E. C. Holt
132	38				River Moy	Ireland	Mr Barrett
133	38		47	26	Lough Derg	Ireland	R. Payne-Gallwey
134	38				Lough Erne	Ireland	Unknown
135	38				Lower Lough Erne	Ireland	Sammy Shaw
136	38		48		Lough Mask	Ireland	H. A. Robinson
137	38				Lough Derg	Ireland	Unknown
138	38				Lough Mask	Ireland	Unknown

Date	Method	Source	Visual evidence
1961	livebaiting	*Fishing Gazette*, 23 December 1961	photo
March 1974	netted (?)	*Angler's Mail*, 27 March 1974	
1898	spiller	*Fishing Gazette*, 31 December 1898	
July 1936	spinning	*Fishing Gazette*, 25 June 1936	
1960	netted	*Fishing Gazette*, 25 November 1961	
March 1909	unknown	*Angling*, April/June 1945	photo
July 1958	stranded	C. G. Smith: letter to F.B., 1977	
ummer 1904	stranded	Dr C. Tate Regan, *British Freshwater Fishes* (1911)	head preserved
March 1911	shot	*Field*, 24 June 1911	
Sept. 1913	spoonbait	Martie Sommerville: conversation with F.B., 1977	cased
Aug. 1928	unknown	*Fishing Gazette*, 25 August 1928	photo
1945	spinning	*Angling*, April/June 1946	
July 1949	spoonbait	Personal interview, 1977	
1963	rod and line	Mr Coucill: letter to F.B., 1970	
March 1963	netted	Mr Coucill: letter to F.B., 1970	photo
Feb. 1967	livebaiting	*Angling Times*	photo
July 1956	spinning	*Stream and Field for Ireland*, February 1957	photo
c. 1875	spinning	Letter from Moore's granddaughter (1980)	cased
March 1901	rod and line	*Field*, vol. 98 (1901), p. 553	
c. 1915	netted	*Fishing Gazette*, 20 October 1923	photo
June 1949	trolling	Hugh Gough: letter to F.B., 1977	cased
Sept. 1950	spinning	*Field and Stream in Ireland*, March 1956	cased
	livebaiting	*Stream and Field*, February 1955	
Dec. 1969	livebaiting	Peter Collins: conversation with F.B., 1970	
March 1973	trailing	Irish Tourist Board: March 1973 news-sheet	
c. 1800	trimmering	Alexander Mackintosh, *The Driffield Angler* (1806)	
Oct. 1871	spinning	The Rev. F. Kilvert, *Kilvert's Diary, 1938–1940*	
Oct. 1895	rod and line	*Field*, 2 November 1895, p. 729	
c. 1864	unknown	*Fishing Gazette*, 31 October 1874	
Jan. 1876	unknown	*Field*, 22 January 1876	
Feb. 1877	spinning	*Field*, 24 February 1877, 10 and 18 March 1877	cased
	unknown	P. J. Martin, *Days Among the Pike and Perch* (1907)	cased
	unknown	D. Barnes: conversation with F.B., 1976	cased
July 1904	netted	*Fishing Gazette*, 25 March 1905	cased
March 1911	netted	*Fishing Gazette*, 18 March 1911	
1911	rod and line	*Record of Sports* (1914), p. 17	

No.	Weight lb	oz	Length (in.)	Girth (in.)	Location	Country	Captor
139	38				Lough Conn	Ireland	H. Mumford-Smith
140	38				Lough Mask	Ireland	Anthony Canney
141	38		45	22½	Overstone Park Lake	England	Captain C. Yarde
142	38				Lough Corrib	Ireland	John Hurney
143	38				Lough Mask	Ireland	Inland Fisheries Trust
144	38				Lough Lene (Westmeath)	Ireland	Unknown
145	38				Lough Corrib	Ireland	Inland Fisheries Trust
146	38		49½		Lough Ree	Ireland	Paddy Earl
147	38				Cong River	Ireland	Brendan Faragher
148	38				Lough Mask	Ireland	Inland Fisheries Trust
149	38				Lough Owel	Ireland	Inland Fisheries Trust
150	37	12	51½	25	Lough Ramor	Ireland	Rev. William Henry
151	37	12			Private lake, Warks.	England	J.R.J.
152	37	12	50		Lough Derg	Ireland	Tom Tiernan
153	37	08	46	25½	Burlington Pool	England	Unknown
154	37	08	44		Dorset Stour	England	Richard Arabin
155	37	08	49	27	Lough Corrib	Ireland	Peter Fahy
156	37	08			Reservoir nr Loughborough	England	Captain Barnes
157	37	08			Lough Conn	Ireland	John Loftus
158	37	08	49	24¼	Hampshire Avon	England	Clifford Warwick
159	37	08			Lough Gur	Ireland	Patrick Higgins
160	37	08	47	19½	Lough Mask	Ireland	J. O'Reilly
161	37	04	49	28	Exton Park Lake	England	Lord Gainsborough
162	37	04	48½	25	Templehouse Lake	Ireland	George Andrews
163	37		48		Hickling Broad	England	Unknown
164	37				Unknown	England	David Foster
165	37		48½	24	River Shannon	Ireland	William Duffy
166	37		49½	26	Lough Conn	Ireland	J. E. Cockburn
167	37				River Arun	England	Mr Allen
168	37		46	26	River Wye	England	Major W. H. Booth
169	37				Lough Ree	Ireland	Edward Strevens
170	37				Lough Mask	Ireland	Michael O'Connor
171	37				Lough Mask	Ireland	Inland Fisheries Trust
172	37		54	21	Glaslough	Ireland	John Killen
173	37				Lochgelly	Scotland	L. Jones

Date	Method	Source	Visual evidence
June 1929	trailing	*Fishing Gazette*, 31 August 1929, p. 212	cased
Oct. 1938	trailing	*Fishing Gazette*, 22 October 1938, p. 526	
March 1941	livebaiting	E. Marshall Hardy, *Coarse Fish* (1943)	cased
April 1954	netted	D. Brennan: letter to F.B., 16 January 1981	
Feb. 1958	netted	*Angling Times*, 14 February 1958	
Aug. 1961	rod and line	Dr M. Kennedy: letter to F.B., 1969	
April 1965	netted	Aer Lingus Office, April 1980	cased
May 1967	spinning	Irish Specimen Fish Cttee, letter, 1973	
July 1974	livebaiting	Irish Specimen Fish Cttee, 1975 annual report, p. 3	
March 1978	netted	Hugh Gough: letter to F.B., 1978	photo
March 1978	netted	Hugh Gough: letter to F.B., 1978	
1876	netted	*Field*, 11 March 1876	
March 1882	deadbait spinning	*Fishing Gazette*, 27 January 1900	cased
Feb. 1976	spinning	Hugh Gough: letter to F.B., 1976	cased
Nov. 1849	unknown	*Angling Times*, 29 April 1966	cased
Feb. 1859	livebait	*Field*, 14 November 1874	
Aug. 1900	trailing	*Field*, vol. 96 (1900), p. 440	cased
1918	unknown	*Angler's News*, 15 June 1918	
July 1920	trailing	Personal interview, 1970	
Oct. 1944	livebaiting	*Angling Times*, 9 April 1954	cased
1945	spinning	*Angling*, April/June 1946	
Sept. 1962	rod and line	Irish Specimen Fish Committee	
June 1796	rod and line	The Rev. W. B. Daniel, *Rural Sports* (1801)	
Sept. 1961	spinning	*Angling Times*, 7 February 1964	
March 1874	unknown	*Field*, 31 October 1874	cased
c. 1880	livebaiting	*Scientific Angler*, 9th edn (1900)	
March 1893	rod and line	*Fishing Gazette*, 25 March 1893, p. 205	
Feb. 1894	trailing	*Field*, vol. 84 (1894), p. 431	cased
	unknown	*Sporting and Dramatic News*, 20 November 1897	
May 1910	spinning	*Field*, 7 May 1910	cased
1953	rod and line	Omar's (O. M. Reed) private papers (1980)	
1954	trailing	Personal interview, 1977	
Oct. 1957	longline	*Irish Press*, 4 October 1957	
Feb. 1966	plug fishing	*Angling Times*, 18 February 1966	photo
Nov. 1970	deadbaiting	*Woodbine Angling Year Book 1973*, p. 86	

No.	Weight		Length (in.)	Girth (in.)	Location	Country	Captor
	lb	oz					
174	36	12			Swallow Lake	Ireland	Unknown
175	36	12			Fonthill Park	England	'An evacuee'
176	36	08	54		Broads nr Yarmouth	England	Unknown
177	36	08			River Barrow	Ireland	Unknown
178	36	08	46		Lough Mask	Ireland	Colonel Allix
179	36	08	48	30	Lough Corrib	Ireland	Unknown
180	36	08	49	33	Vandervell's Lake	England	Colonel Atherton
181	36	08	$47\frac{3}{4}$	$25\frac{1}{4}$	Lough Kinale	Ireland	Hans Schultz
182	36	04			Lough Mask	Ireland	J. O'Reilly
183	36				Sir J. C. Jervoise's pond	England	Unknown
184	36				Sir J. C. Jervoise's pond	England	Unknown
185	36		49	24		England	Lord Darnley
186	36				Luton Hoo	England	George Forbes
187	36		47		Lough Corrib	Ireland	Unknown
188	36		48	24	Haveringland Lake	England	Frank Thorns
189	36				Lough Sheelin	Ireland	Captain Peacock
190	36				Hampshire Avon	England	Unknown
191	36				Lough Carra	Ireland	F. Stanners
192	36		50		Lough Derg	Ireland	Mr Manning
193	36		47	19	Barrow-on-Soar	England	J. Birch
194	36				Lough Ross	Ireland	C. Tinnelly
195	36				Lough Mask	Ireland	Miss Warren
196	36		48	36	Lough Mask	Ireland	Unknown
197	36				Lough Mask	Ireland	James McVeigh
198	36				River Yare	England	Mr Halliday
199	36				Carramore Lake (Castlebar)	Ireland	Sean McDonnells
200	36				Lough Lene (Westmeath)	Ireland	Michael Byrne
201	36				Lake Kilbarron (Scarriff)	Ireland	Michael O'Halloran
202	36				Lough Corrib	Ireland	John McDarby
203	36				Old Bedford River	England	Great Ouse Board
204	36		50		Cloon Lough	Ireland	W. H. C. Blake
205	36				Martnaham Loch	Scotland	Angus Macpherson
206	36		$47\frac{1}{2}$	$23\frac{1}{2}$	Lough Allen	Ireland	James Earley
207	36				Lough Kinale	Ireland	Wilfried Wegner
208	36				Glaslough	Ireland	Unknown

Date	Method	Source	Visual evidence
Aug. 1926	rod and line	*Fishing Gazette*, 7 August 1926	
1945	rod and line	*Woodbine Angling Year Book 1973*, p. 86	
1873	trimmering	*Land and Water*; note in Norwich Museum	
Feb. 1894	livebaiting	*Field*, 17 February 1894	
1901	rod and line	*Field*, vol. 98 (1901), p. 553	cased
March 1919	unknown	John Bickerdyke, *Angling for Pike* (1959), p. 12	
Feb. 1957	livebaiting	*Angling Times*, 15 March 1957	cased
March 1970	livebaiting	*Angling Times*, 19 March 1970	photo
Nov. 1937	rod and line	J. F. Hampton, *Hampton on Pike Fishing* (1947), p. 158	
c. 1835	netted	William Hughes, *The Practical Angler* (1842), p. 240	
c. 1835	netted	William Hughes, *The Practical Angler* (1842), p. 240	
Aug. 1874	found dead	*Land and Water*, 31 October 1874	
1875	livebaiting	*Fishing Gazette*, 10 July 1897	
1877	trailing	*Angler's Note Book* (1880), p. 22	
Feb. 1880	livebaiting	W. Cooper, *Angling in Norfolk and Suffolk Waters* (1958)	cased
June 1895	unknown	*Fishing Gazette*, 13 February 1897, p. 121	
1896	unknown	J. Bickerdyke, *Book of the All-Round Angler* (1900), p. 97	
June 1900	rod and line	*Record of Sports 1911*, p. 18	
c. 1854	rod and line	D. Brennan: letter to F.B., 1977	cased
Feb. 1912	unknown	*Angling Times*, April 1976	cased
Aug. 1928	trailing	*Irish Times*, 7 August 1928, p. 11	
July 1928	trailing	*Sketch*, 7 February 1934	photo
April 1935	trailing	*Fishing Gazette*, 8 June 1935	
spring 1958	netted	*Angling Times*, 4 April 1958	
1939	rod and line	J. Wentworth Day, *Norwich and the Broads* (1953)	
Aug. 1957	spinning	*Fishing Gazette*, 31 August 1957	
Aug. 1959	rod and line	*Angling Times*, 28 August 1959	
May 1959	rod and line	*Angling Times*, 8 May 1959; *Fishing Gazette*, 16 January 1960	
April 1960	spinning	*Angling Times*, 29 April 1960	
winter 1960	electro-fished	C. G. Smith: letter to F.B., 1977	
Dec. 1963	spinning	Irish Specimen Fish Committee: letter, 1974	photo
1964	livebaiting	Letter from captor, January 1980	photo
March 1970	plug-fishing	Irish Specimen Fish Committee: letter, 1974	
April 1971	livebaiting	Irish Specimen Fish Committee: letter, 1974	
Feb. 1972	spinning	Irish Tourist Board: March 1972 news-sheet	

No.	Weight lb	oz	Length (in.)	Girth (in.)	Location	Country	Captor
209	35	08	46½	24	Rapley Lake	England	George Keene
210	35	08	48	25½	Mote Park Lake	England	Alfred Jardine
211	35	08	50½	25¾	Lough Arrow	Ireland	Mr Ballintine
212	35	08	47	29	Heigham Sound	England	A. Jackson
213	35	08	44½		Lough Conn	Ireland	Ed Mulhern
214	35	08	47		River Finn	Ireland	John Mahon
215	35	04	47½	22¼	Lough Creeve	Ireland	N. Crawford
216	35	04	48		Templehouse Lake	Ireland	Unknown
217	35	04			Templehouse Lake	Ireland	A. Klein Henz
218	35	04			Tullynasiddagh Lough	Ireland	Karl Andrée
219	35		45		Barnmeer	England	Mr Bowlker
220	35				River Blackwater	Ireland	Unknown
221	35				Dagenham Breach	England	Major Rhode
222	35				Shropshire	England	Unknown
223	35				River Stour	England	Richard Arabin
224	35				River Shannon	Ireland	Staverton Mathews
225	35		47	25½	Shardeloes Lake	England	Alfred Jardine
226	35		49	23	Private lake nr Coventry	England	Alfred Newsome
227	35				Lough Mullaghmore	Ireland	A. E. Conway
228	35				Lough Conn	Ireland	Mr Roberts
229	35		47	24	Lough Conn	Ireland	Samuel Mossop
230	35				Grasmere	England	Mr Griffin
231	35		45½	23½	Lough Mask	Ireland	H. Conway Belfield
232	35		45½		Lough Derg	Ireland	Unknown
233	35				Lough Nafooey	Ireland	Holmes Leigh
234	35				River Moy	Ireland	Mr Scroope
235	35				Lough Mask	Ireland	Mrs W. H. Goode
236	35				Lough Conn	Ireland	Michael Moylett
237	35				Lough Mask	Ireland	Pat Burke
238	35				Ballyhoe Lough	Ireland	J. W. Gilmore
239	35		50	27	River Barrow	Ireland	Patrick Byrne
240	35				Loch Ken	Scotland	Fishery Association
241	35				Staines Reservoir	England	S. Cannel
242	35				River Barrow	Ireland	James Howard
243	35		46	25	Lower Lough Erne	Ireland	Thomas Maguire

Date	Method	Source	Visual evidence
Oct. 1874	netted	*Where to Fish 1926*, p. xxxv	cased
Feb. 1877	livebaiting	Francis Francis, *Sporting Sketches* (1878), p. 87	cast made
May 1900	handlining	*Fishing Gazette*, 19 May 1900, p. 378	
Dec. 1948	spinning	*Angling*, March 1949, p. 90	cased
	trailing	F.B., 1973	cased
July 1960	spinning	*Stream and Field in Ireland*, July 1960, p. 31	
Aug. 1971	livebaiting	Irish Specimen Fish Committee: letter, 1973	
July 1916	trailing	*Field*, 26 August 1916, p. 325	cased
Feb. 1975	deadbaiting	Irish Specimen Fish Cttee, 1975 annual report, p. 2	
July 1976	spinning	*Urlaug in Irland* (1977)	photo
c. 1750	rod and line	R. and C. Bowlker, *Art of Angling* (1826)	
c. 1796	lifted out	The Rev. W. B. Daniel, *Rural Sports* (1801)	
c. 1800	trimmering	The Rev. W. B. Daniel, *Rural Sports* (1801), p. 324	
c. 1812	unknown	Thomas Best, *Art of Angling*, 10th edn (1814)	
Feb. 1859	rod and line	*Field*, 16 April 1859	
Sept. 1878	spinning	*Fishing Gazette*, 23 January 1897, p. 68	
Sept. 1879	livebaiting	F. Buckland, *Natural History of British Fishes* (1883)	cast made
Feb. 1890	rod and line	*Fishing Gazette*, 22 February 1890, p. 108; *Land and Water*, 8 March 1890	
1893	rod and line	*Fishing Gazette*, 16 January 1897, p. 50	
Sept. 1896	trailing	*Fishing Gazette*, 6 March 1897, p. 164	
May 1898	trailing	*Fishing Gazette*, 19 May 1900, p. 378	cased
1900	rod and line	*Record of Sports 1911*, p. 18	
July 1902	trailing	*Field*, 19 July 1902, p. 117	cased
1902	unknown	F.B., 1977	cased
Sept. 1909	rod and line	*Angler's News*, 18 September 1909	
1909	unknown	*Record of Sports 1911*, p. 18	
1911	rod and line	*Record of Sports 1914*, p. 17	
July 1920	trailing	Patrick Moylett: letter to F.B., 1968	cased
April 1922	rod and line	*Field*, 3 June 1922	
June 1926	trailing	*Fishing Gazette*, 19 February 1926, p. 551	
March 1927	rod and line	*Fishing Gazette*, 14 May 1927, p. 475	photo
June 1935	netted	J. F. Hampton, *Hampton on Pike Fishing* (1947)	
Nov. 1938	rod and line	*Woodbine Angling Year Book 1973*, p. 86	
Feb. 1940	rod and line	*Fishing Gazette*, 8 June 1940, p. 426	
Feb. 1957	longlining	*Impartial Reporter*, 7 February 1957	

No.	Weight lb	oz	Length (in.)	Girth (in.)	Location	Country	Captor
244	35		54		Rooskey Lake	Ireland	Joseph McKenna
245	35		45½		Windermere	England	Freshwater Biological A
246	35		47	24	Martham Broad	England	Reg Pownall
247	35		49		Lough Derg	Ireland	James Minogue
248	35				Lake of Mentieth	Scotland	Charles Cowan
249	35		44½		Horsey Mere	England	Frank Wright
250	35				Pit nr Snodland	England	Stanley Wright
251	35		50		Lough Beg	Ireland	Alan McQueen
252	35				Boreham Mere	England	Terry Hattley

Date	Method	Source	Visual evidence
March 1958	spinning	*Angling Times*, 28 March 1958	
Feb. 1960	netted	Dr W. Frost: letter to F.B., 1969	
Feb. 1961	plug fishing	*Angling Times*, 3 March 1961	photo
May 1961	spinning	Irish Specimen Fish Committee: letter, 1974	
May 1965	deadbaiting	*Fishing*, 7 May 1965	
Nov. 1967	deadbaiting	*Angling Times*, 9 November 1976	photo
March 1971	spinning	*Angler's Mail*, 6 March 1971	photo
Jan. 1976	deadbaiting	*Angler's Mail*, 28 January 1976	photo
June 1979	livebait	*Angler's Mail*, June 1979	photo

S. J. Hurley, whose reports on Lough Derg's fishing and fishermen were regularly published in the *Field* and the *Fishing Gazette*, accompanied the artist James Temple on a visit to Killaloe in 1891. Temple's drawings, captioned 'Pike-fishing at Killaloe', were published in the *Illustrated Sporting and Dramatic News* on 21 November 1891. S. J. Hurley was one of the witnesses to the landing of the 90½ lb world record rod-caught pike by John Naughton at Killaloe in 1861

14 The Big Pike List of Europe and North America

The list of big pike in the first edition was confined to British and Irish pike. During the intervening years I had made friends with a number of foreign correspondents, who have, with no little effort to themselves, helped me gather data on European and North American pike. In the circumstances I thought it worthwhile to start the second list, which follows.

This list is remarkable in that it shows that North Europeans have an addiction for using artificial baits (albeit with great success). It also shows how wrong many British pike anglers are in their thinking – for many have associated themselves with the view that spinning may produce large bags of small and medium pike, but rarely big pike.

I wish to thank some friends who have helped me to gather data on European pike, particularly Arne Broman of the Swedish magazine *Fiske*; Richard Lütticken of the German magazine *Blinker*; D. Maury of the French magazine *La Pêche et les Poissons*; the Belgian Hugo Martel; the Dutchman Jan

Eggers, an indefatigable researcher who on my behalf has written 200 letters in many languages; the German Georg Peinemann, whose magazine *Fisch und Fang* has been a mine of information; and the Rapala Bait Company of Finland. On the 'home front' I would like to acknowledge the debt I owe to David Beazley who, while carefully researching his own passionate interest in fishing reels, has found much that has assisted me.

Converting continental weights and measures

Because of their increasing wealth and readiness to travel in order to fish, European anglers are mixing with each other as never before. With this cosmopolitan approach anglers are becoming more curious about each other and, aided and abetted by the increasing influence of angling magazines, this trend is likely to continue.

Apart from having to cope with our special *bête noir* – foreign languages – we British also have the problem of trying to understand continental weights and measures.

In some countries fish are weighed in grammes and kilogrammes whereas in others the fish are still weighed (rather quaintly) in pounds. Sadly the European 'pound' has a different value to our own: it is one-half a kilo or approximately 1 lb 1¾ oz.

For years, whenever I have needed to convert the weight and length details of some large European pike, I have patiently calculated their British equivalent; and it has always been a chore and a bore. How I longed to lay my hands on conversion tables like the ones that follow – all formulated with considerable misgivings by myself.

Mr Moser, a noted Austrian taxidermist, sent me this picture of Peter Osternacher's 42 lb 15¾ oz pike (no. 81 on the list) which was immensely long – 56 in. The photograph displaying the pike's huge head and long body reveals what its weight would have been in better times – 54½ lb!

Conversion table 1

Kilos	Continental pounds or pfunds	Avoirdupois lb	oz
9	18	19	13½
9·5	19	20	15
10	20	22	00½
10·5	21	23	02¼
11	22	24	03¾
11·5	23	25	05½
12	24	26	07¼
12·5	25	27	08¾
13	26	28	10¼
13·5	27	29	12
14	28	30	13¾
14·5	29	31	15½
15	30	33	01
15·5	31	34	02¾
16	32	35	04¼
16·5	33	36	06
17	34	37	07½
17·5	35	38	09¼
18	36	39	11
18·5	37	40	12½
19	38	41	14¼
19·5	39	42	15¾
20	40	44	01½
20·5	41	45	03¼
21	42	46	04¾
21·5	43	47	06¼
22	44	48	08
22·5	45	49	09½
23	46	50	11¼
23·5	47	51	12¾
24	48	52	14½
24·5	49	54	
25	50	55	01¾
25.5	51	56	03½
26	52	57	05¼
26·5	53	58	06¾
27	54	59	08¼
27·5	55	60	10
28	56	61	11½
28·5	57	62	13
29	58	63	14¾
29·5	59	65	00½
30	60	66	02¼
30·5	61	67	03¾
31	62	68	05½
31·5	63	69	07¼
32	64	70	08¾
32·5	65	71	10½

Conversion table 2

Grammes	Ounces
50	1¾
100	3½
150	5¼
200	7
250	8¾
300	10½
350	12¼
400	14
450	15¾
500	17½

To Use the Key

Example:

For a German pike whose weight is given as 41 pfd (pfunds) 200 g (grammes):
Look in the main conversion table:

41 pfd = 45 lb 03¼ oz

Then look in the second conversion table:

200 g = 07 oz

Weight of German pike 45 lb 10¼ oz

This enormous pike was taken on rod and line by Friedrich Witzany from a gravel pit near Goslar in West Germany, September 1971. It weighed 52 lb 4 oz at the time of capture. Had this fish survived until the following March – when the weight of its fully developed ovaries would have represented approximately 20 per cent of its body weight – it could have weighed as much as 65 lb! (Kurt Tempes)

The Big Pike List of Europe and North America

No.	Weight lb	oz	Length (in.)	Girth (in.)	Location	Country	Captor
1	75				Ilman Lake	USSR	
2	69	08			River Rhine	Germany	
3	62	08	57½		Reuss-Weiher	Switzerland	Jörg Nötzli
4	60	10			Omutinsk Reservoir	USSR	J. Schirschew
5	59	00½	53½		lake nr Hamburg	Germany	Jürgen Brauel
6	58	06	59½	24¾	Grarup Lake	Denmark	C. M. Damkiaer
7	56	03½			Sâkyhan Pyhajarvi	Finland	Unknown
8	55	15¾	54¼		Lipno Reservoir	Czech'l'vakia	Jira Blaha
9	55	04	59½		Günzstaus Lake	Germany	
10	53	05½			Feld near lake	Austria	G. Wunderlich
11	53	04	50½		River Nida	Poland	Waclaw Biegan
12	52	14½	53½	26	Keurafjarden Lake	Finland	Kalle Koskinen
13	52	04	54		Sieversschen pit	Germany	Friedrich Witzany
14	51	12¾	49		River Drau	Austria	Albert Schmidt
15	51	02¼	52	29½	Klopeiner Lake	Austria	Dieter Ladwig
16	51	02¼			Buendia Marshes	Spain	Mr Montes et al.
17	50	12	53¼	27½	Irr Lake	Austria	Helmut Firzinger
18	50	02½	57¾		Tyrifjorden Lake	Norway	Roy Tait
19	49	10	51¼		Mälaren Lake	Sweden	George Lööf
20	49	09½			Baltic Sea	Lapland	Unknown
21	49	09½			Unterbacher Lake	Germany	Friedrich Klein
22	49	06	52	24½	Hörhäuser gravel pit	Germany	Heinz Niemietz
23	48	13½			Old River Rhine	Germany	Theo Vonderschmitt
24	48	11½			Vihti Lake region	Finland	Unknown
25	48	08			Maaninka Lake region	Finland	Unknown
26	48	08			gravel pit	Denmark	Knud Westerman
27	48	08			Moat of Wickrather	Germany	H. Kopp
28	48	08	56¾		River Juutuanjoki	Lapland	Uula Jomppanen
29	48	08			Vesjoloskoje Reservoir	USSR	
30	48	08			Weikerl Lake	Austria	Karl Weisinger
31	48	08	45¼		Baltic nr Tammisaari	Finland	E. Kuusisto
32	48	05				Denmark	Leif Jensen
33	48		62		Moira River	Canada	
34	47	06			Öyeren Lake	Norway	Harry Rode
35	47	04	56¼			Sweden	Cai Burewell
36	47	04	54¾		Greyerzer Lake	Switzerland	René Gremoud

Date	Method	Source	Visual evidence
Jan. 1930		Leo S. Berg, *Freshwater Fishes of the USSR* (1962)	
c. 1850		Robert Blakey, *Old Faces In New Masks* (1856)	
June 1979	plug fishing	*Petri-Heil* magazine, Dec. 1979	photo
Jan. 1972	spinning	*Fisch und Fang* magazine, Nov. 1974, p. 722	
Jan. 1978	spinning	Letter from editor, *Blinker* magazine, 1978	photo
June 1929	trimmering	*Fishing Gazette*, 14 Sept. 1929, p. 275	photo
1905		Letter to Jan Eggers from Sirpa Luostarinen, Jan. 1981	
Dec. 1979	livebaiting	Letter from Rybárstvi magazine	photo
June 1975	found dead	*Blinker* (Der Hetch), 1979	photo
		Fisch und Fang, March 1980, p. 192	
Nov. 1976	livebaiting	Letter from Polish Record Fish Commission, 1977	photo
Aug. 1912	spinning	Letter from Dr Lauri Koli, Helsinki University, 1981	
Sept. 1971	livebaiting	*Bild* magazine, Sept. 1971	photo
Sept. 1974	livebaiting	Letter from editor, *Blinker* magazine, 1978	photo
May 1976	livebaiting	Letter from editor, *Blinker* magazine, 1978	photo
		Spanish newspaper	photo
Nov. 1978	livebaiting	*Blinker* (Der Hetch), 1979	photo
May 1976	trailing	Letter from editor *Villmarksliv* magazine, 1977	photo
June 1973	spinning	Arne Broman: letter to F.B., 1977	
c. 1954	netted	Arne Broman: letter to F.B., 1977	photo
arch 1972	livebaiting	*Fische und Fang* magazine, Aug. 1972	photo
Feb. 1977	spinning	*Blinker* magazine, July 1977	photo
1973	rod and line	*Fisch und Fang* magazine, April 1973, p. 209	
1894		Letter from Dr Lauri Koli, Helsinki University, 1981	
May 1942	netted	Letter from Dr Lauri Koli, Helsinki University, 1981	
Dec. 1952	spinning	Arne Broman: letter to F.B., 1977	
1968	rod and line	*Fisch und Fang* magazine, Jan. 1969, p. 2	
June 1969	plug fishing	Letter from Dr Lauri Koli, Helsinki University, 1981	
1977		*Fisch und Fang* magazine, March 1978, p. 181	
1977	livebaiting	*Fisch und Fang* magazine, March 1978	
June 1979	plug fishing	Letter from Dr Lauri Koli, Helsinki University, 1981	
1970	plug fishing	*Tight Lines* catalogue (1971), p. 17	
		Irish Angling Nov./Dec. 1947, p. 25	
Aug. 1976	plug fishing	Arne Broman: letter to F.B., 1977	
		Arne Broman: letter to F.B., 1978	
July 1978	livebaiting	*Petri-Heil* magazine	

No.	Weight lb	oz	Length (in.)	Girth (in.)	Location	Country	Captor
37	47		52¾		River Peene	E. Germany	E. Pietsch
38	46	13	55¼		Vannsjø Lake	Norway	Per Erlandsen
39	46	04¾	53½		Murten Lake	Switzerland	Pius Tschoppe
40	46	02	54½	25	Sacandaga Reservoir	USA	Peter Dubuc
41	46				River Inn	Austria	Unknown
42	46		52		Rozstepniewo Lake	Poland	Marian Polowczyk
43	45	12			Basswood Lake	USA	J. V. Schanken
44	45	08			Hohenwarte Reservoir	E. Germany	Werner Rudiger
45	45	08			Kriebstein Reservoir	E. Germany	Gunter Peter
46	45	07				Norway	Per Erlandsen
47	45	04	53½		Schlier Lake	Germany	Josef Schrädler
48	45	03¼			pit at Höxter-Godelheim	Germany	
49	45	03¼			Platten Lake	Hungary	K. Spalter
50	45	03¼			Kärtner Lake	Austria	Walter Merzincik
51	45	03			Öyeren Lake	Norway	Harry Rode
52	44	10¼	52		Schalkenmehrener Maar	Germany	Karl Klein
53	44	08	51		Starnberger Lake	Germany	Karl Zeitler
54	44	05	54¼		Irr Lake	Austria	Franz Köch
55	44	04	50½	25¼	Oster Lakes	Germany	Josef Schrank
56	44	04				Sweden	Willy Thune
57	44	02			Neufelder Lake	Austria	Wilhelm Lopata
58	44	01½			Umpilampi Lake	Finland	Unknown
59	44	01½	51			Germany	H. Oestreich
60	44	01½	56¼		Matt Lake	Austria	Mrs E. Rieder
61	44	01½	53¼		Irr Lake	Austria	Mr Hackle
62	44	01½	52¾		Rot (Red) Lake	Switzerland	Lajos Posta
63	44	01½			Kamptal Reservoir	Austria	
64	44	01½			Wörther Lake	Austria	Ludwig Kowatsch
65	44	01½	51		Gleinker Lake	Austria	R. Kriechbaum
66	44	01½			pond nr Grossholzleute	Germany	J. Merz
67	44	01¼			River Donau	Austria	Jaroslav Malek
68	44	01	49¼		Stroms-Vattudal Lake	Sweden	Tor Modin
69	44	01				Denmark	Kurt Ravnsgarrd
70	43	13½			Neufelder Lake	Austria	K. Hiawatsh
71	43	12	48¾		Langen gravel pit	Germany	Kurt Breldert
72	43	10				Sweden	I. Larsson

Date	Method	Source	Visual evidence
Aug. 1969	rod and line	*Fisch und Fang* magazine, April 1970, p. 120	
April 1975	spinning	Letter from editor, *Villmarksliv* magazine, 1977	
Oct. 1965	spinning	*The Sport Fisher*, Feb. 1966, p. 33	photo
Sept. 1940	plug fishing	*Field & Stream*, March 1941	
April 1909	speared	*Field*, 10 April 1909	
April 1970	livebaiting	*Polish Angling News*, 1970	photo
1929	rod and line	*Field & Stream*, March 1941	
1971	rod and line	*Fisch und Fang* magazine, April 1972, p. 204	
1971	rod and line	*Fisch und Fang* magazine, April 1972, p. 204	
1977	plug fishing	Arne Broman: letter to F.B., 1978	
1979	netted	Letter from editor, *Blinker* magazine, 1979	photo
1961	found dead	*Fisch und Fang* magazine, June 1979, p. 500	
1968	rod and line	*Fisch und Fang* magazine, Sept. 1968, p. 296	
1971	rod and line	*Fisch und Fang* magazine, Jan. 1975, p. 6	
Aug. 1976	plug fishing	Arne Broman: letter to F.B., 1978	
Feb. 1975	livebaiting	*Fisch und Fang* magazine, July 1975, p. 440	photo
1979	found dead	*Blinker* magazine, Jan. 1980	photo
July 1972	trailing	*Fisch und Fang* magazine, Aug. 1972, p. 476	
1974	spinning	*Blinker* magazine, Jan. 1975	photo
1974		Arne Broman: letter to F.B., 1978	
1968		*Tight Lines* catalogue (1969), p. 11	photo
1927	spinning	Letter from Dr Lauri Koli, Helsinki University, 1981	
April 1962		*Fisch und Fang* magazine, May 1979, p. 394	
1969	livebaiting	*Fisch und Fang* magazine, Sept. 1969, p. 322	
1970	rod and line	*Fisch und Fang* magazine, July 1970, p. 247	
Nov. 1972	livebaiting	*Fisch und Fang* magazine, Jan. 1973, p. 7	photo
1973	rod and line	*Fisch und Fang* magazine, June 1974, p. 373	
1973	spinning	*Fisch und Fang* magazine, Sept. 1973, p. 568	
April 1979	maggot bait	*Fisch und Fang* magazine, June 1979, p. 474	photo
June 1979	livebaiting	*Fisch und Fang* magazine, Dec. 1979, p. 952	
1972	rod and line	*Fisch und Fang* magazine, Dec. 1972, p. 716	
1953	trailing	*Sportfiskaren* magazine, 1953	photo
1976	spinning	Arne Broman: letter to F.B., 1978	
Nov. 1979	livebaiting	*Fisch und Fang* magazine, Jan. 1980, p. 4	
Nov. 1974	livebaiting	*Fisch und Fang* magazine, Dec. 1974, p. 746	photo
1958	rod and line	Arne Broman: letter to F.B., 1978	

No.	Weight lb	oz	Length (in.)	Girth (in.)	Location	Country	Captor
73	43	10				Norway	Rune Lökling
74	43	10				Sweden	Karl Karlsson
75	43	08			gravel pit, Schermbeck-Bright	Germany	Hans Schoel
76	43	06¾	50½	26	Lamden Vesijârvi	Finland	Kyosti Kurimo
77	43	06¾			Sorpe Lake	Germany	Manfred Goebel
78	42	15¾			Atter Lake	Austria	M. Staufer
79	42	15¾	51½		Feld-Am-See	Austria	F. Kiltzer
80	42	15¾	49½		River Isar	Germany	Georg Beer
81	42	15¾	56		Irr Lake	Austria	P. Osternacher
82	42	15½			Kopenhamn Lake	Denmark	Thrane Nilsson
83	42	15½	51¼		Wierwäld Lake	Switzerland	
84	42	12			Stony Rapids	Canada	Willard Terry
85	42	06	50½		gravel pit nr Porta Westfalica	Germany	F. Niemeier
86	42	05¼				Switzerland	Walter Stübi
87	42	05¼					K. Zajewski
88	42	02				Canada	Robert Hendry
89	42				Lake Simcoe	Canada	Harry Bed
90	42					Sweden	H. Linblad
91	41	14¼	59		Szinkuhner Lake	Germany	F. Weber
92	41	14¼				Sweden	B. E. Jacobsson
93	41	14¼			Platten Lake	Hungary	P. Friedrich
94	41	14¼			Forrgen Lake	Germany	H. Krois
95	41	14¼				Norway	Leif Berg
96	41	14¼			Rur Lake	Germany	Franz Szczechowski
97	41	14¼			Öyeren Lake	Norway	Harry Rode
98	41	14¼				Sweden	H. Andersson
99	41	14¼	51		Bieler Lake	Switzerland	Gottfried Kuffer
100	41	07			Illmen Lake	Germany	R. Eckhardt
101	41	05¼	51		Klopeiner Lake	Austria	Georg Blaczek
102	41	03				Sweden	H. Lindblad
103	41				Kolborn Lake	Germany	W. P. Krüger
104	40	12½			Weser Backwater	Germany	Paul Korf
105	40	12½			River Lahn	Germany	A. Flick
106	40	12½			Mond Lake	Austria	Walter Hutterer
107	40	12½			Weissen Lake	Austria	Johann Friedberg
108	40	12½	51		Happinger Lake	Germany	Paul Lukas

Date	Method	Source	Visual evidence
1974	rod and line	Arne Broman: letter to F.B., 1978	
1976	spinning	Arne Broman: letter to F.B., 1978	
April 1975	livebaiting	*Fisch und Fang* magazine, June 1975, p. 368	photo
winter 1969	jigging	Letter from Rapala Baits to Jan Eggers, 1981	
1973	rod and line	*Fisch und Fang* magazine, July 1973, p. 44	
1968	rod and line	*Fisch und Fang* magazine, Jan. 1969, p. 4	
1975	trailing	*Fisch und Fang* magazine, Nov. 1975, p. 708	
Oct. 1979	livebaiting	*Fischwaid* magazine, Dec. 1979, p. 699	photo
		Fisch und Fang magazine, March 1980, p. 192	photo
1957	spinning	*Napp Och Nytt* catalogue, 1958	photo
May 1978			photo
July 1954			
	livebaiting	*Fisch und Fang* magazine, Jan. 1979, p. 13	photo
1942	rod and line	*Fisch und Fang* magazine, Jan. 1973, p. 7	
1978	rod and line	Letter from Abu to Jan Eggers, Dec. 1980	
June 1948	rod and line		
May 1959	trailing		
1968	plug fishing	*Tight Lines* catalogue, 1968	photo
Feb. 1899		*Allgemeine Fischerie Zeitung*, 1 March 1899	
1957		Arne Broman: letter to F.B., 1978	
1968	rod and line	*Fisch und Fang* magazine, Sept. 1968, p. 296	
May 1970	livebaiting	*Fisch und Fang* magazine, June 1970, p. 198	
1972	spinning	Arne Broman: letter to F.B., 1978	
Dec. 1974	livebaiting	*Fisch und Fang* magazine, Jan. 1975, p. 5	photo
Aug. 1976	plug fishing	Arne Broman: letter to F.B., 1978	
	plug fishing	Arne Broman: letter to F.B., 1978	
		Petri-Heil magazine, 1980	
July 1978	livebaiting	*Fisch und Fang* magazine, Sept. 1978, p. 684	
July 1974	trailing	*Fisch und Fang* magazine, Nov. 1974, p. 690	
1967	spinning	Arne Broman: letter to F.B., 1978	
1971	rod and line	*Fisch und Fang* magazine, Jan. 1972, p. 2	
1975	rod and line	*Fisch und Fang* magazine, Jan. 1976, p. 5	
Dec. 1977	livebaiting	*Fisch und Fang* magazine, Jan. 1978, p. 4	photo
1979	rod and line	*Fisch und Fang* magazine, Sept. 1979, p. 746	
May 1980	spinning	*Fisch und Fang* magazine, Sept. 1980, p. 756	photo
Aug. 1980	livebaiting	*Fisch und Fang* magazine, Sept. 1980, p. 746	photo

No.	Weight lb	oz	Length (in.)	Girth (in.)	Location	Country	Captor
109	40	11	52½		gravel pit nr Draveil	France	M. Lécrivain
110	40	06				Sweden	Johan Ullsten
111	40	05½			Zella Lake	Austria	H. Casapiccola
112	40	04	53½		Brenn Lake	Austria	W. Kaltenpoth
113	40	04			Gurker Reservoir	Austria	B. Krubath
114	40	03	51		Irr Lake	Austria	W. Grünsteidl
115	40	02				Norway	J. H. Berg
116	40	02			Tonkuhle	Germany	O. Baasner
117	40	02	52		Kamptal Reservoir	Austria	Mr Schleicher
118	40				River Inn	Austria	Unknown
119	40				Runn Lake	Sweden	Unknown
120	40		51			Austria	Mr Opa
121	40		51			Austria	German visitor
122	39	11	46¾		Foteviken Lake	Sweden	Voldemar Wilnieks
123	39	11			lake nr Odense	Denmark	A. Oerlsen
124	39	11			Zeller Lake	Austria	R. Wallnstopfer
125	39	11			Schacht Lake	E. Germany	Hans Pohlmann
126	39	11			Forrgen Lake	Germany	H. Feller
127	39	11			River Drau	Austria	G. Löscher
128	39	11			Niedertrumer Lake	Austria	J. Stockinger
129	39	11			Afritzer Lake	Austria	M. Esterl
130	39	11			Irr Lake	Austria	K. Hahn
131	39	11				Denmark	Lars Henricksen
132	39	11	53¼		Mond Lake	Austria	Franz Loidl
133	39	11			Schladener Kiesteich	Germany	Hans-Dieter Boenke
134	39	11	49¾	25½	River Saône	France	M. Viollon
135	39	11	50¾		Vinkeveen Lake	Holland	Gunter Willmsen
136	39	11			Starnberger Lake	Germany	Wolfgang Wendroth
137	39	11	52¼		Rurtal Reservoir	Germany	Manfred Strauss
138	39	11	51½		Bieler Lake	Switzerland	Kurt Vogler
139	39	11	47¼		Traun Lake	Austria	J. Elder
140	39	11	49¼		Rheinhausen Club Water	Germany	August Dossinger
141	39	11			Vomb Lake	Sweden	H. Pohlhausen
142	39	11			Turey Lake	France	Edouard Van Gelder
143	39	11	49¼		River Rhine	Switzerland	Alfred Matzinger
144	39	11	50¾		gravel pit nr Pampel	Germany	Rudolf Weiss

Date	Method	Source	Visual evidence
Jan. 1979	spinning	*La Pêche et les Poissons* magazine	photo
1964	spinning	Arne Broman: letter to F.B., 1978	
1977	rod and line	*Fisch und Fang* magazine, Jan. 1978, p. 8	
June 1975	livebaiting	*Fisch und Fang* magazine, Aug. 1975, p. 507	photo
		Fisch und Fang magazine, Jan. 1979, p. 6	
July 1978	trailing	*Fisch und Fang* magazine, Sept. 1978, p. 695	photo
1968	plug fishing	*Napp Och Nytt* catalogue, 1969	photo
June 1971	livebaiting	*Fisch und Fang* magazine, July 1971, p. 238	photo
1975	livebaiting	*Fisch und Fang* magazine, June 1975, p. 383	photo
April 1909	shot	*Field*, 10 April 1909	
c. 1909		*Fishing Gazette*, 18 March 1911	
autumn 1979		Jan Eggers: letter to F.B., 1980	photo
autumn 1979		Jan Eggers: letter to F.B., 1980	photo
1950	spinning	Arne Broman: letter to F.B., 1978	
1968		*Fisch und Fang* magazine, Sept. 1968	
1969	rod and line	*Fisch und Fang* magazine, Jan. 1970, p. 4	
1971	rod and line	*Fisch und Fang* magazine, April 1972, p. 204	
1971	livebaiting	*Fisch und Fang* magazine, June 1971, p. 192	
1971	livebaiting	*Fisch und Fang* magazine, Dec. 1971, p. 406	
1972	livebaiting	*Fisch und Fang* magazine, June 1972, p. 343	
1972	rod and line	*Fisch und Fang* magazine, Oct. 1972, p. 602	
1972	rod and line	*Fisch und Fang* magazine, Nov. 1972, p. 660	
1972	plug fishing	*Napp Och Nytt* catalogue, 1973	
1973	rod and line	*Fisch und Fang* magazine, Sept. 1973, p. 568	
1975	livebaiting	*Blinker* magazine, Jan. 1975	
Nov. 1975	livebaiting	*La Pêche et les Poissons* magazine, April 1976	photo
Dec. 1975	spinning	*Fisch und Fang* magazine, April 1976 p. 240	photo
Oct. 1976	livebaiting	*Fisch und Fang* magazine, April 1977, p. 252	photo
Sept. 1976	livebaiting	*Fisch und Fang* magazine, Nov. 1976, p. 750	photo
Oct. 1976	trailing	*Fisch und Fang* magazine, Dec. 1976, p. 822	photo
May 1978	livebaiting	*Fisch und Fang* magazine, June 1978, p. 445	photo
1978	livebaiting	*Fischwaid* magazine, April 1979	
	rod and line	*Fisch und Fang* magazine, June 1979, p. 492	photo
Dec. 1979	livebaiting	*La Pêche et les Poissons* magazine, July 1980	photo
May 1979	livebaiting	*Fisch und Fang* magazine, June 1979, p. 470	photo

No.	Weight lb	oz	Length (in.)	Girth (in.)	Location	Country	Captor
145	39	11	49½		Cham's Club Water	Germany	Rupert Schmalix
146	39	07				Germany	R. J. Bouterwerk
147	39	04				Norway	Ludvig Nicolaysen
148	39	04				Norway	Hans Fredriksen
149	39	04				Sweden	Arne Johansson
150	39	04				Finland	Ole Öhrnberg
151	39	04			Schlier Lake	Germany	Hans Hechenberger
152	39				Dodge Lake, Michigan	USA	Larry Clough
153	39					Norway	H. Meyer
154	38	09¼	47¼		Horlachgraben	Germany	W. Fischer
155	38	09¼			lake nr Frankfurt	Germany	G. Pfuffer
156	38	09¼	47¼		Steinbachtalsperre	Germany	A. Vroemen
157	38	09¼	50½		lake nr Utrecht	Holland	Ruud Van Dort
158	38	09				Denmark	Jörn Henriksen
159	38	09				Sweden	Lars Johnsson
160	38	09				Sweden	Jorma Konti
161	38	08	48½		Baltic Sea	Sweden	Lennart Säfstrom
162	38	06				Sweden	Jan Roos
163	38	06				Denmark	Ole Barett
164	38				Mjøsa Lake	Norway	Unknown
165	38				Puckaway Lake, Wisconsin	USA	J. A. Rahn
166	38					Norway	Howard Saether

Late entries

Weight lb	oz	Length (in.)	Girth (in.)	Location	Country	Captor
61	15			Vahojärvi Lake	Finland	T. Pilpola
61	11½			Lynbi Lake	Denmark	
61	11½			Vänern Lake	Sweden	
53	09¼	50		Lake nr Darmstadt	Germany	D. Kralik
52	07¼			Kuivajärvi Lake	Finland	I. Saarela
49				Lake Tschotagama	Canada	
47	06¼				Denmark	Victor Haröm
47				Near Duisburg	Germany	

Date	Method	Source	Visual evidence
July 1980	livebaiting	*Fisch und Fang* magazine, Nov. 1980, p. 914	photo
1967		Abu Contest Register, 1967	
1964	spinning	Arne Broman: letter to F.B., 1978	
	plug fishing	Arne Broman: letter to F.B., 1978	
	plug fishing	Arne Broman: letter to F.B., 1978	
1974		Arne Broman: letter to F.B., 1978	
1977	livebaiting	*Blinker* magazine, June 1978	
1961		Sheldons Inc.: letter to Jan Eggers, March 1980	
1962	spinning	*Tight Lines* catalogue, 1964, p. 9	
Oct. 1972	livebaiting	*Fisch und Fang* magazine, Nov. 1972	photo
		Fischwaid magazine, April 1978	
1978	livebaiting	*Fischwaid* magazine, April 1979	photo
Dec. 1979	spinning	Jan Eggers: letter to F.B., Jan. 1981	photo
1965	plug fishing	*Tight Lines* catalogue, 1966, p. 14	photo
1971	spinning	Arne Broman: letter to F.B., 1978	
1975		Arne Broman: letter to F.B., 1978	
1960	plug fishing	*Sportfiskaren* magazine, Feb. 1961	photo
1966	spinning	Arne Broman: letter to F.B., 1978	
1974		Arne Broman: letter to F.B., 1978	
1904		*Field*, 10 Sept. 1904	cased
Aug. 1952		Sheldons Inc.: letter to Jan Eggers, March 1980	
1965	spinning	*Tight Lines* catalogue, 1966, p. 27	

Date	Method	Source	Visual evidence
1944		Letter from editor, *Suomen Kalamiest . . .*, March 1981	
1857			
c. 1915		*Sportsfiskerleksikon* magazine	
March 1981		*Fisch und Fang* magazine, May 1981	
1953		Letter from editor, *Suomen Kalamiest . . .*, March 1981	
1890		Keen Buss, *The Northern Pike* (1961)	
1911	netted	*Rhein and Ruhr Zeitung*, July 1911	

Weight		Length	Girth	Location	Country	Captor
lb	oz	(in.)	(in.)			
44	01½	51		Starnberger Lake	Germany	Mr Ruderboot
44	00½	49¼		Fort Voordorp Moat	Holland	Bart De Ryk
44				Minnesota	USA	Joseph Stutz
43	13¾	54¾		Eider River	Germany	Helmut Seidenpfennig
42	15¾	52¼		Private lake	Germany	Helmut Seidenpfennig
41	14½	53¼	25½	Haspelschiedt Moat	France	Louis Kriegel
41				Loon Lake, Minnesota	USA	T. E. Nicholls
40	12½	56		Waginger Lake	Germany	Franz Christl
40	09			Traun Lake	Austria	Franz Medwed
40				Minnesota	USA	Harry Glorvik
40				Delay Lake	Canada	Ken Asper
39	11			Virmasvesi Lake	Finland	Ville Kukkonen
39	11			Sorpetalsperre	Germany	H. Dennl
39	11	50		Pit nr Amsterdam	Holland	Geert Trompetter
38	05½			Rheindorf	Germany	W. Kaffka
38	04½				Germany	M. Heil

Date	Method	Source	Visual evidence
1979	found dead	*Blinker* magazine, Jan. 1980, p. 42	photo
Aug. 1977	potato bait	*Utrecht Nieuwsblad*, 24 Aug. 1977	photo
1949		R. Sternberg, Dept of Nat. Resources, Minnesota	
Oct. 1975	livebaiting	Letter to Jan Eggers, April 1981	photo
Sept. 1974	livebaiting	Letter to Jan Eggers, April 1981	photo
Sept. 1980	spinning	*La Pêche et les Poissons* magazine	photo
1948		R. Sternberg, Dept of Nat. Resources, Minnesota	
1980	trailing plug	*Traunsteiner Wochenblatt* newspaper	photo
Oct. 1980	livebaiting	*Fisch und Fang* magazine, Jan. 1981, p. 56	photo
1956		R. Sternberg, Dept of Nat. Resources, Minnesota	
June 1969		World Freshwater Fish Records, 1979-80	
May 1927	netted	Letter from Dr Lauri Koli, Helsinki University, 1981	
1980		*Fisch und Fang* magazine, Jan. 1981, p. 3	
Feb. 1980	livebaiting	Letter from Jan Eggers	photo
1980		*Fisch und Fang* magazine Jan. 1981, p. 3	
1980		*Fisch und Fang* magazine, Jan. 1981, p. 3	

15 A chapter of errors

Now what happens when we take a close look at those fish that survive on my 'possible list'? Well, for one thing we soon find many discrepancies when we compare details given for the same fish by different authors.

Let us take, for example, Alfred Jardine's famous record-breaking pike caught at Shardeloes Lake, near Amersham, in 1879. This pike, No. 225 in my Big Pike List, was said to weigh 37 lb, yet J. W. Martin was apparently not convinced, as is evident from his remarks in *Days Among the Pike and Perch*: for he reminded anglers of an article written by one of Jardine's friends, a Mr Brougham, which appeared in the *Fishing Gazette* in 1879, shortly after the pike's capture. Brougham stated: 'It weighed [he was referring to the same Shardeloes pike] on the club scales of the Piscatorial Society 34¾ lb and was an exact counterpart of

Alfred Jardine's sometime 'record' English pike. It was caught on livebait in Shardeloes Lake near Amersham, Bucks., in 1879. It was said to weigh 37 lb

the 35 pounder captured by Mr Jardine two years previously.'

Another contemporary author, Frank Buckland, in *The Natural History of British Fishes* (1880) confirmed the weight of 34¾ lb: 'In November 1879 [actually it was September], Mr Jardine caught in fair angling, by means of a dace, snap-tackle and a cane rod, a grand pike, which, after having been out of the water twelve hours scaled 34¾ lb, so that it was a good 35 lb fish.'

Martin felt compelled to comment: 'This ought to settle the vexed question as to the exact weight of Mr Jardine's brace, as they have been growing during the interim.'

Martin's mention of the weight details of *a brace of pike* brings into dispute yet another of Jardine's big pike, vide: the pike generally known as the 'Maidstone pike', caught in Mote Park Lake, near Maidstone, in February 1877. For this pike Jardine claimed a weight of 36 lb.

Martin was backed up by Francis Francis, perhaps the most omniscient of the *Field's*

many outstanding angling editors. In Francis's *tour de force, Sporting Sketches* (1878), there is a facsimile of a letter he wrote to his friend 'J'.

Dear J., I've got a day on Lord Thompson's for myself and friend, I mean to go the first open day *in February*, so rig out some big live snaps and watch the weather. I'll take the lunch and I will leave the drinks and baits to you.

Now we know that Jardine had a great reputation as a slayer of big pike, and so unique was his reputation that the next line in Francis's book would seem to provide the strongest circumstantial evidence for the fact that 'J' was Jardine himself.* 'Thus I wrote some years ago to my friend J., a slayer of mighty pike, indeed, his friends call him Jack the giant killer.'

The account proceeds with a record of the day's fishing, which was, judged by any standards, very successful. Towards the end of the day 'J' was invited by the bailiff to use a small pike as bait to lure a huge pike known to be the tenant of a certain pool. The small pike was taken as soon as it hit the water. After a fifteen-minute gorge the fish was tightened on,

---

* Sometime after the first edition was published I noticed that Westwood and Satchell, the bibliographers, state in their scholarly *Bibliotheca Piscatoria* (1883) that Francis Francis's companion referred to in *Sporting Sketches* is '*Alfred Jardine, the noted slayer of big pike, well known to metropolitan anglers*' (my italics).

and a fierce battle ensued, at the end of which the pike gained her freedom by breaking the line just above the float – leaving 'J' in a state of collapse. Francis consoled his companion thus: 'Never mind old man. Take a drop of the '34 and never say die. You fought him splendidly, and had the water been clear [meaning clear of obstructions] you must have killed him.'

Francis reckoned that 'J' would have his fish within a week. And so it proved; for after a lapse of only three days a parcel arrived at 'J's office containing the same pike done up in straw, together with float, gimp and four or five yards of line. The bailiff had seen the float, and pulled out the pike in an exhausted condition. Francis wrote, 'He was hooked in the gullet; and even then he weighed $35\frac{1}{2}$ lb. Our great taxidermist Cooper set him up gorgeously and he is the pride of J's ancestral halls.'

Thus, we must I think concede that Jardine's Maidstone pike was caught by another; moreover it weighed $35\frac{1}{2}$ lb and not 36 lb as claimed.

We are not finished with Jardine yet for he was an obsessive correspondent who often had the temerity to question the weights claimed for pike killed by other anglers and even, as in the following instance, the weight claimed for a pike that was found floundering:

When Whittlesea Mere was drained in the early part of this century in order to reclaim the land and place

... a parcel arrived at 'J's' office containing the same pike done up in straw. ...' By coincidence the pike depicted in this engraving was based on a painting by H. L. Rolfe, a close friend of Alfred Jardine. I found this print in Gilliot Hatfield's scrapbook inscribed in 1881

127

it under cultivation, as the waters receded a huge pike was left nearly 'high and dry' and captured; it weighed 49 lb.

All other writers, including Hampton, have declared the weight to be 52 lb. Perhaps Jardine was a little conservative when describing fish which he did not catch himself!

Now let us look at No. 188 on my list: a 36-pounder recorded by Bickerdyke in his *Book of the All-Round Angler* as having been caught on livebait near Norwich by a Mr Thome in February 1878. These details so closely resemble those given by Hampton in *Hampton on Pike Fishing* that I suspect they represent one and the same fish. Hampton took his reference from *The Anglers' Notebook* dated 15 March 1880, which stated that a Mr Frank Thorn of Norwich took a pike of 36 lb on livebait in the month of February. I now understand from personal communications with Peter Collins (of *Angling Times*) that this fish was set up and is still to be seen; moreover, it was caught in Haveringland lake by a Mr Thorns, not Thorn.

Now let us look at a pike which was referred to in A. L. Ward's fine little book, *Pike – How to Catch Them*. The weight given was 37 lb, and according to the text was taken from the River Thurneat Potter Heigham in 1948. I first became suspicious of the validity of this fish when I realized that I had not heard of a River Thurneat, and as a consequence of my suspicion I contacted Mr Bitton of the Norfolk

River Board who confirmed that no such river existed. I realized that this was probably a printer's error which had transposed the text from *The River Thurne at* to the *The River Thurneat*. In any event I can find no confirmation for a 37 lb fish taken from the River Thurne in 1948, but, of course, there is Mr Jackson's 35½ lb pike (No. 212) which was definitely caught in the same year but from Heigham Sound, which is, of course, very close to the River Thurne, separated only by the length of Candle Dyke.

Now what of Tommy Morgan's fish – the mighty 47-pounder – long recognized as the British record pike, caught by Tommy on livebait in Loch Lomond in July 1945?

Although no great reliance can be placed on Mona's scale (since we know from details given in Chapter 7 that very heavy pike tend to owe their great weight to an expansive girth measurement rather than to a dramatic length increase – which is usually nominal), we can nevertheless obtain from it some means of judging what is possible or impossible by further reference to girth. From a perusal of the details recorded for Morgan's fish we can see that a girth measurement of 19 in. is unacceptable when related to the known weight (47 lb) and length (53 in.). This thought first struck me when I realized that 19 in. was the true girth

Inquiries concerning the whereabouts of Frank Thorns's pike eventually bore fruit. It is to be seen in Norwich Castle Museum where it was photographed by Bill Giles

This fine Norfolk 35½-pounder was taken by Mr A. Jackson of Hemsby. He caught it at Heigham Sound on 10 December 1948

measurement of an 18½ lb pike which I caught in 1943. With Morgan's fish, either an error of measurement was made at the time, or the figure has become transposed sometime during the interim period. The weight of the fish is, of course, genuine, as are the witnesses to it, including Morgan's usual boat companion, the late Mr Jackie Thompson, who had over the years become a personal friend of mine.

It is interesting to record another discrepancy in the accounts written in respect of this great fish. Weatherall, in his book *Pike Fishing*, stated: 'This was caught by Mr Thomas Morgan, in July 1945, whilst livebaiting with a *perch* on Loch Lomond.' Whereas Ward said, 'It is worth mentioning that the livebait used was a *roach* of not less than 14 oz.'

Bickerdyke described a pike of 40 lb (No. 90 in my list) as having been caught at *Epton House*, Edgehill in *1879*; a fish later exhibited at the Fisheries Exhibition in 1883. This is undoubtedly the fish (referred to by Brian Vesey-Fitzgerald in D. Watkins-Pitchford's *Fisherman's Bedside Book*) which was caught in *1865* at *Upton House*, Edgehill, Warwickshire, albeit on a croquet mallet. This fish grounded itself on a mudbank after taking the mallet head which had been tied to a piece of string and thrown into the lake by a three-year-old child. Colonel Purefoy Fitzgerald, father of the child, waded out to the mudbank, and after a short but severe tug-of-war hauled the pike ashore. The pike was weighed within hours by that famous naturalist, Frank Buckland, who found it to be in a starving condition. Vesey-Fitzgerald confirms that although the family pike was exhibited in London on several occasions (as was Bickerdyke's version), it now occupies a position of honour in his study – 'looking very fierce in its glass case'.

According to Hampton, Major Booth's 37 lb pike (the sometime joint English record holder, No. 168), was caught in 1911. Ward, however, tells us that it was caught in 1910! The 35½ lb Rapley pike (No. 209 on my list), recorded at this weight by Hampton, is given the heavier weight of 36 lb when noted by Marshall-Hardy.

I was gravely suspicious of the very existence of the 49 lb pike placed on my first edition list. The fish is described in E. Marshall-Hardy's book *Coarse Fish* as having been caught by B. Browne in 1916 from Lough Conn. I think the confusion arises out of the details of length (49 in.), recorded for a 45½ lb pike (No. 41), caught by B. Browne on Lough Conn in April 1917. I have in my possession Mr Browne's original letter to the editor of the *Fishing Gazette* dated 1 May 1917, so I am sure we can discount the former claim. Hampton, incidentally, describes the captor as M. Browne whereas we know him to be a Mr B. Browne.

I think that I have shown with these few examples how tangled are the accounts which describe some of our biggest pike. My motive in doing so is not to discredit these pike but to draw attention to the ample evidence of human error; not, incidentally, committed by those who are usually the most suspect – the anglers.

Mr Browne's letter. The crossing out is the work of the *Fishing Gazette's* editor

16 The Endrick pike

In the summer of 1967, four anglers, having dined splendidly at the Tullechewen Hotel, made their way back to 'Ayacanora', the home of Mrs Harry Britton. Here they were guests and, as such, were giving expression to a wish made by Mr Harry Britton just before he died. Ironically, and tragically, Richard Walker and the legendary Harry Britton never met, although a meeting between those two formidable juggernauts of the angling scene was a wished-for, and planned, occasion.

Fortunately, Mr Harry, as he was often called, shared a colourful fishing career with his close friend Jackie Thompson. So it was that Mr Thompson now represented Mr Harry, as well as himself, at those after-dinner discussions which were a feature of our daily programme. During these discussions, we would retrace and analyse the events of the day so as to improve our prospects for the next day's sport. Jackie was a salmon and sea-trout fisher who recoiled at the nature of men who came 400 miles to fish Loch Lomond for the 'vermin pike', yet passed over the chance to catch salmon and sea-trout. Nevertheless, our enthusiasm gradually infected him – not to the point that would ever make him fish for pike, but to a point where he shared our desire to understand the place of the pike in the economy of Loch Lomond's fish life.

One evening, when we were talking about the really big ones, Jackie recalled a story that he had heard years ago. It concerned the existence of an exceedingly large pike which had been found dead – marooned in a shallow depression by receding floodwater that was finding its way back to the River Endrick before disgorging itself into the loch.

The story of the pike was hearsay, and Jackie was careful to caution our hopes of seeing the head of this mighty fish. The existence of this pike head, it seemed, depended on the probability of there being a Scot so greatly impressed with the size of the pike's rotting carcass, as to feel impelled to cut off its head and carry it home! Small chance indeed.

Jackie, however, promised to make further inquiries and report his findings to us the next evening.

Yes, the pike story was true. Yes, the head was in existence. Yes, the head was massive, for he had seen it for himself. We were to see the pike the next evening.

Under Jackie's orders we dressed formally, and promised to show the respect that was due to 'The Major' and his wife who were now both twenty years and more beyond the 'allotted span of life'. It was they who owned Ross Priory on Loch Lomond's southern shore and it was towards that ancient building that we drove, beguiled by the prospect of seeing and handling the Endrick head for the very first time.

As we approached the priory we were aware of a tingling anticipation. All the ingredients were there. The history of the ancient property lent something to the atmosphere, and the threatening dark purples of the loch and mountain scene added more as daylight grew weak. We drew up to the front steps, climbed out quietly and squeezed the doors closed, instinctively aware that a banged door would be an affront.

We climbed the steps, noticing the valuable oriental furniture which stood within the canopy leading to the main door. One of us knocked. It was some time before the door was opened – by the lady we knew to be the Major's

Ross Priory, besides being the home of the Endrick pike, has an even greater claim to fame. It frequently gave shelter to one of Scotland's greatest sons, Sir Walter Scott. In 1817, setting out from the priory, Scott and his friend and fellow advocate Hector MacDonald Buchanan, owner of the priory, revisited Rob Roy's cave and the scenes of the outlaw's exploits at the head of the loch. These lines from 'MacGregor's Gathering' are by tradition ascribed to Scott's experience as he stood on the shore at Ross Priory, looking north:

'The moon's on the lake, and the mist's on the brae,
And the clan has a name that is nameless by day.'

wife. We were directed to the Major's trophy room where, in a few waiting moments, our eyes took in more than our brains could sensibly cope with. That small room contained all but 'Nessie' of Scotland's rich fauna, and it looked sideways, upwards and downwards at us.

Soon, the Major joined us and we inquired into the origins of certain of the numerous first world war souvenirs which gave a bizarre touch to his collection. At another time and in another mood these would have been completely absorbing, not least in interest being the German soldiers' first hand-held anti-tank gun, fashioned in reply to the British ironclad monster.

At last he handed us the prize we had come to see – the Endrick pike head – which we then passed round with the care normally reserved for a piece of rare pottery.

In those few questioning minutes, before the Major felt tired, we learned that the pike had been found dead on the Endrick marshes about the year 1934. He had seen bigger pike heads before, long ago when he had lived at the head of the loch by the River Falloch. Yes, that was the place, he thought, for really big pike.

It all added up, for Ardlui was the place that Francis Francis recommended to his readers in 1874, after he had journeyed north in Colonel Thornton's footsteps to write that stirring book *By Lake and River*.

In retrospect I am conscious that at that time our host's vibrant grip of life maintained a living link with that remote past.

There was just time to photograph and measure the head – $12\frac{5}{8}$ in. from snout to gill-cover! But measurement is a feeble means of describing a pike. A photograph is better, as my readers can see for themselves. We needed neither of these means to appreciate what the pike must have weighed in her prime.

As each of us conjured a weight and self-consciously reduced a calculated guess, Walker came out with a big one first time – as the American long jumper Bob Beamon had done at the 1968 Olympic Games – and in so doing he likewise scattered the field.

Seventy pounds!

This out-of-character action was no doubt intended as an object lesson to pinpoint an essential truth about pike heads; a truth first established by Tate Regan when he wrote in *British Freshwater Fishes*: 'Other things being equal, the larger the fish the smaller the head proportionately; growth of the head ceases or becomes almost imperceptible before that of the fish as a whole.' We can infer that when other things are equal a very large head is indicative of a very large body indeed.

We will never know the true facts of the life, or the actual weight, of this magnificent pike, but it is easy to imagine a drama to account for those last days which were a prelude to her death.

She had succeeded at ambush but she was restless. She moved off with the tail of her victim – a spring salmon – still protruding from her jaws. It was April and she was heavy with spawn when the call came to reproduce her kind. With her male consorts, like so many pygmies, following in her train, she pressed her seventy pounds against the floods of Endrick... never to return.

A supreme reign of terror was over.

The age of the Endrick pike

In April 1980 I sent two small scales taken (they were about to fall off) from the Endrick pike head to two different authorities for a reading. Interestingly, in spite of the well-known dif-

The Endrick pike head in the hands of Ken Taylor

ficulty of reading even those scales taken from the preferred region of a pike's body – the shoulder region – the readings matched remarkably well.

Fish ecologist Dr R. H. K. Mann of the Freshwater Biological Association's River Laboratory staff at East Stoke in Dorset, reporting on one scale, wrote:

Dear Mr Buller,
The scale from the Endrick pike has caused much interest here at the FBA River Laboratory. We cleaned the scale in a 2% solution of sodium hydroxide (caustic soda) before mounting it on a

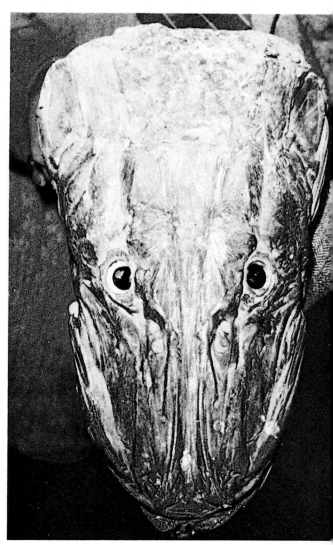

glass slide and taking some photographs. Pike scales are not easy to read because of the presence of false rings and, in old fish, because the rings on the edge of the scale may be very close together and therefore difficult to count. The 'Endrick' scale presents a further problem in that the centre is of scar tissue (the original scale having been lost and replaced early in the pike's life) and there is some surface erosion or pitting in the centre also. However there are 16 annual rings visible (see photograph and pencilled outline) and my guess is that 1, maybe 2, rings are missing in the centre. Also 1 or 2 may be hidden on the scale edge although this is less certain. Please note that the rings on the photograph are not as clear as on the scale itself when viewed under a microscope. My conclusion is that the fish is at least 16 years old and may be as much as 20 – perhaps 17 or 18 years is a reasonable compromise.

I note that Dr Frost estimated that the oldest Windermere pike was about 17 years old, and the same age has been quoted as the maximum for pike in one North American lake. It looks as though the 'Endrick' fish is of the same age although this cannot be determined exactly.

With many thanks for letting us examine a scale from this famous fish.

Alwyne Wheeler of the fish section at the British Museum (Natural History) at Cromwell Road, London, reporting on the other scale, wrote:

Dear Fred,
Thank you for your letter of 18 April. I am sorry if it seemed I was neglecting you but it arrived while I was away from the Museum on a field trip in Greece. The scale focus is 'offcentre' and this makes it hard to read on the shorter side (growth lines being more compressed): I believe that I can see 17

This photograph shows a much enlarged image of a tiny pike scale taken from the Endrick pike's head. The head has now been put on permanent display in the gallery of Glasgow's Kelvingrove Art Gallery and Museum (By courtesy of Freshwater Biological Association)

annual rings on the long side. I have cleaned the scale up a little and re-examination confirms this figure.

As you know pike scales are not usually read for age, but this one seems fairly clear except for a rather opaque centre. It does mean, however, that I have little to compare it with.
Yours sincerely, Alwyne Wheeler

17 The great pike of Meelick

Of all the stories of big pike the one that I find perpetually fascinating is the story of the great pike of Meelick – probably because it affirms my long-held view that a location capable of producing one monster pike is likely to produce another. An example of this phenomenon is provided by Tommy Morgan's 47 lb 6 oz record Scottish pike. Within ten yards of the spot where he caught it in an area so vast as Loch Lomond (a loch some twenty-seven miles long and up to six miles wide), I hooked and had the chance to land one at least as big.

The underlying assumption is that a location which produces a monster pike is by definition an exceptionally favourable habitat, which provides the opportunity for a pike's continuous and rapid growth, and which, notwithstanding the passage of time and providing there was no fundamental change, would do so again.

So far as I am aware the first published account naming Meelick as the home of a monster pike began with the publication of a letter in the *Fishing Gazette* of 28 February 1891. The following is an extract from that letter.

The upper waters of the Shannon, near Banagher and Meelick, also abound with enormous pike; which have been caught as heavy as 50 lb.

This is a great weight, but you will be told that there are even heavier pike in that river. When I was in its vicinity last year, I heard of one that must be – if half the stories told of him be true – the grand, or rather great-grandsire of Irish pike; in fact, the patriarch of the *Esox lucius* tribe. His favourite haunt – for I am informed that he has not yet been captured – is a deep, large pool, below the Queen's salmon gap at Meelick. There he levies blackmail on the shoals of salmon fry as they endeavour to pass through the gap, besides indulging in occasional trout and other fish.

During many seasons, almost every angler who visited Meelick has tried to catch this huge water monster – always, however, with the same result: loss of tackle. Numberless have been the encounters; but, like a giant guarding an enchanted pass, the 'great pike of the gap' has sent back all his assailants shorn of their tackle and honours.

For he is no craven, but stoutly has met each new foe, adding continually to the list of his triumphs. The spoils of these must be rather uncomfortable decorations, if there be any foundation for the assertion solemnly made and corroborated in the most impressive manner by a discomfited angler, who declared that 'if any one took that pike he might set up a fishing-tackle shop with all the hooks and gimp adorning his jaws'.

Meelick on the River Shannon – the home of great pike

The same angler stated that on one occasion when he had hooked this pike he saw his vast proportions, for he had contrived to get him alongside of the boat from which he was fishing. Being asked why he had not gaffed him, he replied: 'Oh, 'tis easy to say "gaff him", but when I desired my attendant to perform that operation the fellow funked, and swore that the pike would upset the boat, and in the meantime the brute dived down like lightning, and carried away my tackle.'

This angler and a brother officer actually journeyed to Dublin for the sole purpose of procuring tackle of extraordinary strength and peculiar construction to capture the 'pike of the gap'.

A relation of mine, a skilful and experienced angler, was tempted to try his luck with the big fish. Accordingly he constructed a trolling apparatus such as is not to be seen every day. It consisted of three large Limerick hooks, but as they were not large enough, my relation had two more constructed, under his own superintendence, by an intelligent country smith. On these five hooks, tied on the strongest gimp, he mounted as bait a trout above two pounds weight, and attached the whole to a stout hemp line wound on a large wooden reel, the concern being far too heavy to be managed by a rod. Thus equipped, he went forth strong in the belief that he was destined to kill the monster pike. Directing his boatman to row slowly backward and forward across the pool, he kept moving his hand, feeling gently as he trolled the line. Suddenly he felt a violent jerk, which from its unyielding nature, he conjectured was occasioned by striking rocks, of which the pool was by no means free. However, the shock was momentary, and he drew in his line to see if all was right. Suddenly he found, with feelings which a brother angler may realize, that his bait was gashed across in four or five places quite to the bone – in fact, regularly 'crimped' – and one of the large hooks was broken off at the bend.

Although the monster pike of the 1890s would have been dead twenty years and more the following report of the finding of a colossal dead pike at Meelick Lock was published in the *Fishing Gazette* in May 1927:

Story of a Monster Irish Pike

The FIELD of April 7 publishes the following story of a huge Irish pike. It is a curious thing that these big pike so often escape notice until it is too late to verify the particulars:

Mr S. G. Parker-Hutchinson, Castle Lough, Nenagh, Tipperary, kindly sends us the news of a very big pike which was found dead at Meelick Lock on the Shannon at the end of 1926, but which does not seem to have been recorded before. As has been the way with so many exceptional Irish pike, there is now no chance of getting enough details to make sure of its weight and it will have to join the big company of semi-legendary monsters, though its story, so far as it goes is thrilling enough for anybody! Mr Parker-Hutchinson wrote to Mr S. H. McGarry, the lock-keeper, about it and encloses his reply, which runs as follows:

'I can truthfully state that a very large pike was found dead at Meelick weir early in December last. He was not weighed, but was measured by a German engineer, a Mr Hasey, and he was exactly 1¾ metres, or 69 inches.

'He evidently got smothered or choked, as he had a salmon partly swallowed and jammed in his gills that had not spawned. The salmon was partly decomposed and when extracted from the monster's mouth was estimated at about 15 lb at least before capture by a fisherman who saw it. The monster must have been dead some days and a strong SW gale landed him dry on the weir wall almost at the end of the sluices.'

It is evident that the enormous pike was not altogether unknown in the neighbourhood, for Mr McGarry goes on to say that during the warm weather of 1925 'a very large pike was seen for some days by Major Lyster and other anglers, but they would not give him any chance of their baits, as he was such a savage-looking shark in fresh water that they believed their tackle would not land him.' Apparently also the fish was nearly responsible for a shipwreck! Anyhow, 'Mr Fleming, Bank of Ireland, Banagher, struck him one night when returning from trout fishing at the very end of the lock, and he drenched him with one splash of his tail, and at first he thought it was a log of timber that he struck with the boat.'

Another letter on the subject appeared in the *Fishing Gazette* in January 1930:

Big Pike

Dear Sir, with reference to the letter in your issue of December 28 about big pike. A pike was found dead in the Shannon at Meelick Lock, some four miles below Banagher, in, I think, 1926. There was an account of this fish in the FIELD. I got the particulars from the lock-keeper, who I know very well, and who I believe to be a trustworthy man. This fish was choked in trying to swallow a small salmon, and was measured by a German engineer employed on the Shannon scheme. It was 5 ft 9 in. long, and was unfortunately too decomposed to do anything with. Unhappily neither the engineer nor the lock-keeper were fishermen, and consequently did not realise the fact that the pike was a unique specimen, and made no effort to preserve the bones. The lock-keeper's name is J. McGarry, of Meelick Lock, Banagher, and the engineer's name is Herr Hassee, of the firm of Siemens Schuckert.

Yours truly, A. E. BANNATYNE.
The Grange, Castleconnell.

The editor of the *Fishing Gazette* commented, 'The weight of a pike of 69 in. would be somewhere about 80 lb in all probability.'

On 11 January 1964 the *Fishing Gazette* published an article, 'Stories of Irish Pike', by Dr E. J. Went, of the Fisheries Department, Dublin, in which he refers to the Meelick pike. Dr Went reckoned that a 69 in. pike would have weighed 102 lb were it in good condition and at least 90 lb if it were not. In *The Domesday Book of Mammoth Pike* I worked out, on the basis of Mona's scale (after taking the unprecedented step of suggesting that Mona's scale was meant to refer to measurements of 'extreme' length rather than 'fork' length), the probable weight of the Meelick pike at 90 lb.

The fighting qualities of big pike

It seems to me that the majority of game fishermen, and for that matter a good many coarse anglers, are under the impression that pike, even big pike, are not great fighters. Even those who admire the pike but whose experience is limited to catching run-of-the-mill, river, pond and gravel-pit pike may have the same impression. Now, to deduce from impressions or experiences of this kind that big

Fog and mist slow down the speed of human travel, and likewise turbid water prevents fish from navigating at full speed. Loch Lomond's waters are crystal clear, which gives a hooked pike leave to travel at great speed, which it inclines to do. An extra large tail and a characteristic streamlined shape give the native pike the extra jumping and fighting power for which they are justly famous

loch pike are likely to fight in the same manner is to make an error of considerable magnitude. Some of the great loch pike of Scotland and Ireland have fought battles which almost defy description. I would like to illustrate the point with a few examples.

In May 1917, Mr B. Browne, secretary of the Loughs Conn and Cullen Fishery Association, wrote to the editor of the *Fishing Gazette* giving details of four salmon taken on the fly in Lough Conn by Messrs William Browne and Gallagher.* It was the custom of the secretary to send reports to the *Fishing Gazette* of salmon taken in the district. On this occasion Mr Browne gave additional details of a 45½ lb pike which he had killed on Lough Conn the previous Sunday. The fish had taken a brown Devon (on a steel trace) meant for a salmon. It fought for two and a half hours and broke the salmon rod in three places before it was eventually gaffed by Mr Browne's companion, Constable Killgallon. The pike was 49 in. long and had a girth measurement of 22½ in. Mr Browne noted that the fish had a very small head for a pike of such great size.

'Silver Doctor', renowned fishing correspondent of the last era, whose rods had taken a set on New Zealand's great rainbows and Canada's huge Tyee salmon, had this to say of his first Irish pike.

We were patrolling the side of a monstrous weedbed when a pull came and at last I was into a fish. At first he made towards the boat, but a mighty swirl and a screaming reel told me this was something sizable. Suddenly without the slightest warning a huge pike leapt clear from the water showing every inch of himself, while with wide open mouth he shook his great head from side to side for all the world like a tarpon. I never shall forget the sight nor Mike's gasp, 'Begob, what a poike!' [Mike was the boatman.] For the next quarter of an hour this Irish pike gave me all I could do and, when he was gaffed aboard, the myth that pike don't fight had gone from my mind for all time. He weighed 23 pounds, a lovely bright fish in grand condition. . . .

* His letter is in my possession. *F.B.*

Well, that fish was only 23 lb but it gives some indication of the fighting powers of loch pike. Master angler Cholmondeley-Pennell had a good opinion of loch pike as will be seen from his description of a skirmish with a Corrib giant.

I recollect once when spinning under the north shore . . . that my spinning bait . . . a whole eel . . . was fast . . . very fast indeed . . . in something. From the perfectly passive, and at the same time utterly unyielding nature of resistance, I concluded I had got hold of a rock, or submerged stump, though how such should be found in water which I knew to be twenty feet deep at least was somewhat unaccountable. I had very powerful new gimp tackle, a strong line, and a stout rod, and I spared neither in my unsuccessful attempts to get clear. Suddenly my bait, began quietly, perfectly quietly to move away!

Unhappily I have to report that Pennell lost his leviathan, but he left us with a simple description of the manner in which a loch pike does battle: 'These Lough Corrib pike fight like demons.'

Morgan's record 47 lb 11 oz Loch Lomond pike, although held on extremely heavy tackle, fought a ferocious battle for forty minutes. Morgan's sometime ghillie, Jackie Thompson, told me that the pike took man and boat right out of the bay where it was hooked and round a point into the next bay and then back again before it was killed. On both trips the pike navigated itself through a narrow deep underwater channel.

Colonel Thornton's account of his sporting tour of Scotland (*Thornton's Sporting Tour*), published in 1804, contains the earliest and perhaps most colourful description in all pike literature of a battle with a great loch pike. It took place in Loch Alva.

I saw a very large fish come at me, and, collecting my line, I felt I had him fairly hooked, but I feared he had run himself round some root, his weight seemed so dead: we rowed up, therefore, to the spot, when he soon convinced me he was at liberty, by running me into the lake, that I had not one inch of line more to give him. The servants, foreseeing the consequences of my situation, rowed, with great expedition, towards the fish, which now rose about

This very fine photograph of an airborne hooked pike was taken by Roy Shaw

This painting of Colonel Thornton playing the big Loch Alva (or Alvie) pike (he described it as 'a perfect monster') appeared in a new edition of *A Sporting Tour* (1896)

seventy yards from us, an absolute wonder! . . . After playing him for some time, I gave the rod to Captain Waller, that he might have the honour of landing him, for I thought him quite exhausted, when, to our surprise, we were again constrained to follow the monster nearly across this great lake . . . frequently he flew out of the water to such a height, that though I knew the uncommon strength of my tackle, I dreaded losing such an extraordinary fish . . . . After about an hour and a quarter's play, however, we thought we might safely attempt to land him, which was done in the following manner. Newmarket, a lad so called from the place of his nativity, who had now come to assist, I ordered, with another servant, to strip, and wade in as far as possible; which they readily did. In the meantime I took the landing net, while Captain Waller, judiciously ascending the hill above, drew him gently towards us. He approached the shore very quickly, and we thought him quite safe, when, seeing himself surrounded by his enemies, he in an instant made a last desperate effort, shot into the deep again, and, in the exertion, threw one of the men on his back. His immense size was now very apparent; we proceeded with all due caution, and, being once more drawn towards land, I tried to get his head

The engraving above depicts Captain Waller holding the rod just as Thornton's pike is being landed. Waller has just walked down the hill that he had judiciously ascended while playing the pike

The engraving below is of Thornton's pike. Both these engravings were executed from original paintings by Garrard. Garrard was hired (as a photographer might be today) to illustrate aspects of Thornton's tour through Scotland

into the net, when effecting which, the servants were ordered to seize his tail, and slide him on shore. He was, however, completely spent, in a few moments, we landed him, a perfect monster! . . . On opening his jaws, to endeavour to take the hooks from him, which were both fast in his gorge, so dreadful a forest of teeth, or tushes, I think I never beheld. . . . His measurement, accurately taken, was five feet four inches,* from eye to fork. . . . The weight of this fish judging by the trones, we had with us, which only weigh twenty-nine pounds, made us, according to our best opinions, estimate him at between forty-seven and forty-eight pounds.

Colonel Thornton caught his pike nearly twenty years before *Thornton's Sporting Tour* was published. I dare say that he relied upon memory for the pike's length, whereas Daniel probably relied on details published at the time of capture.

These new data put Thornton's pike into the category of 'probable', rather than the category of 'unlikely'; where it has been for 200 years.

Finally, in defence of Thornton may I suggest that he could have recorded the figure of 54 in. in his notes and later accidentally transposed it to 5 ft 4 in. It would be an easy mistake for anyone to make – even a printer!

On 16 January 1905 the Rev. Tom Seccombe Gray and friend fished the Herefordshire Wye during a spell of extremely cold weather. Tom's description, in his book *Pike Fishing* (1923), of the hooking and eventual landing of a big fish, is probably the finest account ever written; certainly it is the best account of the landing of a big pike.

The willow opposite has one bough hanging somewhat far out. The silver Devon flies in under this – drops in the water. Spins a couple of yards and

* A weight of 49 lb 14 oz, an extreme length of 4 ft 9 in., and a depth of 11½ in., is given for Thornton's pike in Daniel's *Rural Sports*, published in 1801. Using Dr Frost's formula (page 65) for converting extreme length to fork length, we obtain a measurement of 54 in. (57 ÷ 1·055 = 54).

From the conversion we can see that a more realistic, and acceptable measurement, for a pike weighing 49 lb is obtained.

Readers can confirm this from Figures 18 and 19 (pages 63 and 64), which illustrate the relationship between a pike's weight and length.

stops dead. Ker-chug! Pressure is applied, as much as is dared. And it don't move. That precious (and only) Devon escaped the over-hanging bough to get foul of a root under water. What can be done? Empty that huge punt (look at it!), go across and disturb the water? Or pull and break, or – as I live, it moved! It moved! and sailed along slowly towards the ice.

Then – it's a pike!! All this passed through my mind, and hard on its heels a saying of 'Daddy' Deadman's. 'When you hook a big pike it's like hooking a tree.' I could have showered down blessings on the old man's head had he been there.

It sailed along towards the ice, and I ventured to hit her. Then, near the ice, she turned and swam back again, under and past that overhanging willow. Then she seemed to wake up to the fact that in a measure she was held – an awful spell of head-shaking and jiggering took place. She shook the rod-point (I can see it still, for I glanced at it), till I feared something would go. Then came a rush that made the rim of the reel hot under finger-tip. At its end another jigger which pulled the butt of the rod away from one's body. One had visions of hooks losing hold, or hooks breaking (she did smash one – felt it give, and 'twas not pleasant, that jerk) or the rod being unable to stand up to the tussle. She would shake anything out, so one hit the hooks home again, 'tapped the hooks into her knapper' à la 'Daddy'.

So it went on, R. watching in silence, for which I blessed him. Fifteen minutes passed by, and never a sight of her. Never nearer than 30 yards. It was a succession of rushes and shakings and jiggers. Then the reel got her nearer – she came up and up and up, and away again. The rod was putting on pressure again, and she responded – up and up and up again. She was very deep down – we never saw a swirl or a movement for a long time. She was coming up and then, 25 yards out she showed. A long, long back, like a man's thigh, a big dorsal fin, the upper part of the tail. 'If you *do* come ashore after all this, you go into a glass case.'

Didn't have much time to see her – bang went her tail, as she made for the ice and went under it. A lowered point keeps the line clear of the ice, and slowly round she came.

She was turned always against her will, and slowly. Round and back and nearer in this time. She's coming in – there, now, she is, and we can see her – a whopper – and may we have the luck to land her! Now for a change of tactics.

The Rev. T. S. Gray's 30 lb cased pike, caught at the Horseshoe Bend at Little Court on the River Wye near Hereford. Gray wrote of the cased pike: 'Now she hangs over the fire in the gun-room and has been a delight to possess ever since. Blank days! How many has she sweetened! Come in from one, look at her and say, "We did it one day".'

Do you recollect the agent said 45 foot of water in depth?

Well, she 'sounded' – not a rush under the ice or to the willow – but down and down. The line entered the water about ten yards out, and travelled outwards no further, and the reel sang its song as it yielded. We got her up – and a long way up it seemed! She came into sight again, and we saw her plainly. Across her back a weal as if a stick had struck her. That tree-trunk on the bank suggested trees sunk under water. She may, when she lashed about at the end of her 'sounding', have struck one.

Suppose, horror! she got the line round a branch down there. 'You shan't go down there again!' But she did, and luckily the line kept free. Again up and in, and she sailed parallel along with the water's edge – and – then frost seized the chance of a motionless line, and froze the line in the rings – we dare not reel in. 'R., come and break the ice in the rings with your fingers.' The rod was moved for him to handle. R. was standing behind, upon the bank, and he ran down. Frightened, bang went her tail, and she stripped the ice from the rings – one can hear the breaking of the ice, and see it dropping from the rod!

But the line held, and the reel spoke again. And down she went. Back, and in once more, and again Jack Frost succeeded in locking the line to the rings. R. came quietly this time, the rod was moved, and he broke it successfully. A swirl of mud and she

vanished to come back again. In, quite close in, and now while she's not taking line or the reel recovering it, the handles of the reel move to and fro a couple of inches, and the moving line does not freeze.

Out again she goes, not so hard this time, and in again to our right and along to our left, under the rod-point. Soon she'll be ready, and then comes a sight of blood flowing from her gills. She must have been bleeding all this time, one supposes.

Away and in again: under the point of the rod she makes her last bid for freedom. She gathers herself and comes clean out of the water! Down comes the point of the rod, an uncle's advice flashing through my mind, 'cut your point to a leaping fish,' and over she rolls in the air. We can see the line across her silver belly along the ventral fins. It seemed like a month before the reel moved again. This time she came in head straight to the bank. The rod went to the left hand: R. gave me the gaff – it went in just behind the left pectoral fin, with never even a quiver from the pike. Played right out! She looked like a train coming out of a tunnel as she came out of the water. A pike always looks bigger out than in. And she looked big enough in the water, in all conscience.

Out came the gaff, and in my arms I carried her up to the top of the bank. And began to unhook the silver Devon.

In those days one carried no gag or pike scissors. We opened her mouth with the hook of the big knife and the gaff. She was hooked far down in the mouth, two hooks on the curve of the gills: another hook, broken. She shut her mouth like a vice, and we could not hold it open. But we observed that we could, when open, have dropped a bird as large as a wild duck easily into it.

So the trace was taken off, and leads off trace, gill-cover lifted up and silver Devon and trace pulled out through the opening. The Devon went into the jaws and came out behind it.

We noticed a beautifully deep red in dorsal, caudal and anal fins. Faithfully reproduced in the mounting. Her ventral fins were curiously shaped with a curve forward in the rays of them. And, too, we noted the end of the gimp hitched back in that curious kind of projection in the upper jaw.

My pal told me months after, 'I thought you would bring every ghillie and keeper on the place to see what had happened. You made such a row with your View Hulloos!' That bit remains not a whit in my memories: but no doubt he was right.

Well, we went to some snow-covered objects which resembled a bag and a creel: from the dram flask drank the health of a right gallant fish.

Then we carried her down from the top and laid her near creel and bag, just above the trunk. There she was speedily covered with snow, and her spots and her colours were hidden.

Oh! no – we've not forgotten: her length was 3 feet 8 inches: 44 inches; and her weight 30 lbs.

Part Three

Catching Pike

'. . . I found that pike would come on just at that point of fading light when only the outline of objects could still be discerned.' This photograph of the renowned pike angler Fred Wagstaff fishing the Delph was taken just before our party (which included Michael Prorok) faced the one-and-a-quarter-hour walk back to the Lamb and Flag inn at Welney. Each of us caught two pike, except that one of 'Yankee' Mike's was a 7 lb zander

18 Weather

In my career as a gunmaker and tackle dealer I have become very much aware of the effect that weather has upon angling activities. I suppose my awareness is heightened by the certain knowledge that bad Saturday weather always spells poor business, whereas good Saturday weather usually means bumper business. Many anglers are strangely naïve about weather. They seem to be influenced by weather prospects which affect their *own* comfort, rather than those which affect the comfort of the fish.

Good fishing days come in every conceivable guise – very cold ones, snowy ones, blustery ones, and even very hot ones. A spell of settled weather of one sort or another lasting four days or more makes for good prospects. You may be wondering how to catch a pike on a very hot day. The answer is you don't very often – you wait for the night!

I well remember, one particularly hot summer, fishing the Dorset Stour. The river was very low, the stream weak, and the water temperature high. After fruitless attempts at daytime fishing my friend and I found that pike would 'come on' just at that point of fading light when only the outline of objects could still be discerned. We had capital sport every night for about thirty minutes – fishing with float tackle; relying on our sense of touch to tell us when the pike had taken the bait.

Windy days are an aid to good pike fishing, not because there is merit in the wind itself, but because the wind is apt to cause confusion to the pike's dual senses of vision and hearing. Wave actions, due to high winds, cause a refractive pitch and toss to the light beams entering the water; this may draw off the pike's attention from the angler's clumsy movements. These same winds help to smother the inevitable fish-scaring noises which emit from the angler, and in doing so improve his chances.

Jardine says, '. . . and there, as elsewhere, my best sport has been on windy days' and, 'The ripples on the surface of the water refract the rays of light, and the angler and his punt are but indifferently seen.'

To make certain his point about the usefulness of windy weather Jardine fished Shardeloes Lake near Amersham in Buckinghamshire in September 1879.

He wrote:

The weather was very stormy and tempestuous. My punt was rather small and shallow, and the gale increasing, it was dangerous to keep out in the middle of the lake exposed to the full force of the wind. I therefore shifted to the leeward side of an island, where in ten feet of water I expected to find a monster pike, which some nine months previously had smashed up the rod and tackle of a brother angler, who was then fishing with me. I baited with a half-pound dace and cast it into the open channel between some weeds, and waited but a short while before I had a run, and drove my snap tackle home. The pike immediately made a mad rush, taking nearly a hundred yards of line off my reel, and leaped some feet out of the water, this was several times repeated, but my salmon gut trace held firm. I had the pike well in hand, and in twenty minutes it was gaffed and safe in my punt. The fish measured 47 in. in length, 25 in. in girth, and that afternoon, in the presence of Mr W. H. Brougham, late secretary of the Thames Angling Preservation Society, weighed 37 lbs. *This pike was probably induced by the tempestuous weather to feed fearlessly* and thus lost its life [my italics].

Jardine makes the very point in that last sentence. He does not claim that pike feed voraciously in tempestuous weather, but that they feed fearlessly.

This account of the capture of the then British record pike at Shardeloes has a special significance for me since I have lately had the pleasure of fishing this beautiful Chiltern lake by kind invitation of its owner, Mr J. Brazil. Came the day when I tucked my punt to the leeward of that same island. I had a vision that any true pike angler might have had. I imagined the lake once more filled with shoals of portly redfins, huge bristling perch, and great fat tench – not to mention a few big trout and the odd monster pike – instead of being stocked solely with brown trout and rainbow trout as it is today.

Another reference by Jardine to extreme weather conditions was made when he was fishing the River Frome, where the quieter parts of the river and backwaters were frozen over. He said, 'In the main channel thick slabs of ice were hurrying along the swift flowing current. We fished close to the land-locked ice, and our floats would again and again disappear under the edge of it, as hungered into madness some plunging pike seized our live baits.'

Bill Giles has a more elaborate theory on weather conditions. Although he agrees with the dictum that a period of settled weather prior to a fishing day improves the pike angler's prospects, he goes further. He maintains that a future, and as yet unknown, weather sequence has an equally profound bearing on a pike's current feeding programme. As evidence of this I include the following:

On 3 January 1968 Bill, as usual meticulously recording in his log details of the day's fishing, found a water temperature of 34 °F, some two degrees higher than the air temperature. As a result he expected a poor day with the pike; in the event he caught two 20-pounders, and a 13-pounder. He now believes that had that day been followed by a spell of milder weather he might not have found those fish on feed. The next day in fact heralded the beginning of a very cold weather spell, where the temperature dropped to 8 °F.

Bill believes that a pike is endowed with a

Even a cursory glance at this photograph will make readers aware of the weather conditions, perhaps even before they notice the main characters, the anglers

mechanism capable of being stimulated by weather patterns, which allows it to anticipate a future lean feeding period in order to stock up with food.

This theory is an interesting one and nicely accounts for the occasional flaw in the pattern of pike behaviour, noticed by those who, like Bill Giles, keep an accurate meteorological record of every outing. A broad interpretation of Bill's log data indicates that prospects are good when air temperatures are higher than water temperatures, and bad when air temperatures are lower than water temperatures. This, of course, is a slight oversimplification of Bill's findings since he has noticed that a rising air temperature, even if still below the water temperature, can induce pike to feed.

The fact that pike are disinclined to feed when air temperature is below that of the water probably accounts for the frequently given advice that on hard winter days the middle of the day is best for pike fishing: a time when you might reasonably expect air temperature to climb to a twenty-four-hour peak.

148

J. W. Martin ('Trent Otter'), writing in 1907, held forthright views on the sort of weather likely to provide good sport. He noted that some contemporaries preferred, of all conditions, a gale of wind which rolled the waters up into miniature waves. He agreed that these conditions were often propitious, but gave an example of others which had given him better sport.

Once in particular I remember spinning all one afternoon when the water was clouded and a nice breeze blowing, but not a run did I get; towards evening the wind died away, and the surface of the water was like a mirror, and then the rain came down in earnest; altogether not an evening in which to expect sport with an artificial. However, I had a few casts over a place that several times before during the afternoon I had thrown over without success, but this time I got five fish within the next half-hour, averaging five pounds each.

He went on to say,

There is no rule that can be invariably applied in this matter. I have taken jack in all sorts of weathers – when a gale nearly blew me off the river, and when the softest zephyrs scarcely ruffled the surface of the water; when a north-easter has been roaring down the valleys; when the rain has been coming down in a deluge; when a heavy snowstorm has whitened the whole face of nature, and when the frost has been so keen that every few minutes I have been obliged to suck the ice from the rings of the rod.

Martin made a valuable comment when he distinguished between two good winter-feeding species – the roach and the pike. On their reactions to the same weather he said, 'An east wind with a touch of frost that would drive the roach clean off the feed might make a jack come on right manfully.' If Martin is right, the pike fisher has a point to remember. He must not slavishly follow the lessons learned about weather from his experience with other coarse fish.

Morgan, too, made an interesting point about weather. He reported to a journalist sometime after the capture of his record pike that, in his experience, some of the big Loch Lomond pike (over 30 lb) fed well during a summer thunderstorm. He was also of the opinion that when these big fish were moving the smaller pike were not to be had.

These last two great pike anglers shared another belief. Morgan insisted on a practice of having his boatman row through the weed-beds splashing an oar to drive the pike out from cover, while he livebaited the clear patches from the security and comfort of a small neighbouring island. He maintained (wrongly in my opinion) that pike so disturbed struck the livebait in anger. Martin, on the other hand, although practising the same routine, held a different notion as to the reason for its success.

He wrote:

There are many pike rivers that have small islands, or tiny jungles of reeds and flags with open spaces behind or in front; jack as a rule hide themselves among the roots of these fastnesses, now and again coming out into the open water to feed. A practised pike angler, the very first time he sees the water, can tell whereabouts the pike are likely to lie. Sometimes when a long fringe of flags runs alongside a river, and there is a considerable depth of water for some distance among those flags, the jack back in, and show no inclination to come out into the open water in front. I remember once a gentleman bringing down to the Great Ouse a splendid can of Thames dace; we tried all down by the side of some flags. Two or three hours work resulted in only a four pounder; when I suggested that we should borrow a long clothes-prop, go from end to end of the flags, and bang about as far as we could reach with the pole among them. This we did, and half an hour later those dace again went on a voyage of discovery, and this time we got five right good fish, averaging six and a half pounds each; we had bolted them out of the flags into the open water in front, *where they were more likely to see our baits.*

Walker and I both knew about Morgan's Loch Lomond weed-thrashing routine. In the early days we were sceptical of the benefits claimed for it. However, after some experiment we concluded that once a bay had yielded up its feeding pike to normal, quiet fishing methods, there were more fish to be taken if the latter could be driven from cover.

Coming back to the theme of this chapter – weather. Edward Spence, that intrepid pike fisher, writing in 1928, stated that in his opinion

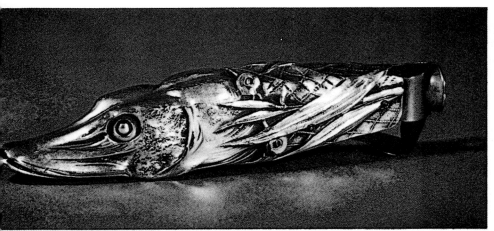

The pike cigar cutter. George Miskin, a member of the Flyfishers' Club, owns what is probably a unique object, namely a cigar cutter with a pike head motif. It is a very solid, probably late Victorian, object of silver plate on Britannia metal. Mr Miskin describes his cutter thus: 'I am very impressed with the accurate likeness and detail that has gone into the craftsmanship. The net mesh with floats and entangled weeds is most artistically incorporated to show the ensnared pike.'

there were three conditions of pike. One, a fiercely feeding hungry pike. Two, a non-feeding sated pike. Three, a pike emerging from a snake-like torpor who might be tempted by a bait properly presented. He maintained that nothing in the way of weather was material to the first group unless it was the closing of the water by ice. He might have added that pike in this condition are but rarely met with, whereas pike in the third condition are all too common, and might be very susceptible to the influence of weather. Spence adds fuel to the thunderstorm theory by quoting from his fishing diary thus:

There was a day at Slapton in September when between tea and dinner I had sixteen runs on livebait and caught thirteen pike from six to fourteen pounds, without shifting the pitch, and the other boats —two of them within a hundred yards of me – did nothing though they stoutly endured a thunderstorm that raged furiously all the time and soaked me to the marrow.

Spence made a magnificent discovery on pike feeding activity (or the lack of it) during very cold spells. At one time he was fishing from a punt on the Royalty water in bitterly cold weather. It was so cold that his punt-pole gathered ice to such an extent that he was obliged to tow the punt up river. Cold slush came down with the stream, and with it went his last chance, or so he thought, of taking a pike. Yet, when after some hours of fruitless fishing, Spence changed from livebaiting with a

float to livebaiting with a ledger, he caught eleven pike from 5 lb to 11 lb. Could it be that in very cold conditions an anchored livebait (or deadbait for that matter), lying close to the bed of the river right on the nose of a pike, will induce it to feed; whereas methods demanding substantial activity from the pike will not?

Dennis Pye made a profound comment on weather when he wrote: 'To my mind a good pike fishing day must be dull, with a slight breeze blowing just enough to put a ripple on top of the water and the air temperature at 50 °F. If I could choose my own time I would prefer to go fishing after three or four days when the air temperature has been steady at 50 °F.' Dennis was not describing essential conditions for good pike fishing, but conditions that were most favourable.

My old friend 'Robbie' (William Robinson), a staffman on the *Angler's News* and *Shooting Times* for most of his life, wrote to me just after the publication of *Pike* in 1971, pointing out certain inaccuracies and omissions. On the subject of weather he reminded me of what Sidney Spencer had written in his book, *Pike on the Plug* (1936).

One thing the study of pike haunts makes clear – they love sunshine.* For every fish that you find on

* Spencer's remark reminded me of three lines in Edmund Blunden's beautiful poem 'The Pike' (reproduced in full on page 47):
He on the sandbank lies,
Sunning himself long hours
With gorgon eyes. . . .

the shady side of the water, under the trees or high banks, you will find three where the light is stronger. In the summer this is less noticeable, but, in the winter the shore on which the sun shines most is always far superior, in my experience.

Robbie also reminded me of a very useful axiom attributed to the Royalty Fisheries' most famous and knowledgeable warden, Mr Haytor: 'They'll come on when the sun hits the water.'

The experience of the best of these old-time professional anglers, bailiffs and boatmen who were out every day gives us a pointer to empirical truths. R. B. Marston, that prince of angling journal editors, was once told by old George Hope, the Thames professional, that 'Pike won't feed well after a moonlight night.' When Marston pressed Hope for an explanation the old man said:

Well, the old 'uns view is this, he says: 'You see Sir, them pikes is werry artful, and they 'as their heyes on the tops of their 'eads, and as they lies deep in water, if the moon's a shinin' they sees the baits a swimmin' over 'em, then they fills themselves, so they don't want nothin' next day.'

When we attempt to assimilate all that has been said up to this point about weather, we may find that we cannot dismiss our chances on any day, unless the water is brown with flood or glazed with an impenetrable barrier of ice.

Perhaps it is a sound angling philosophy to expect less when our experienced reading of the water tells us that prospects are poor, for in this way we may be less disappointed with indifferent days.

Bookmark in the shape of a pike

During the nineteenth century that most easily recognizable of all fish – the pike – was used, or rather its outline was used, as a design motif for numerous practical items, now invariably classified as *objets d'art*. The Victorian cigar cutter (opposite) is one such item, and the bookmark illustrated below is another.

This example of an extremely rare Queen's Head silver bookmark of magnificent quality, made by Thomas Jones of London in 1889, belongs to me. The pike's scales are superbly engraved, albeit stylistically, and the word 'Jack' – an affectionate Victorian nickname for the pike – is engraved within a central frame.

Although the silversmith was an artist he couldn't have drawn the pike from life; otherwise he would have rounded off the edges of the pike's dorsal and anal fins. Mistake or no, the rarity of this item (it came from a shop in the Burlington Arcade) gives it a current value (1980) of £270.

19 Locating pike in large waters

As has been said elsewhere in this book one of the biggest problems facing the loch fisher is the problem of locating concentrations of pike in a large expanse of water. After a period spent gill-netting pike out of Windermere (for research purposes) I became conscious, as did my companions, that under normal conditions the catches from nets set off rocky points, where depth increases sharply close to the bank, were far greater than those from nets placed in other situations. (The exception occurred when nets were placed for pike concentrating to take advantage of char movements into the spawning shallows.) It occurred to me that perhaps pike tend to move along 'lanes' of unchanging water pressure, which is another way of saying that they move generally within the bounds of depth contours. A probable alternative explanation for good catches off deep rocky peninsulas, or points, may lie in the pike's need for economy of movement when navigating from one bay to the next. Whatever the explanation, I submit that anglers can hope for better sport if they fish off these points. Figure 21 illustrates conditions which might be found off a rocky point in a typical mountain loch.

Figure 21 Conditions to be found off a rocky point in a typical mountain loch

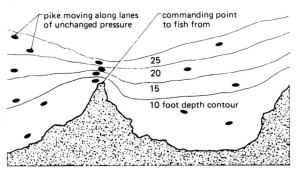

pike moving along lanes of unchanged pressure

commanding point to fish from

25
20
15
10 foot depth contour

The hookless search trimmer
(Figure 22)

Ready access, by way of refrigeration, to spratt, herring and mackerel baits provides a pike fisherman with an opportunity to prebait and groundbait for pike in the remote waters of Scotland and Ireland. Additionally, for those who will take the trouble, it provides the means to bait-up a pack of search trimmers so as to blanket fish and locate pike in one or another of the areas that otherwise would not attract the experienced pike angler.

Tougher deadbaits such as roach or rudd have to be substituted where hungry eels are met with, as eels have the ability to reduce softbaits by constantly tearing at them.

The rig consists of a large, flat, readily visible bobbin supporting a deadbait attached by a 1½ lb BS line. Such a fine line ensures that a break will occur soon after the bait is taken. By using a search trimmer feeding areas can be pinpointed. These locations, once found, mapped and their data properly recorded, can be fished year after year with confidence – providing they are fished at or around about the same time each year.

No better pattern for a trimmer exists than the one that has been in use for centuries. It is shaped like a compressed cotton bobbin with a diameter of about 4½ in. and depth of about 1½ in. The bobbin is deeply grooved to receive a reservoir of strong line (about 30 ft). A tapered peg is fitted in a tight-fitting tapered hole drilled through the centre of the bobbin. A small hole drilled through the base of the peg provides an anchorage for the line which is then wound into the groove on the bobbin. The pointed end of the peg is provided with a split that traps the

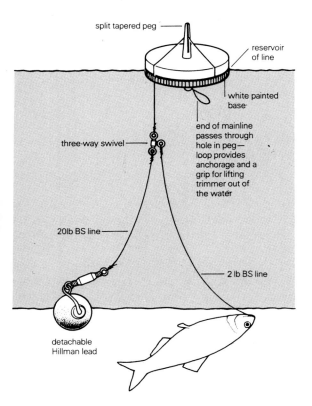

split tapered peg

reservoir of line

white painted base

three-way swivel

end of mainline passes through hole in peg — loop provides anchorage and a grip for lifting trimmer out of the water

20lb BS line

2 lb BS line

detachable Hillman lead

Figure 22 The search trimmer

line so long as the point of the peg is directed skywards.

The terminal tackle consists of a 1 oz anchoring weight fitted direct to the mainline, and a 6 ft link of $1\frac{1}{2}$ lb BS nylon, to which is tied the deadbait: herring, sprat, dace or roach.

A three-way swivel is tied on the mainline three feet up from the anchoring lead to provide an easy means of attaching the bait-link to the mainline.

Directions for setting a search trimmer

Lower the bait over the side of the boat. Then, holding the bobbin in the left hand, lower the lead – releasing enough line for the lead to touch bottom. Pull off another three feet of line and then trap the line in the split peg.

When a pike takes the bait and moves off, it will overturn the trimmer and release the trapped line. The pike can then pull off a further twenty to twenty-five feet of line, which will allow time for the bait-link to break before the pike becomes alarmed by resistance of the trimmer.

If the underside of the trimmer is painted white and the topside red, an angler will know instantly from a distance when he has had a run.

In fact it is a good plan to carry a pair of 10×50 binoculars so that one can 'inspect' the trimmer bobbins – or 'foxhounds', as Scotland's first pike angler, Colonel Thornton, called them when he fished Loch Lomond during the late 1790s – without having to move to see if any have been overturned.

20 Do pike shoal?

Shoaling is a group behaviour pattern whereby an unspecified number of fish move, feed, rest or spawn together. Sometimes they do all these things in such close contact with each other that it would appear to an onlooker as if their movements were under the direction and control of one fish. The advantages of shoaling must be enormous, since the aggregate value of the senses of each individual fish can be put at the disposal of the shoal. There can be little doubt that individual security is greatly improved when all eyes are strained against the common danger.

But as well as being defensive, shoaling is sometimes offensive in character. I once witnessed a dramatic example of this latter type of behaviour in Acapulco Bay off the coast of Mexico. During a period of hot, unrelenting sunshine, the only shelter afforded to a great number of herring-like fish came in the shape of a shadow cast by an anchored ship. Just below and beyond, a large shoal of barracuda patrolled up and down, preventing these little fish from mass escape as individual barracuda made lightning thrusts into the packed ranks to snatch a victim.

I sat in a cutter which was tied to the ship and noticed that its smaller shadow attracted another shoal of herring-like fish. These fish, too, sought relief from the blazing sun and were in turn patrolled by more barracuda. The cutter moved off, followed by the small fish still anxious to retain the benefit of its cooling shadow. Momentarily the barracuda were nonplussed, for in that instant they were all swimming in the opposite direction. But not for long. Within seconds, like a hundred torpedoes, they returned *en masse* to tear into their fast disappearing food supplies.

We in the cutter were soaked by the eruption of fish and water. Yet, in as little time as it took for the water to settle, the only evidence left at the scene of carnage was a cloud of scales sinking like silver confetti in the clear coral seas.

It is said by some experienced anglers that from time to time pike come together in a shoal. If this behaviour pattern exists in reality, then presumably it is offensive in character as it is with barracuda. One man who believed passionately in the pike shoaling theory was the late Jackie Thompson, a veteran Loch Lomond salmon angler, whose observations on fish behaviour had been gleaned from a lifetime of study.

Mr Thompson did not claim to have seen a shoal of patrolling pike which could be compared to, say, a shoal of rampaging perch; but for him the circumstantial evidence points very definitely to the existence of pike shoals. He told me that when the Loch Lomond Angling Improvement Association put out pike nets it is usual for them to catch a considerable number of pike cheek by jowl in one net, and few or none in others set at the same time. On several occasions he had witnessed a series of strikes directed at a passing powan shoal, thus confirming his belief in the pike's shoaling habits – especially since these attacks have been close together in proximity and time.

Bill Giles, another worthy observer of fish behaviour, declares: 'The first observation is that pike do shoal! Not for the same reasons as gregarious fish, of course, but, like a gang of thieves who will turn on each other if they get the chance, they realize that they will benefit if they round up the suckers – the poor sheep – like shoals of roach and bream.' In a letter to

me, Bill goes on to give an account of a particular incident:

It is noticeable how many times anglers will be sitting around in their boats fishless, then almost as though at a pre-arranged signal pike will all come on the feed together. As I have mentioned before, many regular pike anglers have noticed that a large bream shoal will have its attendant marauders on its fringes. Maybe much of the time they will follow it passively then suddenly the signal is given and they swing into the attack – that is when they are really hungry and are out hunting.

I remember one occasion on a small broad into which I had over the years popped many a pike of over 10 lb to improve the fishing: I had been sitting for a couple of hours. All was still; the only sign of life – a coypu grunting away to itself along the reedy edge of the lake. Then suddenly a boil on the surface here, a convulsion there – as pike swung into my section of the broad. In seconds my left-hand float shot under and I was into a pike of 6½ lb. As I slid it into the landing net I glanced at my other float. To my amazement it was careering along the surface

Do pike shoal? You would think so judging by the photograph. On this trip, organized by *Angling Times*, the anglers caught thirty-three pike averaging 15 lb apiece. As a matter of fact the pike *were* shoaling in the sense that they were congregating in a spawning area prior to spawning – on and in the area of Loch Lomond's Endrick bank

pulled by some force which lay about halfway between my rod tip and float. Much mystified I tightened up and eventually landed another six pounder on top of the other one which was still in the net. It must have come into the bay with the remainder of the pike 'shoal' and was chasing roach fry with its mouth wide open. It was about ten yards away from float tackle and hooks and had merely caught my line round its teeth!

These then are the opinions of two highly respected observers. By my own opinion is that pike do not shoal; nor do I believe that they co-operate with each other to secure for themselves some common advantage, as other group hunting species like perch and barracuda will do. I am firmly convinced that pike are non-filial, non-territorial, and non-co-operative (other than at spawning times). Nevertheless, I think we should recognize that where pike share the same environment, experience will probably teach them the same object lessons, so that it should come as no surprise to us if they react in the same way to the behaviour of those fish which form their basic diet. As a consequence, there will be times when pike will attack a shoal of gregarious fish, as if by agreement, simply because individually they understand that it is the right time and place to press home an attack. No doubt there will be other times: when distress signals released by a shoal of fish under attack by one pike may be picked up by other pike in the locality and so trigger off their desire for intestine satisfaction. Hence, we are able to witness what appears to be a concerted effort by the pike on a shoal.

Finally, I think we must acknowledge that pike are unlikely to be spread evenly in any water that does not offer the same ambushing prospects in all locations. This must be an unlikely prospect since the character of a location varies with its component parts of depth, fertility, turbidity, oxygen content, weed growth and bottom strata. Furthermore, the character of a location is in a constant state of flux due to wind, temperature and light variations.

21 Introduction to rigs, tackles and methods

Before attempting to explore in detail the various methods of fishing for pike, I think it would be useful to study the means by which pike satisfy the demands of their appetites. Once we have a better understanding of the processes by which pike locate, select and succeed in capturing their prey, we will be able to fish more methodically and with greater success. Also, it will help towards a dramatic improvement in the design of artificial baits, and we will be relieved of our dependence on empiricism as the sole means of achieving an occasional breakthrough.

I can give an example of what I mean.

Supposing an older generation of pike fishers had been told that pike obtain at least one-half of their food requirements by the simple expedient of picking up dead fish which lie on the bottom. Given that information, they would surely have tried a deadbait ledgering method. In which case, the post-war generation of pike fishers would not have been kept waiting until the Taylor brothers initiated the method from an accidental experience.

Frank Wright holding his biggest pike – the 35-pounder that he took from Horsey Mere in November 1967

Senses and feeding habits

A pike's awareness of a bait, and ability to locate it, depends on the use of one or more of three senses: sight, smell and hearing. If an angler suspects which of these senses he is appealing to on any occasion, he should be able to present his bait with a good deal more confidence than he has felt hitherto.

A pike tends to use the minimum of effort in hunting its food. Its eyes are set high in the head and provide an extensive field of view forwards and upwards. Many of its attacks on other fish are made from ambush. Once a prey fish swims into the striking zone, even if it is a wary and speedy trout, it has little chance of eluding the pike's short but powerful dash from the bottom.

The pike, then, is well equipped to hunt by sight. But it is certainly not vision that plays the *major* part in the pike's feeding routine. The netting of a totally blind but otherwise healthy pike in Lake Windermere proved that it is possible for pike to obtain sufficient food by the use of senses other than sight.

It is possible to evaluate the degree with which the pike's different senses are used for the purpose of getting a meal? One thing is certain: a livebait has a much greater chance of being taken by a pike than a freely swimming fish of the same size and species. Is the attraction of the livebait simply visual, or does the pike become aware of the bait's presence because of some emitted sound or scent? Does a tethered livebait cause distress signals (vibrations) which are picked up by the pike's listening equipment? Does it emit a fear substance which a pike can home on by sense of smell? Is it merely a display of physical distress which catches a pike's eye?

Vigorous livebaits are more effective than ailing ones. Perhaps their signals are more

The Piscatorial Society, established in 1836 'for promoting friendly intercourse and mutual information among the lovers of the Art of Angling', is still extant in 1981. During its long history the society has acquired many articles of interest, including the 'president's chair' (*below, left*), the arms of which are carved to simulate the body of a pike, while the backrest has a bas-relief figure of a pike head. The president's gavels (*below, right*) are surely unique – silver-mounted stuffed matching pike heads

vigorous, and extend over a greater range.

Like other fish, pike do not possess hearing organs similar to mammals. The 'ear' seems to be used mainly as a balancing device. Nevertheless, many species of fish emit underwater sounds. The meaning of these sounds is not yet known; but it seems reasonable to suppose that they have some specific function, and that in some way or another they can be received and understood by other fishes.

What is beyond doubt is that most species of fish are extremely sensitive to vibrations. And the pike is no exception. If a bait is cast so that it falls a little way behind a stationary pike, the pike may swim away – presumably frightened – or it may *turn round and face the bait*. Both reactions demonstrate the pike's ability to 'hear', but the latter indicates that the pike's sense of 'hearing' may sometimes help it to locate its prey.

But what of ledgered deadbaits? They emit no vibrations whatever. And yet deadbaits fished stationary on the bottom are extremely effective. Why? The answer is, almost certainly, smell.

The sense of smell in most fish is exceptionally acute. It has been demonstrated that salmon, returning from the sea to spawn in fresh water, detect their 'home' rivers entirely by scent.* The ability of sea fishes to follow a scent trail is equally well established: as a result the rubby-dubby bag has become a valuable item of sea-angling equipment. During the breeding season, a male pike is able to track down a female pike by sense of smell.

Since there is little doubt that a deadbait (of any kind) gives off a stronger scent than a livebait, it seems probable that pike approach deadbait as a result of picking up the trail of

* Although it has been proved only lately that salmon detect their home rivers 'entirely by scent', it must not be thought that the idea is new. The Rev. Henry Newland of Plymouth, in *The Erne, Its Legends and Its Fly-Fishing*, published in 1851, anticipated the facts over a century ago:

. . . when they the salmon come home from their cruise they merely make the coast somewhere, it may be a good hundred miles from the mouth of their river; and that they discover their port at last by coasting along with their noses close to the shore till they begin to smell their native waters.

this scent – in the same way that a shark picks up and follows the scent of the rubby-dubby, although, needless to say, over a very much shorter range.

This may explain why, in locations which allow satisfactory presentation, deadbait often proves more successful than livebait. As regards proof of pikes' attraction to the smell of herrings, Dr Barrie Rickards (who has done much to devolop pike deadbaiting techniques) experimented with a number of pike traps, some baited with herrings, others unbaited as a control. These traps were set in ditches (where there were no pike) well away from the pike-holding dyke to which the ditches were connected. Baited traps set the previous evening were often full of pike the next morning, whereas unbaited traps were almost always empty.

Pike in River Rede and how they are trapped

Dear Sir, The River Rede [a tributary of the North Tyne] has in certain of its sluggish stretches held a number of pike for many years. The origin of the pike in this water, so the story runs, was that some live pike were sent to Otterburn Tower for the fish course of a certain bishop who was being entertained, but as the good man did not arrive the pike were placed in a small pond, which flood water broke away, carrying the pike to the River Rede.

In course of years the pike population multiplied and spread from their deep haunts into the streamy trout water, with an almost complete destruction of the finer fish.

The late Howard Pease, of Otterburn Tower, in conjunction with the Tyne Conservancy Board, netted the river in the spring for a number of years and killed from twenty to one hundred pike per year.

Netting, however, was not continued after his death, and three seasons ago I commenced spinning with a Fairy rod and Illingworth reel, with good results.

This spring the Tyne Conservancy Board were given a 'Troutconserve' pike trap, which is rather like a wire cage rat-trap in two compartments about 6 ft long.

With this trap I experimented with various lures without, or practically without, result. Odd fish did actually get into the trap out of curiosity when no bait was inside.

However, a jar of goldfish, with a muslin cover, placed in the inner compartment, brought at the first setting a catch of four fish, and since then a five and a six have been obtained. The round jar magnifies the goldfish, and their bright colour proves irresistible to the pike.

The goldfish are fed each second day, but so far the life of them has been about three weeks.

Three more traps have been purchased, and during the summer upwards of seventy pike have been killed in the traps.

Owing to the difficulty of maintaining goldfish supply the insides of rabbits have been suspended in the inner chamber, with good results. Pike, in common with eels, have a strong sense of smell.

I am hopeful that with the steady use of the traps the pike nuisance in the Rede may be greatly abated.

The traps are looked at once a day, and pike have been found in the traps within half an hour of being set in a fresh place.

The enclosed photo of one of the pike taken in the nets may be of interest. The fish, when empty, was not more than 6 lb.

Yours faithfully,
GEO. WADDELL.
The Mill, Otterburn, S.O., Northumberland.

Above Using a baited trap to take pike is, of course, a very old method. It has been used mostly in attempts to rid pike from trout and salmon waters. A letter on the subject published in the *Fishing Gazette* (19 October 1935) gives us a very clear picture of pike behaviour, of their dangerous potential as predators in trout waters and their response to a strong scent (in this instance of rabbit paunches)

Below Twenty salmon and sea-trout smolts were taken from the stomach of one 6 lb pike

160

During the early years, when the deadbaiting method was being experimented with by more and more pike anglers, most of them used herrings or dead roach or some other indigenous fish for bait. During this period of development anglers found difficulty in casting these relatively heavy baits until rod designers started to produce rods that could cope with the weight of the baits.

The more difficult problem was to find a way of securing the bait so that it didn't fall off during the cast, while at the same time finding a method of bait attachment that would allow the hooks to pull out of the bait and into the pike at the moment of the strike. Various ingenious systems were put in service and in the 'instant strike' rigs (Figures 23 and 24, page *173*) we have what is probably the best of them. It has been noted by experienced anglers that pike generally respond better to a ledgered or float-ledgered deadbait in areas· where the bottom is clean and that where the bottom is weedy or foul a suspended deadbait (Figure 25, page *175*) is the only deadbaiting method that can be fully recommended.

For preference then deadbaits should be ledgered on a leadless tackle over a hard weed-free bottom. Unlike herring or mackerel, whose bladders are collapsed, roach, rudd and other members of the carp family sink slowly and are superior when fished over soft weed or a soft bottom. There are times when you have to stick a knife into the bladders of roach, etc., in order to make them sink. This procedure allows you to fish without having to resort to using a lead weight.

Once deadbaiting became popular it was soon realized that many more pike were dying as a result of having been deeply hooked even though their captors made every attempt to treat them gently. This problem has been mitigated to some extent by the amount of

Manhandling a pike in the manner depicted here would not be tolerated by British pike anglers. These Canadians, on the other hand, would be highly critical of British (mostly English) pike anglers who, when their own pike fishing is closed to them, fish in Scotland (where there is no close season) *while the pike are spawning*. This duality reminds me of what Anthony Burgess said of the British who, seventy years after the death of Oscar Wilde, laid an Epstein-carved tombstone over his French grave: '. . . it's a supreme monument to British hypocrisy.'

publicity that has been given to the dangers of delaying the strike and to improved means for removing hooks from a pike's throat or stomach. The problem existed when lots of anglers initially failed to realize that a calculatedly delayed strike, though necessary for livebaiting methods, was not necessary (indeed it was harmful) while deadbaiting.

The reason for this is quite simple when we consider why a pike holds on to any sizeable live victim instead of attempting an immediate swallow. The function of the pike's large canine teeth is primarily to nail its victim securely across the jaws. Their secondary function is to hold on to the victim with those same teeth until the punctures made by the teeth have paralysed the victim's nervous system. The pike knows partly by instinct and partly by experience that a large victim has to be held for a longer period of time before it becomes paralysed. Any premature attempt to spit out and turn a large victim in readiness for the swallowing operation, namely head first, may result in the victim being lost. By the same token a smaller victim can be swallowed more quickly.

When a pike picks up a dead fish it knows that the victim cannot struggle or escape so that it almost invariably starts to swallow it straight away. From this it will be seen that a pike picking up a deadbait should be struck or tightened on as soon as it moves away or, alternatively, if it doesn't move away it should be tightened on within half a minute of the first indication of a bite. If this pattern of timing the strike is not followed, the baits will be swallowed, resulting in the deep hooking of the pike with a correspondingly high proportion of fatalities ensuing.

Anglers who intend to return their pike make sure that their baits are hooked in the tail section rather than the head section. This simple device ensures that fewer pike are hooked in the throat or stomach, since the tail end of the pike's victim is the last to be swallowed.

Some years after deadbaiting was well under way some angler somewhere started to use half

a herring or half a mackerel instead of a whole bait. Such a practice is common when sea fishing for skate or tope but it was a most unlikely bait to use in freshwater. None the less it worked. Once it was realized that a pike would take a half bait (incidentally, the tail half seems to be more attractive to pike) just as well as a whole bait, the big problem of not losing the bait during the cast, while at the same time being able to strike the hooks home effectively, seemed to diminish.

The tackle that I use for bait attachment has proved itself over a wide area of England, Scotland and Ireland and I recommend it above any other that I have tried. In my experience the most successful baits in their order of merit are trout, mackerel, herring, roach and dace. The first and last I use whole, whereas mackerel, herring and roach seem to be more attractive to pike when used in halves.

The relative ease with which mackerel, herring and trout can be bought is very much in their favour. Anglers can buy them when they are cheap and deep-freeze them. It is more convenient to freeze them in packs of four. Several packs can then be transferred to a portable freezer box, taken to the fishing area, and used one at a time; any unused bait can then be returned to the freezer.

In practice a pike angler can manage two rods when deadbaiting. If it is necessary, owing to the character of the water, for the two rods to be fished some distance apart, the angler should remember to point the rods straight up into the air so that he can see both: by this means a run can be discerned at long range.

Summary

Pike fishing methods can be classified and listed under five main headings, and each will be discussed in the following chapters.

Deadbaiting

Deadbaiting with ledger tackle.
Deadbaiting with float paternoster.
Deadbaiting with paternoster.
Deadbaiting with float ledger.
Deadbaiting with gorge, trimmer or long-line. (These days considered to be illegal, unsporting, or both.)
Deadbaiting with float drift tackle.

Livebaiting

Livebaiting with free-line tackle.
Livebaiting with float tackle.
Livebaiting with paternoster tackle.
Livebaiting with float paternoster tackle.
Livebaiting with ledger tackle.
Livebaiting with gorge, trimmer, or long-line tackle. (Same comments apply.)

Baitcasting

Nowadays, baitcasting is represented by any method which requires the casting of an artificial or natural bait, when the bait is kept on the move to simulate a live but possibly wounded fish. It includes:

Spinning with a revolving or wobbling artificial bait.
Spinning with a revolving natural bait.
Plug fishing.
Wobbled deadbait casting.
Trolling with natural bait (sink and draw).

Trailing

Trailing with a revolving or wobbling artificial bait.
Trailing with a revolving natural bait.
Trailing with a livebait.
Trailing with a wobbled bait.
Trailing with a plug.

Fly-fishing

This photograph of the fisherman's boathouse on Turkey Lagoon, near Maidstone in Kent, gives some idea of the placid beauty of that water – placid, that is, on the surface, for below there is perpetual turmoil orchestrated by the 'tyrant of the watery plains'.

22 Deadbaiting

Pike fishing with stationary deadbaits

Historical

Although many claims are made for new pike fishing methods and tackles, most are simply old ones rediscovered. In Britain several anglers claim to have introduced the ledger method of fishing a stationary deadbait, and not a few claim to have been the first to use herrings for this purpose. But the method and the bait were described by Dame Juliana Berners in her 'Treatyse of Fysshynge wyth an Angle' (part of the *Book of St. Albans* published in 1496):

Take a codling hook, and take a roach or a fresh herring, and a wire with a hole in the end, and put it in at the mouth, and out at the tail, down by the ridge of the fresh herring; and then put the hook in after, and draw the hook into the cheek of the fresh herring; then put a plumb of lead upon your line a yard long from your hook, and a float in midway between; and cast it in a pit where the pike useth, and this is the best and most surest way of taking the pike.

For many centuries her method was neglected; indeed, its existence was forgotten until it was rediscovered by Fred J. Taylor in 1954. In that year he wrote an article in the *Angler's News* and gave details of an experience he shared with his brothers:

We had been spinning for several hours and sport had been spasmodic, and Joe, who had been round the far side of the lake, returned for a match for his cigarette. Instead of leaning his rod against a tree, for some reason he flicked his deadbait, with which he had been spinning, out into the lake and put his rod into one of the many forked sticks, which some other anglers had conveniently left stuck in the bank.

He came over to me, lit up, and we chatted for a bit, and then Joe returned to his rod. His reel handle was revolving, the rod top was thumping and line was being slipped off in no uncertain manner! Joe gave a chortle, said something about 'Must have taken it on the way down' and struck! He encountered a resistance and brought pressure to bear on a pike of about 7 lb which, on reaching the bank, spat out a very mangled dead rudd with treble hook attached and parted company with Joe. He tried again, and after the bait had been out about ten minutes, the rod started thumping again and the same procedure followed, only this time Joe landed a pike of about 8 lb. *We had now come to the conclusion that the pike were picking up the deadbait from the bottom....* Now every angler has heard of the occasional pike being taken on a deadbait, but regards it more or less as a fluke. When one stops to think, however, there is nothing unusual about it. *The bottom is the natural place for a dead fish to be* (as opposed to midwater – I know many of them float) and it requires little or no effort on the pike's part to pick it up.

Taylor went on to prophesy: *'I am confident, however, that this method will eventually produce the longed-for twenty pounder.'*

Taylor, having rediscovered that fishing with a stationary deadbait could be a certain method for catching pike, wrote, 'If there is a shortage of bait – and there often is on pike waters – *herrings can be used with deadly effect.'*

In Britain some twenty-five years after Taylor wrote his article the stationary deadbaiting method has developed into a major method in the pike angler's repertoire – indeed it is likely that deadbaiting now accounts for more big pike than any other method.

Why, we might ask ourselves, was the method so readily accepted when for generations practically all pike anglers believed in the old maxim that 'stationary baits catch no pike'?

Konrad Lorenz, one of the greatest naturalists of our time, tells us about the nature of the general acceptance of a new truth. He wrote in his book *On Aggression*: 'A new truth has really convinced when the hearer exclaims, "How silly of me not to have thought of that."'

Since we know that deadbaiting was first described nearly five centuries ago we could ask ourselves why didn't it catch on then? Once again another of Lorenz's observations gives us the essential clue: 'At best he can flatter himself that he has something to say that is "due" to be said at the moment. *His teachings* will be most efficacious if his ideas are only a short head in front of his hearers.'

Apparently, then, Fred Taylor's reintroduction of deadbaiting had that quality of perfect timing, and since its introduction the method has been developed and refined to a remarkable degree.

Perhaps one of the most astonishing discoveries made by anglers from all over the country was that the average weight of the pike caught by this method was greater than of those caught by the livebaiting or by the spinning method.

After my own conversion to the deadbaiting method I sought an explanation as to why deadbaiting should (a) be such a deadly method, and (b) why it should, on the whole, attract bigger pike than other methods.

I had a flash of insight into the probable feeding behaviour of pike after I read an account of some studies on the behaviour of the lions of the African plain. The African lion, previously thought by all to be the epitome of the killing kind (just like the pike), who is said to murder all he meets with, is in reality a scavenger as well as a killer; an animal that prefers to clear up the dead or steal another's kill rather than go to the bother of making its own kill. Perhaps the pike is like the lion in that it doesn't extend itself unnecessarily.

Dr B. Rickards, whose experiments prove that pike are attracted to the smell of herrings, with a finely marked 32 lb pike

165

Pike fishing from a punt on the River Thames at Wallingford, twentieth-century style

I gained an insight into what might be going on under the surface of one of Britain's biggest lakes, Loch Lomond, where pike feed to a considerable extent on powan (*Coregonus*), by reference to a scientific paper, 'Studies of Loch Lomond', written by Dr H. D. Slack:

'Fish as young as eighteen months and as old as ten years were examined but scale readings showed that three- and four-year-olds predominated.'

From this I began to speculate on the fate of the flourishing four-year-old fish who nevertheless seldom survive to become five-year-olds. What happens to them? The most simple explanation is the most likely one: they die and sink to the bottom. A few get washed up on the banks but thousands, even tens of thousands, do not. They just disappear. Where? I suspect they go down the throats of pike and eels as do the casualties of all the other species inhabiting the loch.

To help get this matter in focus we should remember that if the mean turnover of fish life in a fishery is five years then each year practically one whole year class, possibly 25 per cent (by weight) of the population of fodder fish becomes available in the form of dead or dying fish to the pike and other scavengers. In a large lake we can be sure that the total weight of

The powan is the staple diet of Loch Lomond pike. I caught the one shown here

Playing a pike on one of
Ireland's best pike loughs –
Lough Allen in Co. Leitrim
(By courtesy of Angling News
Service)

these fish can be measured in tons rather than hundredweights.

If the figures given reflect a reasonably accurate picture of the true situation that obtains in a fishery, then they indicate why pike readily accept deadbaits: such behaviour is routine, based on the pike's economic preference.

In English pike-angling literature the pike has been referred to as the 'fell tyrant of the watery plain'. There is no doubt whatever that pike in the northern hemisphere, in situations where they face no competition from the Wels catfish or the muskie of North America, are at the apex of the predator food chain. And, from what we know of their scavenging habits, they are probably at the apex of the scavenging chain as well.

Jordan, an early American fish biologist, stated that 'pike are mere machines for the assimilation of other organisms'. Jordan's statement is so carefully worded that it still makes sense even though we know (though he probably didn't) that pike are great scavengers.

From our new-found evidence (although so far as I know no scientific study of the pike's diet, *vis-à-vis* the proportionate intake of dead

or live food, has been conducted), we can speculate as to the pike's *preferred method* of feeding – although we are still unable to describe the pike's preference for individual food items since the pike may, for all we know, prefer to eat a trout (dead or alive) rather than a perch in either state.

1 The pike's first preference is to pick up any worthwhile fish or food morsel found dead in its path. Reason for this behaviour: maximum economy of effort.
2 The pike's second preference is to strike at any worthwhile injured or sick fish or food morsel that it chances upon. Reason: assured success with economy of effort.
3 The pike's third preference is to ambush a live food item of *preferred* size (15–20 per cent of its own weight). Reason: to preclude the need for further effort in the immediate future.

A whole series of descending preferences can be imagined until we reach a point where a very hungry pike would be desperate enough to search, chase and strike at the most uneconomic food morsel in order to keep body and soul together.

167

In answer to the question of why the deadbaiting method should tend to produce catches of a higher average weight than any other method, I can only offer the most obvious and simple explanation, namely that the composition of a pike's diet varies with its advancing age (or weight). From scientific observation it seems that newly hatched pike feed exclusively on live food and probably continue to do so for the first two or three years of their life. At a later period of their life they begin to scavenge and as time goes on scavenging becomes increasingly important for the *continuity* of the larger pike's food intake. If few pike weighing under 5 lb take deadbaits, then these smaller fish will be absent from the catch, leaving the sample of fish that *is* caught of a higher average weight.

A story of a lost pike

My own conversion to an absolute belief in the effectiveness of stationary deadbaiting came after an unfortunate experience of failing to land a probable record pike which I hooked in Loch Lomond in 1967.

Many theories have been compounded on the possible location of Britain's biggest pike, and Morgan's catching of the British record pike from Loch Lomond in 1945 was a sound basis of support for that water. Morgan's account of the capture of his monster, as related to a reporter of a popular but now defunct fishing magazine, and his description of the tackle used to catch it, fired my imagination.

Years later, through the kindness of London rodmaker Robert Myslik, I secured a letter of introduction to two stalwart Loch Lomond anglers closely associated with Morgan. My friendship blossomed with these men, namely Harry Britton and Jackie Thompson, and with their aid I was able to build up a picture of pike movements in the loch and locate several places where I could catch livebait. Other problems were solved over the years, including the problem of transporting across the loch

enough livebait for a full day's pike fishing to satisfy a party of pike anglers.

I then made plans to invite those formidable fishing companions, Ken Taylor, Pete Thomas and Richard Walker to join me in a pike-fishing expedition to the loch in the summer of 1967. We had taken great care (or so we thought) to be properly equipped with tackle suitable for dealing with pike of 60 lb, should we have the good fortune to connect with such fish. All of us were using powerful rods of some $3\frac{1}{2}$ lb test curve, complete with large centre-pin or multiplier reels holding not less than 200 yards of 25 lb BS line. Our choice of terminal tackle was individual, and to some extent experimental, but a trace strength of at least 20 to 30 lb was characteristic.

The first few pike caught were killed in order to examine the stomach contents and in this way we obtained confirmation of my previous findings, namely that powan were always present. The powan is a plankton-feeding whitefish, similar to, though somewhat larger than, a herring. Although the powan is confined to Loch Lomond and neighbouring Loch Eck it is closely related to pollan, vendace, gwyniad, schelly and other whitefishes.

I had long held a theory, born out of an appreciation of the character of this particular pike-fishing location, that the powan followed a 'sheep track' round some islands into what (for want of a better description) I called the 'hotspot'. To me this was the natural point of ambush. No other reason could fully explain the presence of so many pike in such a small area within the vastness of Loch Lomond.

Walker, who was with Ken Taylor in a boat close to mine, fished with deadbait to take his first loch fish of $16\frac{1}{2}$ lb and was pleased to confirm that it fought with a tenacity rarely found in its southern cousins. Due to a shortage of livebait and being somewhat stimulated by Walker's success with deadbait I decided to fish a deadbait rig myself – baited with a $\frac{3}{4}$ lb roach.

Almost at once my roach was picked up, and Pete Thomas cleared the decks for action. He also raised the anchors, according to a prear-

Peter Thomas and the author fishing at Portnellan, Loch
Lomond

ranged plan, so that we should be ready to
follow the pike out of the bay if it were
necessary. (This was Walker's idea to minimize
the risk of losing a really big one.) In the event it
was the smallest pike we had yet taken – a mere
6-pounder.

We settled ourselves once more. I cast a fresh
deadbait to the same spot, and turned to call
my excuses to Walker for the smallness of my
capture – since I had told him that we were
unlikely to catch small pike. At that moment,
Thomas nudged me to call attention to the
disappearance of my float.

This time the pike took 20 yards of line
without stopping, so I tightened on it.

Tightening proved to be an explosive
measure. It made the pike shoot off like a
rocket from a launching pad, and this was
despite my most extreme pull in the opposite
direction (Thomas afterwards described the
rod curve as frightening).

After running some 30 yards the fish stopped
just short of a large submerged boulder which
we knew to be in its path. It turned and came
back at me, and it was only a hurried lifting of
the anchors which deterred it from going under
the boat (this time we had failed to carry out
our routine). Instead, it turned again and

169

rushed off towards Walker's boat which was moored close to a large weed-bed. Once again, extreme pressure from my end did not appear to influence the pike's direction at all. But, after 20 yards it did at least bring the pike to the surface. At this point the pike kited* and stopped for some three seconds before making its next turn. From a distance, Thomas and I could see the back of the pike and noted its considerable length. Walker and Taylor had an even better view of the fish, for it was by then almost within gaffing distance of their boat.

Realizing that I was into a very large pike indeed, I determined to play it at half pressure as long as it was going in a safe direction.

During the very next run, for no obvious reason, the line broke where it had been joined to a swivel!

I now understand that braided nylon and terylene is greatly reduced in strength by any knot other than the hangman's noose, due to

strangulation. Alas, I did not know it then – and sat helpless with disappointment.

Walker and Taylor, who had seen the depth of the pike's flank, said that it was the biggest pike either of them had ever seen. Ken Taylor (witness of the landing of a 32-pounder) said that if his life depended on a guess he would put the weight at 50 lb. The more cautious Walker thought it must have been at least 40 lb, might well have been 45 lb, and if we caught it the next day with my hook in it and we found it weighed 50 lb, he would admit: 'Ah well, you never quite know with these very deep fish.'

Two days later, when the loch went calm for the first time, we were privileged to witness a shoal of powan come finning their way towards us (powan poke their dorsal and caudal fins out of the water when feeding in the surface layers). They followed straight through the 'sheep track' defined in my theory, passing the place of ambush before a breath of breeze stole them

* 'Kiting'. A pike tends to swim in a straight line. When changing direction it usually stops and re-orientates itself, before setting off again. In my experience, this behaviour is not common to other species, but I have found it very significant of big pike.

'Instead it turned again and rushed off towards Walker's boat which was moored close to a large weed-bed.' Richard Walker and Ken Taylor in their boat viewed from the boat I shared with Peter Thomas

from our vision. That my theory was doubly confirmed was exciting, and did much to console me for the loss of that wonderful pike. But by the end of a week's fishing, although we had caught pike up to 22 lb, we were still numbed by the tragedy of losing the 'big fellah'.

Our long drive home began with an inquisition, and ended with plans for the next Scottish foray.

We are not retiring beaten! One of us will catch a big fish there within the next few years, for we are convinced that Loch Lomond shelters many 50 lb pike – perhaps some a good deal bigger.

The account that you have just read of the loss of this fish was written in 1968 before I had recovered from the recurring nightmare of constantly regretting the way I had handled the big pike – after all the years of patient build-up and research.

It was Hugh Falkus who helped me get the thing in perspective after I relived the incident with him in 1970 when together we enjoyed the magic of fishing Portnellan Bay for the last time.

My old friends Harry Britton and Jackie Thompson are dead and it was they who put me on to the big pike that lived in the bay. They saw it frequently and wanted me to catch it and I failed. The 'big fellah', for that is what they called it, was never seen again after it was hooked. In 1970 there was one that weighed 32 lb, but that is another story that Hugh Falkus intends to tell one day; that reminds me of Bacon's remark, 'Things graceful in a friend's mouth, which are blushing in a man's own.'

Having mentioned Tommy Morgan's 47 lb 11 oz pike earlier I should point out that many people, myself included, believe that his pike – the biggest caught in Britain by fair means – *is* the British record for the species.

In my *Domesday Book of Mammoth Pike* (1979) I assembled all the evidence that supported this view, and since publication I have come across yet another letter corroborating the record. It was published in January 1950 in the *Sportsman's Magazine* (now defunct):

A 47½ lb Pike from Loch Lomond

To the Editor of *Country Sportsman*

Sir, I heard the story of the capture of this lovely fish from the angler and also from his gillie.

They were fishing from a small dinghy in the bay just opposite East Port Nellan Farm and were using as bait a large, live roach mounted on a snap tackle and buoyed by two large red floats.

When the floats disappeared under the water the angler, who is an expert pike-fisher, waited a moment or two and then struck vigorously. The rod immediately curved over alarmingly and line was stripped off the reel at a terrific rate; as he played the fish the angler noticed a violent threshing on the water a good distance off and, almost at the same moment, he realised that it was caused by his fish, and that it had almost stripped his reel of line. The commotion on the water was caused by the fish charging through a shallow weed-bed.

The anchor was immediately lifted and the gillie pulled the boat after the running fish as best he could in an effort to regain some line. It was a relief when a considerable amount was recovered, and the fight now took place in the more open waters of the bay.

The rod and tackle were stout enough, and after some time, during which the pike made several jumps, the angler managed to bring the fish alongside. The pike was utterly exhausted and as it lay there on the water it was gingerly lifted into the boat; the angler never used a gaff at any time when he went pike-fishing.

The party had come up by motor-boat and that evening they went down to Balloch some miles away at the foot of the loch. The fish was brought ashore and was weighed at the well-known boating station of Thomas Lynn & Sons, where so many big fish from Loch Lomond have been weighed in the past. Here the pike tipped the scales at the remarkable weight of 47½ (forty-seven and one-half) pounds. A wayside photographer took a picture (which I have seen) of the pike, but it was almost valueless.

GEORGE McGREGGOR

A monster Thames pike

In December 1890 the *Fishing Gazette* published a photograph of a pike's lower jawbone. The memorandum attached was written by Mr

171

W. Deacon, sometime owner of the Ray Mead Hotel.

Jaw-bone of a jack, 4 ft 5 in. from nose to tip of tail; 10 in. across head, i.e. depth. Picked up [presumably dead] below Ray Mead Hotel, Sunday afternoon July 3, 1887.

Commenting on the find of this great pike (it probably weighed at least 45 lb sometime during its life), Alfred Jardine said that the bones indicated that a

giant pike existed as recently as 1887, either in the deeps of Boulter's Weir pool, or the waters between there and Cookham; which pike no doubt caused much loss of tackle and discomforture to anglers who happened to have hold of the fish, they little dreaming – after 'a break in the attachment' – what was its actual weight and dimensions.

Rigs and tackles for deadbaiting

Although the individual rigs and tackles used by pike anglers for deadbaiting are many and varied it seems that only a few basic types can be fully justified. From what I have seen and used myself in a wide variety of situations, I have selected four basic types that cover all my needs. These are:

1   the instant strike rigs, Nos. 1 and 2
2   the drifting deadbait rig
3   the Fred J. Taylor tackle
4   the Universal snap-tackle

When I make up my tackles I invariably use cabled wire. I never use single strand or piano wire. Although it is often recommended by pike anglers I have found it totally unreliable.

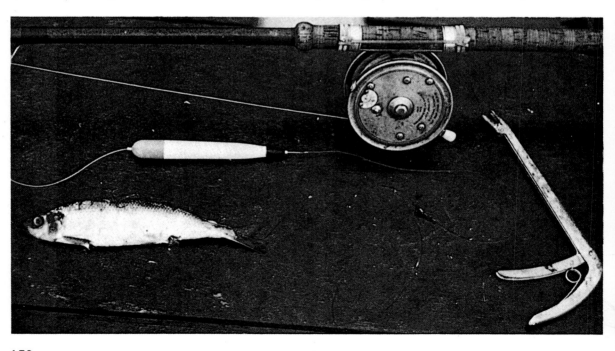

Lean's instant strike deadbait rig No. 1
(Figure 23)

Peter Lean invented a fine deadbait rig, which *Angling* published in October 1976. In essence Lean described a rig that would allow a pike angler to cast good distances without losing a bait, but with this difference: if a pike took the bait the hooks could be pulled home with ease, because in Lean's rig the hooks were not bait-supportive.

The device consists of a simple hook made from aluminium or any non-corroding metal which supports the bait, independently from the trace, via a nylon sling round the tail. This link simply falls apart during the splash. In the case of head-halves and whole baits, the sling is laced through mouth and gills.

Long artery forceps are useful here. When assembling for use, note that the trace is left slack to avoid pulling the hooks out when casting, because to be fully effective, the bait will be only lightly hooked anyway, having just enough purchase for that gentle retrieve to be made; particularly gentle when using trebles with straightened-out points.

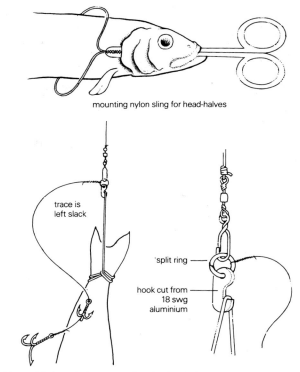

mounting nylon sling for head-halves

trace is left slack

split ring

hook cut from 18 swg aluminium

Figure 23 Lean's instant strike deadbait rig No. 1

The Oxford instant strike rig No. 2
(Figure 24)

This instant strike rig was designed by an Oxford group of pike anglers who fish mostly in gravel pits. The rig has become essential for pike fishing in these pits where, owing to the pressure of fishing, pike have become very wary and as a consequence often drop a bait after making only a short run.

With the instant pike rig the strike is made as soon as the pike picks up the bait. The bait, usually the tail half of a herring or mackerel, is armed with two hooks (size 2), which are so

slightly nicked into the bait's skin, that on 'reeling in' the bait is expected to fall off.

How then, a reader may ask, can you cast a bait which is apparently so lightly secured? The answer is to be found in the use of a second link – in reality a bait-supporting link – which frees the hooks from one of the tasks associated with their twin functions of (a) hooking the pike,

Figure 24 The Oxford instant strike rig No. 2

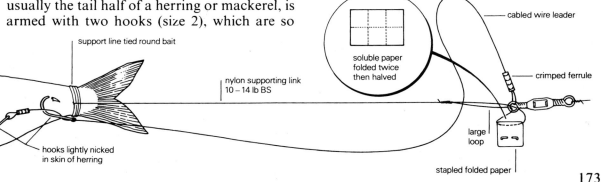

support line tied round bait

soluble paper folded twice then halved

cabled wire leader

crimped ferrule

nylon supporting link 10 – 14 lb BS

large loop

hooks lightly nicked in skin of herring

stapled folded paper

This photograph, of the late Bill Keal, captures that instant when a rod is fully compressed and is about to launch a herring into space

and (b) supporting the bait during casting operations.

A piece of *water soluble* paper ($1\frac{3}{8} \times 1$ in.) is folded (as shown in Figure 24) round the loop end of the support link. A staple secures the folded paper which in turn prevents the loop of the support link from passing back through the eye of the swivel. On casting out the support link takes all the strain. Before the bait reaches the bottom the paper usually dissolves, freeing the support link as it does so (the loop of the support link invariably catches on the hooks and is retrieved on reeling in). As a result of their instant striking the Oxford anglers find that the pike they catch are nearly always hooked in the 'scissors'.

Although a float could be used in conjunction with the instant strike rig the Oxford men usually ledger their baits.

The drifting deadbait (Giles) rig (Figure 25)

During the 1960s two famous English pike anglers (Bill Giles and Reg Sandys) developed a method of deadbaiting on the Norfolk Broads which subsequently they and other pike anglers used successfully in many parts of Britain. Using either herring or mackerel as bait, they drift a float-rigged tackle about 1 foot off the bottom on local broads averaging some 5 ft in depth. The bait is suspended at a point of balance so that it will drift on an even keel. Giles reckons that mackerel are superior to herrings for this purpose because the back of a mackerel stays straight, whereas the herring is apt to bend under its own weight. The anglers each gently cast the bait a short distance across the wind from either side of the boat. They allow the wind acting on the floats to drift the baits slowly away as they pay out line. They have developed a special tackle for this style of fishing which is described in Figure 25.

The 15 lb BS mainline nylon is attached to a diamond-eye link swivel. A 15 in. length of 20 lb BS wire joins the swivel to a split ring. The bait-supporting treble hook, embedded in the back of the bait by two of its limbs, is attached to the same split ring. The second treble is again

174

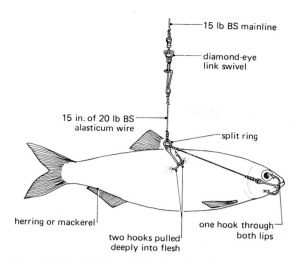

Figure 25 The Bill Giles drifting deadbait rig

15 lb BS mainline

diamond-eye
link swivel

15 in. of 20 lb BS
alasticum wire

split ring

herring or mackerel

one hook through
both lips

two hooks pulled
deeply into flesh

mounted on 20 lb BS wire and is pulled through the lips of the bait leaving two hook limbs free. The wire on this forward treble is cut to suit the bait's length before being attached to the split ring.

Considering the limited time they have allowed themselves to develop this routine, Giles and Sandys have had considerable success. The reasons for the deadliness of this method are not fully understood. In all probability, the slow drift of a level-mounted deadbait simulates the heedless and dilatory movements of a preoccupied fish. Some of us who have kept aquaria will have witnessed the curious antics of fish preoccupied with some tasty food item – or even with nature's most dangerous preoccupation, sleep – and we can imagine how dangerous these preoccupations must be in pike-infested waters.

The F. J. Taylor deadbait tackle (Figure 26)

Take a 2 to 3 ft length of 14 or 20 lb alasticum wire (I prefer cable wire), bend it over and slip the bend behind a size 2 or 4 treble hook (see Figure 26). Pass both ends of the wire through the eye of the treble, from opposite sides (c). Pull tight and twist the wire (d) right up to the second treble, slipping the bend of the wire behind it in the same way as the first. Push the

ends of the wire through the eye of the second treble (e), pull tight and finish off with a twisted section of about 1 in. (f).

The distance between the trebles should fit the size of the deadbait. Half a dozen tackles made up with varied distances between hooks will accommodate any variation in the size of the herring or other deadbait used.

Taylor prefers to pass the end of the wire through the fish with the help of a baiting needle (dotted line in g). This prevents the bait from being flung off the hooks during the cast.

Finally, trim the emergent wire to between 9 and 12 in., before connecting up to a swivel on the mainline.

For anglers who blench at the mention of a baiting needle, Taylor suggests the rig illustrated in (h). The business end is the same as before, but the free end of the wire is twisted

Figure 26 The Fred J. Taylor deadbait tackle

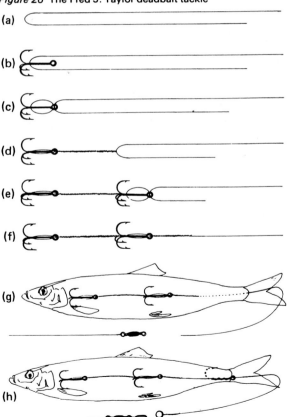

(a)

(b)

(c)

(d)

(e)

(f)

(g)

(h)

four times round the shank of a large Model
Perfect hook before it is passed through the
eye. The hook is slid along the wire according
to the length of the deadbait, then pulled
through the fleshy part of the tail.

A split ring is twisted on 12 in. or so up the
leader and the wire trimmed off.

To allow for the quick changing of mounts a
link-swivel is attached to the mainline.

The Universal snap-tackle

Before describing the Universal snap-tackle we
should take a closer look at a tackle that has
had a universal appeal for five generations of
pike anglers.

Richard Walker and Peter Thomas fishing at Portnellan, Loch
Lomond, in the 1960s, on the spot where I failed to land the
enormous pike referred to in the Foreword. It was here that
Tommy Morgan hooked and landed the British record pike of
47 lb 11 oz

The *Jardine snap-tackle* (see photograph on
page opposite) was first described in the *Fishing
Gazette* in 1882. Now almost a hundred years
later it is still the most popular livebait tackle in
use.

Here is Jardine's description:

The Perfected 'Jardine Snap' for Pike Fishing

The dorsal-triangle has a large rider-hook, which is
to be put through the base of back fin, thus
obtaining a firm hold on the live bait. The small

176

rider-hook on the end triangle is to go into the base or joint of pectoral fin, thus lying close to the bait, but without injuring it.

I have my snaps made in three sizes, so as to suit bait of various lengths, and on copper gimp, because it is not so showy in the water as brass or silver.

This tackle can also be used for 'snap paternostering' (a very killing method) by putting the large dorsal rider-hook through the lips of live-bait, and the small pectoral rider-hook through the back fin, as illustrated in models herewith.

If preferred, the dorsal triangle can be made to slide up and down the gimp, like the lip-hook of a Thames spinning flight, but bound to the gimp is a neater method.

This original description of his famous tackle raises a number of interesting points. First of all the editor of the *Fishing Gazette* was obliged to apologize for making two mistakes in the illustrations: the middle drawing should show the rider-hook inserted at the front end of the base of the dorsal fin rather than at the rear; and the bottom drawing should show the rider-hook passing through both lips of the bait and not just through one lip as shown in the photograph.

Notice also that in this extract Jardine spells 'rider' with an 'i'. Sixteen years later, in the first edition of his book *Pike and Perch*, he changed the spelling to 'ryder'. Again, in his early version he prefers the upper triangle to be whipped (and of necessity fixed) in its position on the tackle but by 1898 he preferred the upper triangle hook to be a sliding one. In the early version he recommends pulling the rider-hook into the base of the pectoral fin but, later, he was to suggest placing the hook into the top corner of the bait's gill cover.

Long before Jardine came on to the scene pike tackles for snap fishing were being designed by the dozen, and since his time quite a few more have made their appearance; but none has found favour with pike anglers – possibly because they are all inferior.

Like many other contemporary pike anglers, I have experimented with a design for an improved snap-tackle and the one that I have

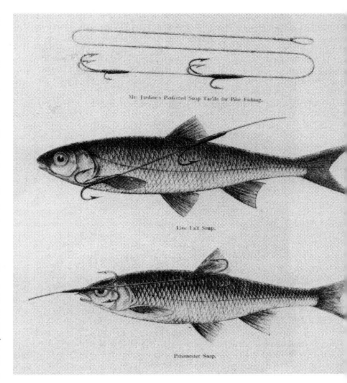

Mr. Jardine's Perfected Snap Tackle for Pike Fishing.

Live Bait Snap.

Paternoster Snap.

found to cover *all* my needs, I call, not unnaturally, the Universal snap-tackle.

The tackle is based on a discovery I made many years ago when I found that a deadbait could be held much more securely during periods of prolonged casting if a single hook of the Beak type was used as the 'holding' hook of the tackle.

The Beak type of hook has a curved-in point and a turned-down eye and for some reason, as yet obscure to me, is *vastly* more efficient at gripping the bait.

The sliced-shank feature in the Beak design, so far as pike fishing is concerned, plays no part in bait-holding but the two upstanding slices on the shank act as bollards for the two turns of wire taken round the shank before the wire passes through the special dorsal eye incorporated in my hook design (see Figure 27).

Since modern pike anglers prefer not to use a wire-trace (necessary to complement the short length of wire used in commercially produced snap-tackles) I have lengthened the wire on the Universal tackle to 20 in.; and, instead of

finishing with a normal loop for attachment purposes, I have incorporated a ball-bearing swivel.

Like the later version of the Jardine snap-tackle the Universal snap-tackle can be adjusted to accommodate variations of bait length.

This tackle comes closest to the ideal sought by all anglers – a tackle that will hold the bait securely so that it won't come off with repeated long-range casting – while ensuring that every pike is well hooked.

For those anglers who prefer to make up their own pike tackles I now describe a DIY way of making a Universal snap-tackle, which originally appeared in a piece I wrote for the German angling magazine *Blinker*.

Making a Universal snap-tackle (Figure 27)

Nowadays I use this tackle for nearly all my livebait and deadbait fishing. It supports and secures the bait during casting operations

Robert Templeton with a 14 lb pike taken on a spoon. You will seldom see such a cheerful-looking pike fisherman or a more apprehensive-looking pike. The pike had no need to worry, for his captor is a member of the Pikers, Northern Ireland's skilful band of pike fishermen who put pike back unharmed

better than any other tackle I have tried; it can be made to accommodate baits of varying sizes; it is the best hooker of pike that I have encountered; and it is simple to make. The essential ingredient of the Universal snap-tackle is the uniquely designed Sliced-Beak hook matched with a treble hook of the appropriate size.

The slices on the shank of the Beak hook (made by Edgar Sealey in England and by Mustad in Norway) are not used as the makers intended, namely, to secure the bait and prevent it from slipping, but as bollards for the two forms of trace wire taken round the shank.

Take a 2½ ft length of stainless cabled wire

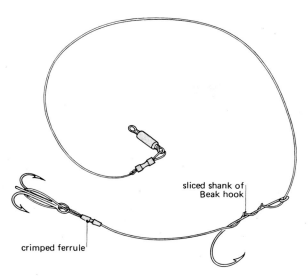

sliced shank of
Beak hook

crimped ferrule

Figure 27 A Universal snap-tackle. Although not shown in the drawing, I now whip a metal eye to the shank of the beak hook just behind the rear-end slice. This modification ensures that the beak hook does not over-readily slide back towards the treble

from 15 lb to 30 lb BS (it can be plain or nylon covered) and pass one end through a brass ferrule of the appropriate bore. Pass the same end through the eye of a treble hook and then take the emergent end of the wire round the back of the treble before passing it back through the eye of the treble hook from the opposite side. Pass the end of the wire back into the ferrule and tie a knot in it where it emerges from the ferrule. Slide the ferrule up to the treble before crimping the ferrule with special crimping pliers (the ones sold by Abu are very good).

Pass the free end of the wire through the eye of a Beak hook and slide the hook down the wire to within about 2 in. of the treble hook. Holding the treble hook in the left hand and the Beak hook in the right hand start a wrapping motion with the left hand until three turns of the wire between the hooks get wrapped round the shank of the Beak hook. The slices on the shank of the Beak hook stop the wire from unravelling.

Pass the free end of the wire through a second ferrule and then through one end of a ball-bearing swivel before passing it back through the second ferrule once more. Tie a knot in the emergent wire: slide the ferrule back to the swivel and crimp the ferrule into place with the Abu crimpers.

The tackle is now complete and the Beak hook can be moved up or down (by unwrapping, sliding and rewrapping) the trace wire in order to accommodate baits of varying sizes.

Note that I give instructions to tie a knot in the ends of the wire where they emerge from the ferrules. This is an insurance against the wire pulling through a ferrule that has not been crimped perfectly.

When I designed the Universal snap-tackle many years ago I found that Sliced-Beak hooks were vastly superior to any other as the holding hook and I found by experiment the best combination of hook sizes to be:

No. 4 Beak with a No. 8 treble hook
No. 2 Beak with a No. 6 treble hook
No. 1 Beak with a No. 4 treble hook

23 Livebaiting

Before discussing in detail the various tactical aspects of presenting a pike with a livebait it might be useful to summarize the four recognized major methods:

1 Float fishing
2 Paternostering
3 Ledgering
4 Free-lining

None of these methods is an entity in itself. Each usually comprises of many variations on a theme and the angler chooses a particular variation in the hope that it will be the one to meet the situation.

Float fishing

Of one period in Britain, that is from the end of the last century until the 1960s, I think it fair to say that livebaiting had become pretty uninspiring. The majority of pike anglers were resigned, and yet seemingly content, to use the conventional float rig devised and perfected by the very successful Victorian pike angler, Alfred Jardine. The rig he designed is still in use today. It consists of a round pilot float, a Gazette pattern mainfloat incorporating a line-locking peg and a wire trace (to which a Jardine spiral lead of appropriate weight to balance the float is attached), joined to a Jardine snap-tackle. Although the float can be adjusted to allow the bait to be fished at varying depths, in practice the limit to this adjustment is fixed by the length of the angler's rod (for example, it is impossible to cast a fixed float rig comfortably with a 10-foot rod if the float-to-bait setting is more than 7 ft or so).

The revered Jardine lived during the first

Figure 28 Alfred Jardine's float rig (*left*). This old-fashioned Allcock's banana-shaped sliding-float (*right*) was, until recently, the most efficient design of sliding-float known. It eliminated the sliding-float's greatest bugbear – drag due to line friction against the body of the float. It was customary to tie a rubber float cap, or matchstick, on to the line to provide a stop. In their turn rods had to be fitted with much larger rings to allow passage for the stop

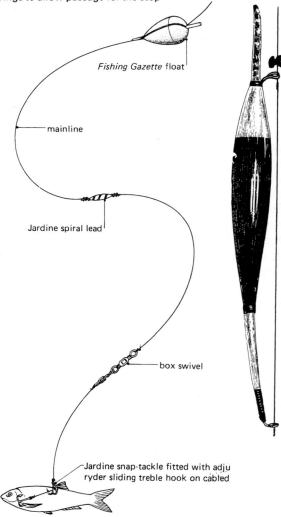

Fishing Gazette float

mainline

Jardine spiral lead

box swivel

Jardine snap-tackle fitted with adju ryder sliding treble hook on cabled

golden age of pike fishing, when there were many methods in use; but because he was so successful and caught so many big pike, generations of new pike anglers were content to copy him. This proved to be a snare and a delusion because those who copied him often used his method in situations that demanded different methods entirely. Quite simply it is forgotten (or not realized) that Jardine caught most of his big pike in small man-made lakes (made by damming streams), which were all alike – alike, that is, in the sense that they were all relatively shallow. Now that pike anglers can use an efficient slider float, which can be put to use in any depth of water, Jardine's float-rig (Figure 28) is outmoded – even for fishing on those private decorative lakes, sited nearby the stately homes of old English country estates, most of which Jardine was uniquely able to fish.

The successful development of an efficient slider-float during the late 1950s was due to a discovery made by Billy Lane, some-time world champion match-angler. In order to understand Lane's achievement it is necessary to describe the old-type slider-floats, which were unpopular, crude and limited in application. The old style of sliding-float had its side fitted with two large rings for the line to run through. It was banana-shaped in order to reduce the sliding-float's greatest bugbear – drag due to line friction against the body of the float. Billy, at a stroke, discarded the upper ring altogether – which eliminated line contact with the side of the float – and replaced the bottom ring (which had hitherto been big enough to take a 200 lb BS line) with a ring just big enough to allow the line to slip through.

He fitted a small *sliding* stop-knot, made from a short length of 6 lb BS nylon, and fixed it on the mainline above the float so that it could be slid to a point that would set the *float-to-bait distance* required by the angler (Figure 29). This tiny knot replaced the matchstick or other clumsy equivalent (which severely inhibited casting) used with the old sliding-floats. Here then was a big breakthrough: float fishing will never be the same again.

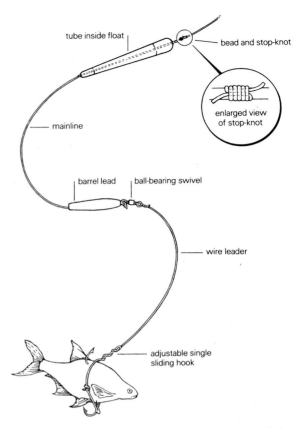

Figure 29 The modern sliding-float livebait rig. Essentially, a livebait fished on float-tackle should be free to tow the float and explore a wide area of water. To facilitate this free movement the line *must* be made to float (a sunken line catches up on underwater obstacles and effectively anchors the bait). Grease the line to make it float before passing it through a bead (which has a bore diameter slightly larger than that of the line). Then pass it through the tube of the float. For the sliding-float livebait rig *do not* use the Billy Lane bottom eye-only type of float attachment (see float paternostering for recommended use), because it pulls the line near the float underwater and by degrees this results in the rest of the line sinking. The diagram shows the elements of a sliding-float ledger deadbait rig with the bait mounted on my Universal snap-tackle

Of all livebaiting methods the float-fished method is the most popular, and deservedly so, considering the services a float renders to an angler: (a) it acts as a bite-indicator; (b) it suspends a bait at a given depth; (c) when aided by current or wind it carries a bait to the fishing area; (d) it acts as a supporter of the casting weight that may be required to reach the fishing spot.

These days most pike anglers agree that the profile of a pike float should be slim rather than bulbous, as it used to be, because a slim float passes through weeds with greater facility and causes less disturbance when it hits the water.

As to the size of the float it is always sensible to relate the buoyancy of the float to the power of the livebait. If the float is too small an angler is not always able to tell whether a pike or the livebait is pulling his float under. But to use an undersized float is the lesser of the two evils: the greater evil is to fish with a float that is too large for the bait. To appreciate this it is necessary to understand what happens when a pike takes a livebait.

Having struck from ambush (usually from below) and grabbed its victim, the pike does one of two things: it either returns to safe cover or sinks slowly back to the depths from which it originally struck. In either case the victim is held across the jaws, and crushed in a vice-like grip until the shock of its wounds prevents any chance of escape.

The float, of course, has been pulled under. But during the period when it is holding its victim, the pike lies motionless. When a pike is motionless it is very delicately balanced in the water and the extra buoyancy of a large float will affect its equilibrium. A large float will bring a small pike head-first towards the surface again. A big pike is not likely to be brought up in the same way, but its suspicions are likely to be increased rather than diminished by the buoyancy pull of an over-large float.

As a general rule, if an angler sees his float resurface after a take he can be pretty sure that his float is too large. The dropping of a bait by a

A master pike angler float-fishing with livebait on the pike fisherman's Mecca, Loch Lomond. Here Frank Wright is just about to gaff one of the pike pictured in a group on page 155

suspicious pike, through the use of an over-large float, happens more frequently on heavily fished waters.

It is customary for a pike angler to argue with his friend as to how long, after the disappearance of his float, he should wait before tightening or striking. This is an argument that will never be resolved. I remember vividly, once discussing the problem when I was fishing with Britain's best known angler Richard Walker. We were fishing on Loch Lomond together in an area where a 47 lb 11 oz pike had been caught some years previously – and where, some few days before, I had hooked, played and lost one as big. My bait on this occasion, a $\frac{3}{4}$ lb roach, had been taken and after some two almost unendurable minutes had dragged by, I said to him nervously, 'Do you think that I should hit the pike now?' He replied 'You do what you like, my old cock, but if you tighten now and fail to connect with the pike you can be sure it isn't the one you've come all this way to catch – so it won't matter much really, will it?'

He was right, of course, because a very big pike would make short work of a $\frac{3}{4}$ lb roach. Walker's indirect comment on bait size introduces a very important aspect of livebaiting: how big should a livebait be if you hope to attract a big pike – or, shall I say, a very big pike?

Many good pike anglers go through a period in their development when they are convinced that in order to improve their chances of catching a really big pike they must use very, very big baits. In time they discover (as I did) that the attendant problems of using a huge livebait far outweigh any advantage such a bait may have in luring a monster pike.

Very simply it is a problem of scale. To cast out a bait weighing several pounds requires tackle of enormous strength. Everything has to be scaled up – even the livebait container, and who would have the strength to carry it? Last, but most importantly, the business of getting hooks out of such a livebait and into the pike's bony mouth cannot be solved by the normal process of striking or tightening. No, forget

VIATOR (F.B.): Do you think that I should hit the pike now?. PISCATOR (Richard Walker): You do what you like, my old cock, but if you tighten now and fail to connect, you can be sure it isn't the one you've come all this way to catch . . . so it won't matter much really, will it?
Piscator and Viator are out from Balloch on their way to the pike grounds at Portnellan

huge baits and settle for baits that are easier to catch; baits that are not too big to cast; baits that are convenient to transport; baits that are still enticing enough to attract a 40-pounder.

In my estimation where much casting has to be done baits weighing from 4 oz to 10 oz are best, although slightly heavier baits weighing up to a pound are good providing no long casts have to be made.

When it comes to choosing tackles for livebaiting (or deadbaiting) it must be remembered that we are attempting to reconcile two virtually irreconcilable requirements, namely, to secure a bait so well with hooks (so that it will not fall off during the cast), and yet to have these same hooks clear the bait and hook the pike at the moment of tightening.

One of the most elementary mistakes made by anglers is to equate the size of hooks used on spinners with those used on livebait tackles.

Remember that hooks used on livebait tackles *must be much smaller* than those used on the equivalent-sized spinners, because unlike the hooks on spinning baits the hooks on livebaits *have to be pulled out of the bait* – before they can be pulled into the pike.

Treble hooks, sizes 6 or 8, will suffice for all livebaiting tackles where more than one treble hook is used. A size 4 treble can be used if it is used by itself. Single hooks on the other hand can be much larger up to sizes 1/0 or even 2/0. My own favourite tackle consists of one single (No. 2) and one treble hook (No. 6).

Pike tackles should be made up on cable laid wire; never single wire which is treacherous due to its tendency to kink. I use wire of between 20 to 30 lb BS to make up my hook tackles and I make them at least 2 ft long so that I can dispense with a steel leader.

Great care must be taken when livebaiting with float tackle to make sure that the line floats properly. I used to have special floating level lines (bubble fly lines) made to order in America, but I now find that monofilament that has been put through a press and made oval-shaped floats just as well when dressed with a good flotant. A line that sinks is a curse – it always impairs the free movement of the livebait and it makes it impossible for the angler to straighten his line without partially retrieving the bait. Moreover, a running pike may feel the line drag (if it gets caught in weeds or underwater snags) and drop the bait.

My collection of pike floats, any of which can be used as a sliding or a fixed float. One of them is fluted, the value of which design nobody described more succinctly than Fred J. Taylor when he wrote: 'It has been said that the fluted shape offers less resistance to a taking fish than a conventional round-bodied float, but this is not strictly true. Where the fluted float scores is in trotting downstream against an upstream wind. This I think was the purpose of its original design, as outlined by the late Major Smalley, its inventor.

'A non-fluted float will not move downstream against a strong wind, but a fluted one will. The reason is the much greater surface area of the float to the current. The round-bodied float offers a streamlined shape to the current and the current passes round it. The fluted float offers at least one of its concave depressions to the current and is therefore moved along by the flow of water which cannot pass round it.'

Sliding stop-knot (Figure 30)

For use when fishing a sliding-float. To tie the stop-knot, lay slip of nylon alongside the mainline with the end at point C on Figure 30, then proceed to lay coils as indicated. For ease

Figure 30 Sliding stop-knot

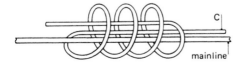

of tying, hold each loop as it is formed between thumb and index finger of the left hand. Pull tight, so that a determined pressure is needed to slip the knot up or down the line. Trim off, leaving $\frac{1}{8}$ in. stub ends.

The Captain Parker fast-water livebait rig (Figure 31)

The late Captain Parker designed a livebaiting pike rig which overcame the difficulties hitherto associated with float fishing for pike in fast-running rivers. The terminal tackle of his rig has a sliding single front hook which is adjusted to the length of the livebait (by sliding up or down the trace), before being inserted into the bait's top lip. The treble hook of the tackle is slung below the bait to act as a keel, and is very lightly nicked into the belly. The rig is com-

Landing a pike taken on sliding float tackle from a small lough near Tulla, Co. Clare (By courtesy of the Irish Tourist Board)

Figure 31 Captain Parker's fast-water livebait rig

pleted with a slim float and the appropriate lead. Swanshots are most useful leads for this purpose because their numbers can be adjusted to suit the bait and the conditions.

The hook arrangement of Captain Parker's tackle is designed to induce the bait to swim at the proper fishing depth. Without this arrangement a pike would only get a fleeting glimpse of the livebait passing overhead. With fast-water livebait fishing little casting is done as the fishing is usually carried out from a boat or a punt. Consequently the single anchor hook on Parker's tackle is just sufficient to secure the bait and it therefore offers only token resistance to the force of the strike needed to drive the treble hook into the pike's jaw.

With this style of fishing it is usual to trot the livebait down the stream on the edge of the

185

current swirl, close to the bank. The bait is rarely retrieved but may be held whilst the punt is moved down for the next trot. In this way good distances are quietly and quickly covered by the livebait. A skilful angler usually takes great care to fix his rypecks, or anchors, quietly and will even wear slippers so as to keep fish-scaring noises down to a minimum. The boat style of fishing is essentially a two-man operation. The second man is needed to bring the punt downstream, or to put a companion ashore, if he wishes, once a good fish is hooked. Of course, a small pike can be brought upstream with little difficulty.

In summertime, in spite of prolific weed growth, there are usually some clear runs which can be fished. Sometimes there is open water to be found below and to one side of a run. In these circumstances the bait is first trotted down through the run and then the rod is held up high to one side (the angler stands up to do this if necessary), so that the bait can investigate this open water. Captain Parker's rig is useful for fishing stillwaters when these are fished from a boat.

Paternostering

Although the origin of the generic term 'paternostering' (there are several ways of paternostering) is lost in the mists of time – or, more precisely, although the connection between the method and the name itself is lost – it is nevertheless very probably the most deadly of all basic methods of catching pike.

Perhaps the most telling advantage of the paternoster lies in the practical significance of having a bait properly located, properly presented and patiently waiting until the pike come on the feed. This is very different from the more usual practice of being obliged to search for fish which are already on the feed. We could say that this style of pike fishing is a contemplative style; yes, but a deadly one just the same. So deadly, in fact, that many of my friends, once introduced, count it as their favourite method! Moreover, it is a ubiquitous style, as effective in rivers as it is in lakes and ponds.

The paternoster has many distinct advantages over most other basic methods. When set up a baited paternoster fishes a chosen swim, hole or run effectively over an extended period of time *without further disturbance*. In this way the vigour of the bait is retained and not squandered, as it might be with the constant casting associated with other methods. Additionally, a bait can be fished a calculated distance up from the bed of the lake or river regardless of any variations in the depth of the water. Furthermore, the anchored bait is unable to foul up the tackle by swimming into weed-beds or other obstructions. With the paternoster there is a close ratio between the number of baits used and the number of pike caught; this saving of baits is no small consideration.

There are many variations of the paternostering theme but I shall describe the five most important ones:

The standing pike paternoster
Brown's paternoster
The float paternoster
The green cork paternoster
Count De Moira's beam paternoster

The standing pike paternoster (Figure 32)

We are all, I think, familiar with the sea-angler's beach-casting style of setting up his rod high in a rod-rest. Strangely, the freshwater angler disdains to emulate the sea-fisherman; yet I have found his style, with certain modifications, perfectly suitable for pike fishing.

Method

Choose a rod, of 10 or 11 ft, that will support the casting of a bait weighing a half-pound or so. The rod should be flexible enough to use in conjunction with a 12–14 lb nylon monofil line. Whichever rod you use, try to avoid all those short, stumpy, stiff pike rods beloved by generations of pike fishers. For preference, fit to the rod a centre-pin or a multiplier reel rather than a fixed spool reel (it is an advantage

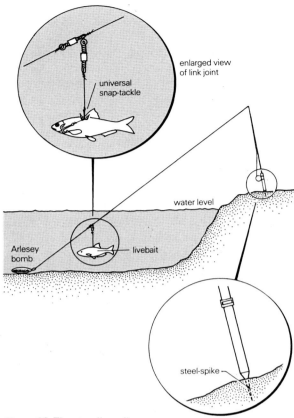

Figure 32 The standing pike paternoster

to have a type of reel which incorporates a check mechanism) that will give line to a running pike and when doing so emit a noise that attracts the angler's attention.

Tie a 1 oz Arlesey bomb on to one end of a 5–8 ft length of nylon, and on to the other tie on a swivel. Pass the mainline through the second eye of the same swivel before attaching by means of a second swivel any preferred type of bait-holding tackle (the total length of which should not be greater than $2\frac{1}{2}$ ft). The rig is completed with the most important item, a tapered pointed 6 in. steel spike threaded so as to screw into the rod butt cap. Choose a swim, and cast out the livebait with a long, slowly accelerated swing. As soon as the lead settles, stick the spike into the ground so as to support the rod in a vertical position. Wind in the slack line until the line is tensioned between the rod tip and lead. Set the drag on the reel to support

the check so as to maintain the tension on the line.

You will observe the tugs of the fresh bait on the rod top, but these will settle down. From then on there is no need to sit behind the rod in a mood of concentration unless the sport is exceptionally fast.

The standing pike paternoster is really a variant of the classic running paternoster rig. The latter was used by Richard Walker and Bob Rutland in those great days during the 1950s when they caught fifty-six perch over 3 lb, which included seven over 4 lb (best fish 4 lb 13 oz), from Arlesey Lake in Bedfordshire. They found this rig particularly useful *when fishing at long range in deep water*.

For pike fishing rig up the running paternoster just as you would the standing paternoster but this time lay the rod in rests, close to the surface of the water to minimize wind interference. Deadbaits are preferable where long casts need to be made but livebaits can also be used where long casts are deemed unnecessary.

This drawing, captioned 'Jack Fishing – Lea Bridge' (*c.* 1850), was the work of Henry Heath Jnr. A closer look at the drawing reveals a large livebait can, the absence of a float, and a spike fitted to the butt of the rod. These clues indicate that the successful angler was livebaiting with a standing (floatless) pike paternoster rig (By courtesy of Walter Spencer)

you are to allow a taking fish free line during its run. Walker overcame this problem by passing the line round an empty nylon spool laid on the ground between the reel and the butt ring. The open side of this empty spool was filled with sand – just enough sand to balance the pull on the line. This way the rig was made sensitive, and the line dislodged from the empty nylon spool as soon as the bait was taken, thereby allowing the fish complete freedom to run line off the reel with the bale arm left open. The running paternoster rig allows the angler to cover great areas of water, using a wind, stop, wind, stop routine. Additionally, the bait can be jiggled up and down to simulate a wounded fish, a useful trick to induce a surfeited, or circumspect pike to strike at the bait.

Brown's paternoster (Figure 33)

When strong wind makes it difficult to use the standing paternoster, Brown's paternoster keeps the bait high in the water and is unaffected by wind.

This 45 lb Corrib monster might have fallen to a proud angler had it not been caught on a longline set by Peter Lydon (on the left) who was the last man to make a living on and around the shoreline of Corrib with net, trap, longline and gun. He was also the last of a famous Irish breed – the professional otter-killer

When the bait is taken, the strike should be delayed; in fact Walker uses the word run to indicate the pause needed before tightening and striking. Another significant discovery made by the two anglers was that they caught the majority of their deep-water fish when the light penetration to the bed of the lake was at its maximum.

In order to make the paternoster work properly, the angler has to maintain a tight line from lead to rod tip. This creates a problem if

Figure 33 Brown's paternoster – (a) shows how the line is completely shielded from the wind, and (b) is an enlargement of the terminal tackle. Note that the bubble float is *always* attached to the middle eye of the three-way swivel to ensure that the strain of a hooked pike is in line with the axis of the swivel

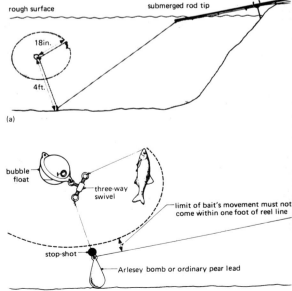

F. B. at Salthouse Bay, Lough Corrib, holding a 25½ lb pike taken on a spoon

The float paternoster (Figure 34)

This method of paternostering, which has survived from the nineteenth century, has been improved considerably in recent years. The advent of the modern sliding-float has brought about the improvement because it not only allows deep water to be float fished in comfort for the first time but it also allows a pike angler to fish in varying depths of water with the minimum amount of tackle adjustments (he only needs to slide the stop-knot up or down).

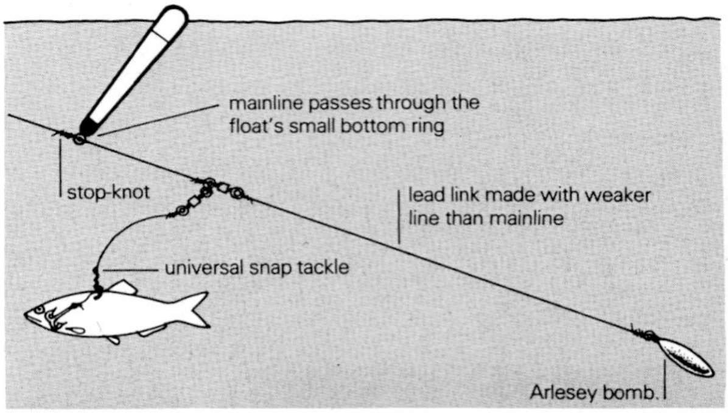

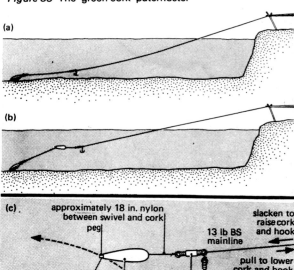

Figure 34 The float paternoster

The 'green cork' paternoster (Figure 35)

The rig is most useful when we require to fish at long range and keep a paternostered bait well off the bottom. Inevitably, at long range the line sags between the rod tip and the lead – regardless of the angler's efforts to straighten it by further tensioning. This curve in the line is known as a catenary curve.

Figure 35 illustrates the phenomenon and indicates the difficulty of keeping the bait off the bottom except in very deep water. (We might consider a lead link of perhaps some 10 yards together with a very short hook link; but such a rig would be impossible to cast.) The green cork rig overcomes the difficulty. Figure 35(b) demonstrates the raising of the hook link by way of a buoyant cork. Figure 35(c) illustrates the elements of the rig in more detail. Apart from the cork, the rest of the rig is similar to the normal classic running paternoster rig. The cork need not be as streamlined as the one shown, but some concession to streamlining is useful to facilitate casting. A cork about the size of a medium cigar is about right for use with 10 in. livebaits and should be painted a dull green to make it unobtrusive. It is bored to facilitate the passage of the line through to the Arlesey bomb. A peg is fitted to trap the line, and this should be pushed in the cork at the lead end so that it is less inclined to catch on weeds when retrieved. With a normal running paternoster the line is tightened to raise the bait, but with the green cork paternoster it is slackened to raise the bait and tightened to

lower the bait. The green cork pivots about the lead to the extent indicated by the dotted line, depending on the tension applied to the mainline once the stop-shot reaches the eye of the swivel.

Figure 35 The 'green cork' paternoster

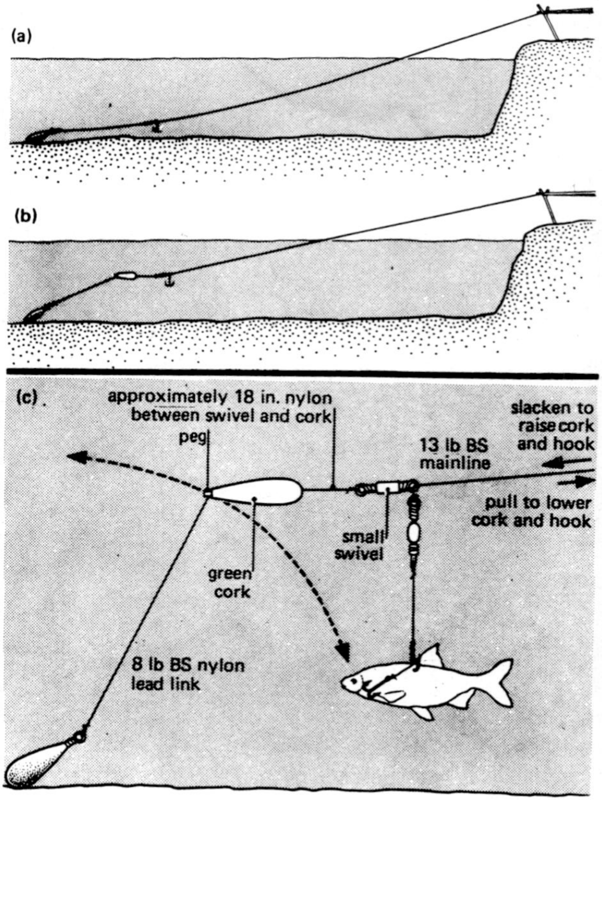

The most impressive picture of a big pike that I have ever seen. The pike weighed 46 lb and it was 52 in. long. When it was caught in 1970 by Marian Polowczyk it constituted the Polish record for the species. I would like to thank Tadeusz Andrzejczyk, the Polish angling writer, for the extraordinary lengths to which he went in order to secure the negative from which this print was made

For bite indication divert the line running between the reel and butt ring round an empty nylon spool and balance the latter with lead weights to counter the pull of the livebait.

The pike feels little resistance from the green cork, since it can take line freely from the reel. To make this possible the bale arm should be left open on a fixed-spool reel, and a light check applied to a centre-pin or multiplying reel.

One of the problems associated with fishing the great lochs of Scotland and Ireland is the difficulty of knowing where to fish to make the best use of one's time. In other words, there is the problem of locating pike. We know from experience that fish cannot move rapidly from deep to shallow water, or from shallow to deep water without incurring swim-bladder troubles. This being the case, there is good reason to suppose that ranging pike take notice of depth contours and follow them for comfort. Such behaviour could account for the fact that gill nets set on Windermere (where the Freshwater Biological Association has done much research on pike and pike behaviour), usually produce heavier catches of pike when placed off rocky points, where depth contours plotted on a chart run very close together (see Figure 21, page *152*). A close study of depth charts may reveal places where depth contours converge close to the bank. When these are found I believe that the green cork rig offers the most effective way of presenting the bait to the pike, especially since we know that deep-swimming pike on Windermere strike the gill nets some 5 ft up from the bottom. Furthermore, we know that a pike's vision is accented forward and upward which again indicates the need for a raised livebait in deep waters.

Count de Moira's beam paternoster
(Figure 36)

Numerous beam and boom paternosters have been advocated for pike fishing. This particular rig was described in *The Book of the All-Round Angler* and is considered to be old-fashioned; but old-fashioned or not, *it works*. The description is so clear that I give it verbatim. (The

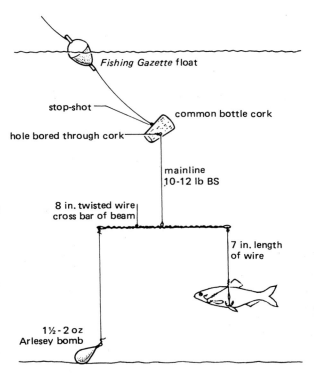

Figure 36 Count de Moira's beam paternoster

rig in Figure 36 has been re-drawn in terms of modern materials):

It is obviously important to have the cork just the right size to support the bait and the wire beam in horizontal position. With this tackle the bait has great freedom, pirouetting round the plumb which anchors it at the proper place and depth. It is altogether so novel, and apparently so complicated, that it is not likely to be viewed with much favour; but the Count de Moira says he kills more fish with it than his friends do on other tackle. R. B. Marston wrote of this tackle:

'You often come across breaks and bays in beds of weeds and reeds which line the bank; they are often too small to try the ordinary livebait tackle in, because the bait would swim into the reeds at once. It is impossible to keep the bait on an ordinary paternoster at the exact depth, unless you are almost over the spot, and hold the line taut all the time; directly the line slackens, the bait fouls the weeds at the bottom, and might remain there a month without attracting the notice of a fish. With Count de Moira's invention your bait must swim round, supported (at any depth you please) by the cork, and anchored in one spot.'

Another Corrib giant – 43½ lb – held by Danny Goldrick

Ledgering with livebait (Figure 37)

As with all types of fishing there are many ways of presenting a bait. For some reason, not always known to the angler, on one particular day one method is more rewarding than any other. Whereas deadbait ledgering is very popular in Britain it is probably true to say that few anglers ledger with livebait – and yet on the day when baits need (for some reason or other) to be presented ledger-style this method can be deadly indeed.

From my own experience the ledger method is likely to be more effective than other methods when water temperature is very, very low or when pike have been pushed into small pockets to avoid heavy water during floods. In both instances, I think it is the close proximity

Figure 37 A sample layout of a livebait ledger rig

between prey and predator (in a situation where pike may be disinclined to search or hunt for their prey), that makes all the difference. Needless to say, pike may take a ledgered livebait well in normal conditions.

Free-lining a tethered livebait

Because neither float nor lead is used with this rig the livebait can range about in any direction or depth available to it at the time – subject only to the amount of line paid out by the angler. The method is usually referred to as free-lining, which is a misnomer. The bait on a tethered tackle has the same freedom to range about as a float-fished bait but with these differences:

1 It can swim to any depth.
2 It can swim on an even keel (note that a bait which tows a float cannot).
3 It does not have to exhaust itself dragging a float and lead about.
4 It can accelerate in an attempt to avoid the attentions of an approaching pike – behaviour that might well entice a suspicious pike, especially a pike that lives in heavily fished waters.

I use the term 'tethered bait' because it reminds me of the way in which generations of farmers have tethered goats, ponies and cattle with a long rope fixed to a peg.

My own experience of using this method goes back twenty-five years and I have found it to be particularly useful when fishing from a boat anchored in the centre of a bay of the type found in most big lakes. My first experience was when I used such a powerful livebait that it kept pulling down my biggest float so that I kept thinking that I'd had a run. I responded by taking off the float and lead and gave the fish free reign. This particular bait went a record distance from the boat before it was taken by a big pike right at the surface.

Hooking arrangements for tethered-livebait fishing are the same as for ledgering.

24 Spinning and wobbling

The origins of spinning

The origin of spinning with artificial baits is obscure but the method may be many thousands of years old. In all probability it started in northern Europe soon after the development of the hook which occurred some 11,500 years ago. The finding of the remains of deep-water fish (cod) at a Neolithic site at Hemnor in Gotland (Denmark) implies the use of lines of considerable length. Perhaps the use of pieces of shell in the form of sinkers to sink the Stone Age fisherman's baits attracted the attention of some boat-fishing troglodyte angler who pondered the significance of his sinker being attacked as it sank through the clear waters.

There is little doubt that it was from an earlier shell-fashioned lure that the most famous and killing cod-lure, the Norse pirk, originated.

This conjecture fits in nicely with the record we have of a 'trowling lure of Bryte shel' being used by a Dane on Hyckelyngge (Hickling Broad) in the ninth century and of Captain Cook's observation that the South Sea Islanders used shell lures to catch sea fish.

The pike spoon used in modern times is said to have been invented by one of the Duke of Exeter's servants after an incident that occurred sometime between 1846–56. While emptying a pail of slops into the River Exe, this servant saw a pike dart out from under the bank and take a spoon that had been inadvertently left in the pail. Being a fisherman, he had a local tinsmith fashion a spoon bait with appropriate hooks (I bet he stole some of the duke's old spoons). See Figure 38.

Figure 38 The Duke's spoon. A plain spoon, it seems, was the forerunner of all metal artificial baits. The first notice, and illustration (from which the above was taken), of this type of artificial being used in Britain was in Cholmondeley-Pennell's *The Book of the Pike* (1876)

It is said – and I am sure it is true – that a pike takes a spoonbait because it mistakes it for a sick or an injured fish. This feeding ploy, were it not for human deceit, normally improves a pike's chances of making a kill. Unfortunately for pike the flashes emitted by a spinning or a wobbling spoon exactly imitate the flashes of a sick or an injured fish when it is unable to maintain normal orientation – dark side up and reflective sides away from direct sunlight (Photo: W. S. Berridge)

194

Spinning

Make no mistake, spinning proper – that is, casting with a natural or an artificial bait designed to spin on its own axis or, in the case of artificials only, revolve or flutter round a bar when retrieved – is an art.

Understanding this art and becoming skilled in it is every bit as difficult to achieve as is the artistry associated with even the most lauded branch of angling.

Unfortunately, many anglers after only limited and mainly frustrating experience, excuse their own failure – with that timeworn alliterative phrase 'It's only chuck it and chance it.'

They are wrong. Had they persevered they might have discerned the faint outlines of a pattern that would solve the enigma of their few successes and many failures. During my own apprenticeship I found a pattern emerging after a year or two, and now after forty years of spinning I am able to read, albeit with a signal failure or two, water that is quite new to me – by building up a composite picture with jigsaw pieces remembered from more familiar places.

In my view, the terms used in angling books to describe the recognizable features of rivers and lakes cannot be used effectively to describe the areas worthy of the spinner's attention. You know the sort of terms I mean: 'by the camp sheathing', 'below the bridge support', 'on the edge of the current', 'in the eddy', etc! The same places are recommended for every sort of fish and as a result are usually overfished. And, what is more to the point, pike rarely lie cheek by jowl with their fodder fish. Hardly surprising, really: it would be like soldiers of opposing armies sharing the same trench!

Having made a statement it behoves me to support it with corroborative evidence. To start with, I have made a point of asking many skilful pike fishers of my acquaintance the same question: 'Are the best roach swims, or, for that matter, the best dace, chub or bream swims, ever particularly productive swims for pike?'

Spinning the modern way – with a properly designed 10 ft glass-fibre or carbon-fibre rod matched to the appropriate fixed-spool or multiplying reel – is a joy. Seen fishing the River Lune with just such an outfit is ex-Lune water bailiff Albert Shuttleworth, whose best bag was seven pike to 28½ lb, making a total of 90 lb (Photo: Adrian Czarnecki)

The answer has always been in the negative. The really good roach swim, it would seem, may produce a pike or two, as may the best dace or bream swim, but the pike hotspots are generally to be found elsewhere (although, frequently not very far away).

Over the years having spent much of my time

195

looking through the crystal clear waters of my favourite river the Dorset Stour (now sadly ruined by those who have altered its shape and character in the name of progress), I have witnessed scenes which, when assessed from a mere glance, indicate that pike are sometimes 'allowed' to share a swim, or a run, with other fish, such as roach or dace, without the latter appearing to take particular notice or alarm.

Some anglers think that this indifference on the part of roach and dace to the presence of pike occurs only when pike are not actively feeding. In my view this is the wrong inference to draw; or, at least, it is an oversimple interpretation for what can be only one facet of a complex behavioural pattern. Indeed, I think it is quite wrong to infer that fish are capable of assessing the intentions of the inscrutable pike just because it happens to be lying still. In situations where there is a constant threat to small fish, as there must be where pike remain in close proximity to the fish which constitute their diet, the food fish must always remain on the alert in anticipation of that threat. Thus, the essential element of surprise is lost to the pike, and such loss is likely to deprive it of its reward.

Surely, when shoal fish congregate in favoured holes, runs or swims, it is to enjoy the greater overall safety offered by these locations in the face of a multitude of dangers – be they from pike, gulls, cormorants, ospreys, otters, mink, man or any other source. Should the essential character of these locations change from a favourable to an unfavourable one, from the security point of view, then I am sure the shoal will move on to new pastures. Fish are obliged to take risks in order to fulfil essential functions like feeding and breeding, but at other times personal security must remain an unending preoccupation.

Because favoured sites enjoy concentrations of fish for extended periods (generally during the daylight hours), they are likely to be over-grazed and offer little in the way of food to the tenants. On the other hand, some adjacent areas, rested as they are for longer periods of time, must, subject to the degree of their

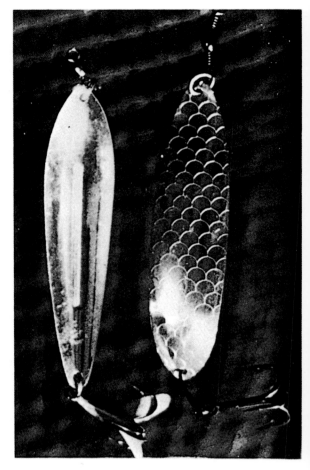

The Jim Vincent spoon (*right*). This famous pike spoon, made by Hardy Bros., was named after England's master pike fisherman, Jim Vincent. Although nowadays made of chromed copper, it was originally made of hardwood. Jim copied an Indian-made original which he brought back from Canada, where he had seen it used for pike with deadly effect. A good spoon for deep-water pike fishing

Williams's Wabler (*left*). You can see the generic similarity of this modern Canadian pike and musky spoon to Jim Vincent's original. However, there is an essential difference – the wabler bait is made of light alloy, which permits its effective use in shallow water

productive capacity, offer better grazing prospects to the shoal fish. The diurnal movements of shoal fish to and from these feeding grounds give pike the opportunity to press home their attack from ambuscade.

In my experience the most productive water

lies in the 3–6 ft contour. There are many exceptions, of course. In summer, pike may be found in very shallow water, and in some lakes pike are taken well down, although 12 ft is as deep as I would ever want to spin.

An incidental piece of intelligence on the relationship of food to the colouring of pike comes from a friend, Mr John Spear, who has observed that a pike about to strike, or having struck at a bait, usually turns a shade paler in colour. Mr Spear made his original observation at Farlow's lake near Iver in Buckinghamshire, but has confirmed this phenomenon elsewhere.

There is little doubt that light values play a big part in the relative effectiveness of the pike fisher's artificial bait. For example: a few years ago I was privileged to fish an excellent pike lake, in the company of two good friends. It was our custom to fish from a boat. With three of us drift-spinning from one boat, and all using different baits with various rates of retrieve, it usually worked out that one of us would start building up a good catch while the others would be catching few or none. After a time, whenever this happened, the two less successful ones would change their baits over and do their best to emulate the style of the most successful. These tactics usually made for team success. As soon as sport declined we would start experimenting with other baits until one of us again found the answer.

During the day the pike's requirements in terms of a spoon pattern, or style of retrieve, would change, and if these demands were not met the sport flagged. Any sort of stubbornness on the part of one angler to relinquish a favourite spinner – persevered with, perhaps, because of some strongly held notion as to the bait's super pike-catching potential – usually resulted in the eventual extinction of his former loyalty to the bait.

The apparently fickle changes of the pike's taste in artificials seemed to be related to the changing light conditions. I am fairly sure that it was not a matter of colour, although we used various coloured spoons with mixed success. It was more a question, we thought, of the bait's light-reflective value in changing light conditions. The only thing I am certain of, regarding the effect of the actinic value of daylight, is that it is necessary to experiment with many different baits during the course of a day's fishing, for this is the only way to capitalize on the true pike-producing potential of any water.

I would like to see a bait manufacturer make a series of baits of the same basic type and size with different light-reflective values. We could

Spoon plug (*top*) Primarily designed as a deep-trailing (trolling) lure, it will fish fifteen feet down from the surface. If this lure picks up weed it will turn over on its back and surface
Colorado (*second from top*) This has probably accounted for more pike in England than any other artificial bait
Mepps Giant Killer (*second from bottom*) Together with the Devon minnow, the Mepps has probably killed more predatory fish throughout the world than any other artificial bait
Ellips (*bottom*) A new pike bait that will probably feature in the future record of big pike catches

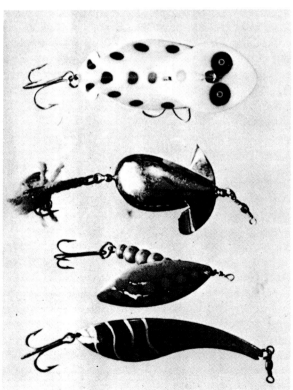

then buy, say, a 2 in. spoon with bright, medium or dull finish. Armed with a variety of patterns each with three shades of brightness it might be possible, on a day when we catch forty or so pike, to draw certain tentative but interesting conclusions.

I have already mentioned speed of retrieve. This is very important in pike fishing. Retrieve a spoon or spinner as slowly as possible. Never let the consideration of losing a bait influence you. If you are a person who means to start a day's spinning with six spinners and return home with the same number, you will never be a good pike fisherman. Build up a large collection of baits by buying them three at a time of a type and size. This will allow you to fish on with a pike-taking spoon even though you have just lost the one which has caught a lot of pike.

The bait, if it is being fished properly, should bounce on the bottom. If it comes in with weed on the hooks, clean it – again and again if necessary – and don't worry. The slower a bait is fished the longer it will remain within the pike's striking zone. The longer the bait takes to pass through the pike's striking zone the more time the pike has to make up its mind to grab it. And again, the closer the bait is to the bottom the longer it will remain within the pike's striking range. This will be appreciated if you draw a quarter circle (see Figure 39) on a piece of paper and imagine a pike resting at the point where the compass sticks in the paper. Supposing the radius of the quarter circle represents a distance of 8 ft, and that in given circumstances 8 ft represents the limit of the pike's natural striking zone, then if two lines are drawn parallel to the baseline, the first, 1 ft above the baseline (representing a bait drawn close to the bottom), and the second 7 ft from the baseline (representing a bait drawn high through the water), you can measure both lines from the points where they intersect the vertical and the periphery. From these measurements it can be seen that a spinner drawn close to the bottom will have a longer traverse through the pike's striking zone than the one drawn high through the water.

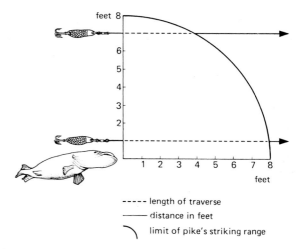

----- length of traverse
——— distance in feet
⟍ limit of pike's striking range

Figure 39 The closer the bait is to the bottom the longer it will remain within the pike's striking range

Now we begin to see how important it is to retrieve slowly. I can illustrate the value of slow spinning by recounting an experience on the River Test. I have fished this river for salmon on several occasions. During these operations I have caught five pike and, I am sorry to admit, only one fresh-run salmon. The pike in this chalk stream are scarce since they are wired, netted, trapped, shot and generally harried at all times by the river keepers. Another fisherman was most surprised to see one of my pike, for he had yet to catch a pike on the same reach even though he had fished it quite successfully for salmon for upwards of twenty years. The point I am making is that my bait retrieve has become conditioned by years of pike spinning, so that I am able (without intent) to catch a few pike on water where the pike must see and resist countless spinners thrown across them by salmon anglers who, perhaps, retrieve them at a faster rate.

Having reread the foregoing prior to publication, I was struck by my statement, 'retrieve a spoon or spinner as slowly as possible'. I realized that it was capable of misinterpretation because sometimes a pike angler has to retrieve quite quickly! Perhaps it would be safer to aver 'Never retrieve more quickly than you have to.'

198

A note in my diary implied that long casting and/or slow retrieving was useless when fishing the very shallow and weedy Cloon Lough in Co. Mayo:

Pike Fishing, Cloon Lough (12–16 Dec. 1976)

Trout returning from spawning in the Aille River. A seven pound pike had a 2 lb trout kelt in its throat. Spin spoons very fast – as one sprig of weed on the bait wastes the cast. Also make short casts; with long casts the bait is soon into weed. Best baits – copper & silver or red & silver (large). Colorados didn't take a fish but a jointed plug took 3 fish.

There is an old saying that goes: 'Those who keep their bait in the water catch most fish.' Perhaps this old saying draws attention to some essential truth, but as with all other sayings there is an underlying supposition that other things are equal. With spinning, other things are *not* equal. It is more important to fish thoughtfully and selectively with a spinner so that you make every cast a measured one. From time to time it is necessary to rest for a spell so as to rebuild nervous energy. Never fish despairingly. For my part, if everything I know about spinning tells me that it is a waste of time to continue, then I stop, for experience has taught me that it is bad to carry on and become demoralized.

At some time in a pike angler's career, he usually gets a notion that a huge spinner will be more attractive to a very large pike than one of normal dimensions. I am afraid this notion is erroneous. In my experience, very large spinning baits catch small pike or nothing. Certainly most of Ireland's big pike have been taken on Devons or other small artificials.

Mr Hogg, a Loch Lomond boatman, told me recently that one of his salmon-fishing clients caught a 42 lb pike on a Devon; and we know that the largest Wye pike was caught on a Wagtail bait. I believe there is an optimum size for each and every pike spinner, and if this size is exceeded the attractiveness of the bait is diminished. For instance, I have used $2\frac{1}{2}$ in. Colorado baits for pike with great success, whereas larger ones have been a great let down.

Another very impressive photograph, this time of a 42 lb $15\frac{1}{2}$ oz pike caught on a spinner by Thrane Nilsson of Copenhagen

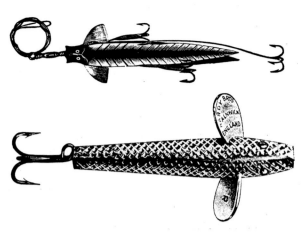

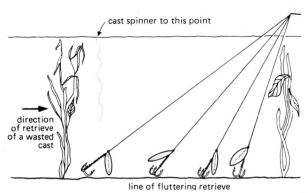

Figure 40 Use of a fluttering-type spinner in weedy waters

The Wagtail bait (*top*) has probably accounted for more big pike, albeit when used as a salmon bait, than any other artificial

The Devon Minnow (*bottom*) probably the most used and possibly the most successful artificial bait of all time. Countless thousands of pike have fallen to the Devon Minnow, most of which surprised their captors, who were fishing for other kinds of fish

I am not suggesting that we fish with small salmon baits. On the contrary, I think that salmon baits owe their success as good pike catchers to the fact that in many salmon waters they are the only spinners the pike ever see.

Finally, I would like to mention a small point about the gaffing of pike. Most people hold a gaff incorrectly. To be effective, the point of a gaff should be lifted in the vertical plane. This way, the soft skin between the lower jawbones is easily penetrated without harming the pike. A gaff held incorrectly and brought up at 45 degrees delivers a glancing blow to the pike's chin and may do a great deal of damage. Hold the gaff handle as you might a dagger. This will allow the angler to lift the gaff in a vertical plane. Never hold a gaff as you would hold a broom or a rod – most people do, but it is the wrong way to gaff a pike!

Spinning in weedy waters (Figure 40)

An angler who prefers to spin rather than fish plug seldom attempts to operate throughout the season, because weeds rarely die down sufficiently for him until late November. A

season can be extended for a few more months if an angler uses a fluttering type of spinner like the large Mepps. Looking at the arrow in Figure 40, we can see the fate of a spinner cast to full range in weedy conditions. The spinner is inevitably pulled into the first weed tresses at the onset of the retrieve. The rest of the retrieve represents time wasted, as no self-respecting pike takes a weed-covered bait; whereas numerous short casts into clear patches, where the bait can be swung through in pendulum fashion, can be quite productive. Large Mepps, together with other baits of similar design, have a low-friction-bearing attachment to the blade of the spinner. This allows the blade of the spinner to flutter when pulled sideways even at very low speeds, unlike a traditional spoon which could cease to function.

Deadbait spinning

While contemplating the description of a particular deadbait spinning tackle, I made a discovery that although the term *deadbait spinning* is a precise term, and indeed one which perfectly describes a particular pike-fishing method, it is often used with less precision to describe many other methods. It would seem that whereas the word 'deadbait' always has a valid application to these sundry methods, the word 'spinning' has not. I think that we should remember that the words 'spin' and 'spinning' are descriptive of a specific action. They should be reserved accordingly, and not used to describe methods which involve casting a bait and retrieving it without the function of spin.

Flights and mounts for deadbait spinning and wobbling

The terms 'flight' and 'mount' are often confused. There is, however, an important distinction. A spinning 'flight' is an arrangement of hooks which will put a curve in a natural bait, and so cause it to revolve when

drawn through the water. A spinning 'mount' uses means other than a curve (vanes, etc.) to induce the bait to spin or wobble.

Note: Most of the flights and mounts described here have not been marketed during recent years. This is not the fault of the tackles themselves. The reason why they are not on offer in a modern catalogue is *not* because they are wanting in appeal either to fish or fishermen, but because of the harsh modern commercial climate that demands a reduction in tackle items. The tackles used so successfully by our grandfahers will, given the chance, kill fish equally well today. Hence my illustration and description of spinning flights and mounts which the unthinking angler might otherwise reject as being 'out of date'.

The Bromley-Pennell deadbait flight (Figure 41)

Until recently there existed a spinning flight which has been condemned by almost every writer on the subject: the Thames flight. It

Although the French keep no official list of record fish it is thought that this pike, caught by M. Lecrivain in a gravel pit at Draveil, is one of the biggest ever caught on rod and line in France. It weighed 40 lb 11 oz and was 52½ in. long. Many anglers had hooked the same pike, nicknamed Albert, only to be broken. The fish was caught spinning on a No. 2 Suissex bait – a bait not unlike the Voblex which has a plug head and low-friction spinning blade. This photograph with its typically French background – an avenue of trees – was taken by M. Maury, the editor of France's finest angling magazine, *La Pêche et les Poissons*

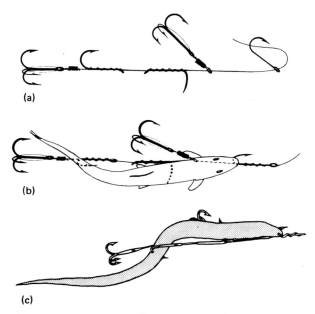

(a)

(b)

(c)

Figure 41 (*a*) The Bromley-Pennell flight; (*b*) with hooks set for the bait to spin; (*c*) mounted with eel-tail bait. On Corrib, H. Cholmondeley-Pennell, fishing with eel-tail, hooked and lost the largest pike he contacted during his lifetime

deserves a brief mention for its historical interest since it taught our grandfathers and great-grandfathers how to attract pike with a natural bait – even though their pike frequently came unhooked!

The Bromley-Pennell spinning flight, legitimate heir to the Thames flight, incorporates only two trebles instead of the Thames flight's outmoded four. Both these trebles are free-flying – which allows them to find an attachment in the pike's mouth the moment the angler strikes.

This is not the case with most other flights (including the Thames flight), where the strike power has first to overcome the hold which the trebles have in the bait, before freeing them to find an attachment in the pike's jaw.

The Bromley-Pennell flight, although no longer available commercially, can easily be made up with cabled wire, the trebles being attached in the way described for the Nottingham flight (page *206*). The curiously shaped 'holding' hook, seen in the illustrations, is a normal hook straightened out and trimmed

with pliers. The lip hook is put on after the wire has been pushed through the gill cover and out through the mouth. It is secured in the correct position by a few turns of wire on the shank before being pulled through both lips of the bait. Should extra casting weight be needed, a barrel lead is pushed down the throat of the bait before the lip hook is fitted.

If the bait is required to spin, it is curved by setting the hooks as shown in Figure 41 (b); otherwise, very good results can be obtained by setting the bait 'straight', and employing a jerky retrieve. This excellent deadbait tackle will probably regain its former popularity when more anglers take up loch and reservoir fishing and become conscious of the need to cover a lot of water.

Cholmondeley-Pennell had this to say about the preparation of a natural eel-bait for use on his mount.

The fresh eel (and tail) makes an excellent spinning bait, tough and enduring. I have used fresh eel-bait dressed in a great many different fashions, from the whole eel (where the latter is not above seven or eight inches long), to six inches or so of the tail cut off a larger specimen. In this case the eel from which the bait is taken, is best rather small, and should not, for ordinary river and lake spinning, exceed a foot in length (9 in. better). For great lochs, like L. Corrib where pike are scarce and run sometimes to an extra-ordinary size, larger eels may be used with advantage. The most perfect eel-tail bait for pike spinning is, I consider, one about 7 inches long, made from an eel of say, three-quarters of a foot, an artificial head – which is more durable than the natural head – being formed out of the turned-back skin. This turned-back skin, besides being so much stronger by being doubled, has a blue colour which looks thoroughly fish-like in the water, and has apparently an appetising effect on the pike's taste.

In forming the head, skin the eel backwards towards the tail as far as the point where the bait is to commence, trimming off the flesh round the spinal bone 'cone-shaped'. Then tie the skin tightly round, close above the bone, and cut it off to within about an inch and a half of the ligature, turning the flap then downwards again, towards the tail. The pin-hook will eventually pass through both the turned down flap and the under-skin, and keep the flap fixed.

Deadbait spinning mounts

Like most of the commercial deadbait pike spinning mounts manufactured during the last 100 years, the Archer mount (Figure 42) is really a modified version of the original Chapman mount.

The Chapman mount (Figure 43) consisted of a wire spike, sharpened at one end to facilitate penetration of the bait, and leaded at the other to increase casting potential. The mount incorporated two spinning blades or vanes which fitted close to the head of the bait. Since the efficacy of the vanes depended on the size of the bait they were expected to set in motion, it was vital to have either a bait which suited the mount, or a mount which suited the bait.

The mount was armed with a complement of up to six trebles. Gradually, over the years, it became evident that although a lot of trebles ensure a secure grip of the bait – which means

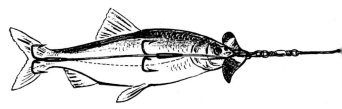

Figure 43 The Chapman spinning mount

that the bait lasts longer – a correspondingly heavy price is paid in lost fish. The chances of a pike being firmly hooked are greatly reduced when the force of the strike is dissipated by a forest of trebles. On the other hand, although the use of fewer trebles means that a bait is less securely held and needs replacing more often, it also results in a higher proportion of hooked fish being landed.

As these mechanical difficulties became more widely understood, the Archer mount, incorporating just three trebles, found universal favour. Or perhaps it might be truer to say that the Archer's popularity was due to the greater facility with which a bait could be put on. At any rate, Jardine spoke highly of it – which was praise indeed.

As can be seen in Figure 42, the spinning-blades are hinged forward prior to the bait being mounted. When the vanes are pushed back into position they grip the bait behind the head. The trebles are then attached to the bait with cotton-elastic, or by pressing in lightly.

In this convenience-orientated age of ours the problem associated with the catching and the preserving of natural baits, prior to a day's piking, seems to be a stumbling block to that style of fishing (namely deadbait spinning and wobbling), for which *trouble-taking* is a prerequisite.

Given the indolence of the modern angler, and the high cost of manufacturing mounts and flights I am not surprised to find that everything mitigates against their continued use. Although I accept this decline in the use of natural baits it would be wrong to suppose that artificial baits have superseded natural baits because they are superior; they are not.

Properly presented natural baits are superior

Figure 42 The Archer spinning mount

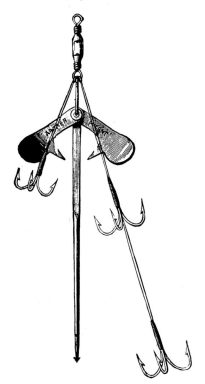

because pike, and any other fish for that matter, hold on to them (because of their natural softness) longer than they would an artificial bait.

Because of the difficulties alluded to, the Archer mount and many others that once graced the tackle catalogues are with us no more, but a version of the Chapman mount (with celluloid fans) is still made.

In the context of the decline and disappearance of natural baits my experience when meeting a Tweed boatman (on the Sprouston beat near Kelso), who practically insisted that I use a natural bait (a golden sprat) rather than an artificial, was refreshing. What was of even greater interest to me was my discovery of a mount that was quite the best that I have ever used.

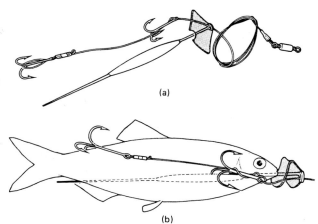

Figure 44 The McElrath (or Tweed) mount

The McElrath mount (Figure 44)

Albert McElrath's mount is a superior piece of tackle. Uniquely, so far as a deadbait mount is concerned, it is not attached directly to the hooks, so that a pike, or any other fish for that matter, cannot use the mount and bait as a lever. Indeed, like the shell of a Devon Minnow, it can be blown right up the trace or leader (the Devon Minnow is known to be the best hooker of all artificial baits for this reason).

Since I have been unable to trace the inventor of this fine mount henceforth I shall know it by the name of its most ardent advocate – Mr McElrath; and, because this mount for pike (and even for salmon fishing, for all I know) cannot be bought I shall append details of its make-up.

Figure 44(a) shows the leaded body of the mount and displays the feature which is at the

heart of the mount's superior hooking efficiency, namely the double-coiled ring at the nose of the mount through which the wire leader (to one end of which is attached a team of treble hooks) passes to join up with the main line.

To make up a McElrath spinning mount, take the middle of a 12 in. length of stiff copper wire (20 SWG) and wind it twice round a nail ($\frac{3}{16}$ in. diameter) to form a nose loop (this double loop eliminates the prospect of the leader-wire jamming) before doubling it back on itself. Push a celluloid, or suitable plastic, spinning fan between the wires – right up to the nose loop. Mould a barrel-shaped piece of lead around the two wires about half an inch back from the fan. Solder together those parts of the wire not covered by the lead and finally trim off the end of the wire to make a mount of the required length.

To make up the hook rig take a 12 in. length of suitable cabled wire and tie a knot at one end before slipping on a brass ferrule. Pass the free end of the wire through the eye of a treble and then take the wire round the back of the hook before passing it through the eye again from the opposite side. Slip the wire back through the ferrule and slide the ferrule right up to the eye of the hook before crimping off. Pass the free end of the wire along the shank of another treble before passing it twice through the eye of this second treble. The distance between the

Opposite:
Some of the author's essential piking equipment
Top Wire-cutting pliers (*left*); the Abu crimping tool (*middle*); electric outboard, Seafarer echo-sounder and deep-water thermometer (*right*)
Bottom Hardy thermometer (*extreme left*); coil of lead wire (*left*); Hardy serrated scissors (*middle*); handwarmer (*right*); Hardy specialist balance weighs up to 40 lb by 8 oz (*bottom middle*)

two trebles can be varied by merely loosening the double loop of wire that passes through the eye of the *second* treble.

Pass the end of the wire through the nose loop of the mount before attaching it to a ball-bearing swivel by means of another ferrule duly crimped.

Figure 44(b) shows the bait *in situ* on the mount. After the bait has been mounted, secure it by winding a 12 in. length of fine copper wire round the bait (so as to keep the armed leader pressed up to the bait) and tie off. One point of each treble can be pushed into the bait, to keep the weight of the hooks close to the bait's centre of gravity, thus facilitating a good spin at slow speeds.

The Nottingham flight (Figure 45)

If you are looking for a tackle which will hold a herring firmly while it is being fished, allow it either to tack and dive or to spin, give good hooking power and allow you to fish for long periods without renewing the bait, you will find all these qualities in the Nottingham flight.

This splendid flight was developed early in the nineteenth century by the Nottingham pike anglers. It is one of the few flights which will make a roach spin well – a bait otherwise considered inferior to dace, sprats, gudgeon and bleak, whose more streamlined bodies are more conducive to a regular and even spin (although nowadays pike anglers put less store on such matters).

To make a Nottingham flight with cabled wire is a simple matter. Take a 30 in. length of 14 or 20 lb BS (plain or nylon-covered) wire and pass about 10 in. of it through a brass ferrule of the appropriate bore. Pass the same end through the eye of a treble hook (No. 2, 4 or 6) and then take the emergent end of the wire round the back of the treble before passing it

back through the eye of the treble hook from the opposite side. Push the end of the wire back into the ferrule and tie a knot in its emergent end. Slide the ferrule up to the treble hook before crimping the ferrule with special crimping pliers.

Pass the free end of the wire twice through the eye of a second treble so that the two trebles are fixed some 2½ in. apart.

To complete the tackle a ball-bearing swivel can be attached to the free end of the wire – once again using a ferrule to secure the joint.

Pull *one* arm of the bottom treble deep into the side of the bait, below and behind the dorsal fin. Bend the body of the fish to the required shape (it is this bend which causes the bait to spin), before pressing *two* arms of the top treble into the bait just to the rear of the gill cover.

Pass the swivel through the gill and out through the mouth before tying on the mainline.

Fred Wagstaffe, one of the most successful pike anglers of modern times, used the Nottingham flight in pursuing his favourite sport – the catching of big pike on spun and wobbled deadbaits.

The flight that Fred used was a variation of the original Nottingham flight. He added a lip hook to the armoury of the two trebles which gave the flight better bait-holding characteristics and the added facility of being adjustable to suit baits of varying lengths. He also slid a barrel-lead down into the bait's mouth before fitting the lip hook.

This is sound advice, for, as he says, it gives an attractive wobbling and diving action to the bait. This, of course, applies when the flight is used as a wobbling tackle. When the flight is used as a spinning tackle, put the lead up-trace where it is more accessible for adjustment.

In fact, Fred Wagstaffe was anticipated by Bickerdyke, who said, 'The tackle is improved by a fixed lip-hook, which has to be passed through the gill and brought out at the mouth – a delicate operation; or a sliding lip-hook can, of course, be passed down the gimp after the triangles are placed', and '. . . you can, if you please, slip a pipe-lead down the gimp, and so into the belly of the bait. . . .'

Figure 45 The original Nottingham flight with hooks *in situ*

The sprat wobbling deadbait tackle
(Figure 46)

During a spell of activity on any given water, pike may react negatively to one method of fishing and positively to another, yet we dare not draw definite conclusions from their reactions since we know that these may be reversed on other days. I can think of an example that illustrates this curious behaviour quite clearly. One October day, Ken Sutton (a man with a penchant for pike spinning) and myself were spinning a Lincolnshire lake where during the morning we had taken at least a score of pike, including several double-figure fish, using our normal so-called 'proven routine'. (This is a simple operation in which we both experiment with a series of spoon baits of a different weight, colour and size, until one of us finds a bait which is acceptable to the pike. Having found a spinner which the pike relish, it is our custom to fish hard for a period with identical baits until such time as the sport falls off, and when this happens we repeat the whole procedure.)

During the morning our boat companion, F. J. Taylor, persevered with a wobbled-sprat method which produced only two very small pike (which I claimed and used successfully for livebait later in the afternoon). None of us could account for the failure of the natural bait.

A few weeks later, however, F. J. Taylor and his brother Ken again fished the same water using the 'proven routine', but on this occasion they found our method wanting and themselves unrewarded, until they changed over to wobbled sprats. With the sprats they were able to amass a bag of pike which was even bigger than ours.

F. J. Taylor's great interest and preoccupation with the wobbled sprat gave him an opportunity to try out all the established methods of mounting the bait – none of which proved satisfactory in the long run. As a consequence of his experience he developed a new rig which although simple in character

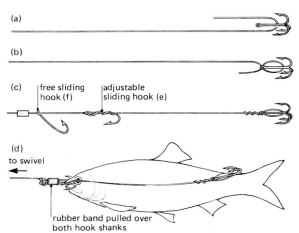

Figure 46 The sprat wobbling deadbait tackle

represents a considerable step forward in the design of deadbait wobbling tackles. This tackle is not available commercially, but for those who can make up a tackle for themselves the following instructions are included.

First choose a treble hook which is as long in the shank as the intended deadbait is deep in the body. Bend 2 in. of a 2 ft length of alasticum wire (14–20 lb BS) round the back of the treble as shown in Figure 46(a). Pass both ends of the alasticum through the eye of the treble from opposite sides (Figure 46(b)); twist off the emergent ends of the alasticum wire until the short end is used up (Figure 46(c)). Slide a large, long-shanked, single-eyed hook on to the alasticum (so that the distance between the single hook and the treble is the same as the distance between the eye of the deadbait and the fleshy root of its tail). Hold the shank of the single hook (Figure 46(e)) in the left hand and wind the alasticum (that which stretches from the single hook to the treble hook) round the shank of the single hook five times. Slide the other long-shank hook (Figure 46(f)) on to the alasticum and follow it up with a half-inch piece of float-cap rubber. Finally, put a swivel on to the end of the alasticum and twist off.

To bait up. Pull the first single hook through the eye of the deadbait (sprat, bleak, dace or gudgeon). Slide the second single hook up the trace before fixing.

25 Plug fishing

Some years ago I enjoyed the company of an impecunious fisherman whose pleasure it was to fish for salmon. Year by year this gentleman augmented the few invitations that came his way by contriving to afford a few days' salmon fishing on one of the poorer Avon beats. I must confess that I thought the prospects of reward from this sort of fishing were pretty bleak, but he, with a painstaking and intelligent approach to his chosen sport, was able to kill a few salmon each season.

He caught most of his fish on plugs, and, as a result, naturally held very strong views about the plugs he used. One day he made what I now believe to be a very good point about tackle in general, and plugs in particular. Having first emphasized the limitations of his purse, he nevertheless seriously maintained: 'I can only afford to fish with the most killing baits on the very best tackle available, for it is imperative that I make the most of my limited opportunities.'

His words impressed me. If a poor man cannot afford to use cheap gear, who can? My friend said that Avon salmon would take genuine River Runt plugs, but not the cheaper and seemingly identical copies of them. I think he thought that he would have difficulty in convincing me of the truth of this statement, but in fact he had no difficulty at all; for I already held similar views.

I suppose I made up my mind about plugs in 1948. In that year, I was having my first extended fishing holiday since the seven-week marathons of my schooldays. I was fishing the Stour in the area of Durweston, Bryanston, Blandford, Langton, Charlton Marshall and Spetisbury. It was November, I seemed to have the river to myself and, better still, the pike were taking like mad. What a revelation it was to fish a plug on this queen of pike rivers.

Nobody else in the area, as far as I knew, fished with plugs at all in those days, for anglers were more conservative than they are today and tended to stick to tried and trusted baits, like Colorado spoons, kidney spoons, Canadian bar spoons and their like. At the time, I had a dozen Bell jointed plugs, gleaned from several swoops on London tackle shops, after I had found that pike took them well. During this period, I began to form pretty strong conclusions as to which of the features combining to make up the plugs' total appeal were responsible for my success, for I was taking as many as twenty pike in a day. Indeed, on one occasion, I caught twenty-seven.

Broadly, my conclusions were:

1 That medium-length plugs were better killers than small or very large plugs.
2 That jointed plugs were more effective than single plugs.
3 That each plug, regardless of the maker's attempt to produce a standard product, had an individual action.
4 That it was this action that determined whether one plug was a better killer than another.
5 That pike would take a plug with a good action regardless of colour.
6 That with other things equal, green was the most attractive colour for a pike plug.

I took these two sleek December-caught Irish lough pike (22½ lb and 16½ lb) on a surface plug. Success with this method probably confers on an experienced pike angler the ultimate in pike-fishing excitement and enjoyment

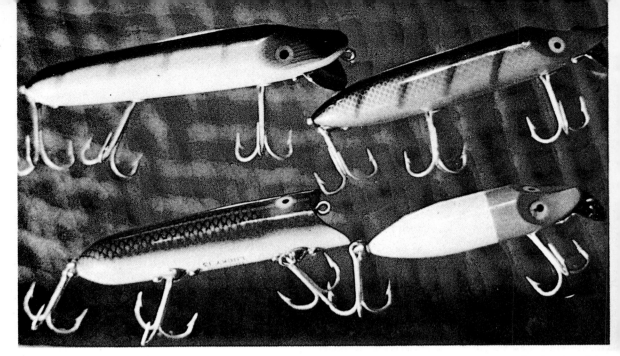

7   That a good plug, though naked of paint through the scraping action of pikes' teeth, would retain most of its killing properties without being repainted.

8   That the good plug would soon lose its killing qualities, to a greater or lesser degree, if the plastic diving vane were damaged, or if the hooks were replaced by hooks of a different size or weight.

9   That it was better not to use up-trace leads.

10   That a plug worked best on a short wire trace of about 5 to 9 in. long.

11   That alasticum wire was the best material with which to make the pike traces.*

12   That a plug was much deadlier if it was allowed to swing on an open looped trace.

Referring back to item 3 in my list on conclusions, I have stated that no two plugs were ever identical (although meant to be). These differences were caused by minute variations in the specific gravity of the samples of wood used in plug production. These

---

* Nowadays I no longer use single wire for making leaders: I have found it treacherous once it gets in a kink. However I have never been let down when using a short plug leader made of alasticum.

variations change the balance of the plug, be they ever so small. And, of course, any variation of shape from sample to sample further exaggerates the difference in the plug's action.

Now I come to the point that my friend made on the killing properties of the River Runt plug. Although he was very conscious that Runt plugs were much more effective salmon baits than cheaper imitations, he probably had no idea why they should be so. I am sure the reason for the River Runt's success is due to the fact that the plastic material content of the plug is standardized. With plastic material, once a

This remarkable photograph shows a pike in the act of striking a plug bait from ambush – or so I thought. Now turn the picture upright and you will see that the pike was photographed hanging in the air (Photo: N. Weatherall)

I caught this fine Lough Mask pike in December 1977 on about the tenth cast after which my companion, William Blake of Totnes, and myself fished all day for just one more pike. This one was 42½ in. long and weighed 25½ lb. Mr Blake once caught a 36½ lb pike, the story of which is told in *The Domesday Book of Mammoth Pike*

killing pattern is established after testing in the field, it can be the model for any number of true copies.

Plug fishing enjoys numerous advantages over spinning. It can be entertained throughout the season. Summer weedy conditions can often be met by fishing just a few inches below the surface. Patches of open water in an otherwise weedy swim may also be investigated with a floating plug. The plug is cast just short of the far weed-bank; made to dive sharply by means of a few quick turns of the reel; retrieved normally through the extent of the open water, and then allowed to surface just short of the near weed-bank, where a fierce pluck, reminiscent of a lion trainer's whip crack, retrieves the plug in the manner of a retrieved fly. Due to the buoyancy of a plug it can be fished successfully with an upstream cast, whereas a spoon or Devon has to be retrieved very fast (too fast) under the same conditions – otherwise it falls to the bottom. I have had pike up to 17 lb on an upstream plug.

A floating plug can be made to fish beneath a tree overhang shielding a likely pike hold. The technique is to stand about six yards upstream of the tree. Cast the plug well out and let the stream carry it down; meanwhile, hold the rod well out until the plug has drifted beyond the offending branches. Dip the tip of the rod in the

water and give the reel a few quick turns to make the plug 'bite'. Retrieve normally once the plug is at the right depth, still keeping the rod tip below water level. The drag of the line will bring the plug towards the bank and right underneath the tree.

It is possible to manipulate a plug in all manner of different ways by altering the speed of retrieve, the direction of retrieve, and the frequency of the vibration, or wriggle. The principle means of achieving this variation of action is by altering the direction of the cast relative to the stream, manoeuvring the rod tip during the retrieve, and by altering the rate of recovery.

Although the Americans favour a short single-handed casting rod and multiplier reel for plug fishing, I prefer a fixed-spool reel with a rod of not less than 8 ft 6 in. My choice of line is a monofilament of about 10 lb BS. I try to avoid using leads whenever possible and make frequent inspections of my alasticum trace for the slightest signs of a kink. I cannot over-emphasize the importance of maintaining an open loop at the point where the plug swings on the trace. So important is this feature that I inspect the trace each time the plug gets caught up on weeds or on the bottom, so that I can open the loop again if it has pulled tight.

The mouse plug

The Americans make the most lifelike mouse plugs. After I first read the account that follows I felt sure that a mouse plug, properly fished, would achieve equal success – and without forcing the angler to endure the grisly prospect (albeit prefaced with the words 'loving care') of baiting up with a live mouse.

In *A Fisherman's Log* (1929) Major Ashley Dodd describes the lack of response or dour-ness of pike: 'At times they will utterly refuse to look at the most tempting lure, however near it

Swim Wizz (*top*)   An excellent musky or pike plug. Two attaching eyes; top fixing makes the lure swim shallow. The inventor has caught over 5000 muskies on this bait. A strawberry finish is the most killing if perch are present as forage bait. This information comes from my Canadian correspondent, John Tollady

Rapala (*middle*)   A deep diver. I have taken many pike on this plug in Irish waters

Kynoch Killer (*bottom*)   Without doubt the deadliest bait of all for salmon on Scotland's River Tay. In June 1977 I was trailing this bait over the char beds on Ireland's Lough Mask in the hope of connecting with a trout like the 13½-pounder my companion, Des Elliott of Dublin, had recently caught (see photograph opposite). Almost immediately I caught a small pike and on the next run connected with a fish that 'played' for twenty minutes on powerful salmon tackle before it was lost. Des Elliott, Robbie O'Grady (Lough Mask's finest fisherman) and I still argue about 'the fish that was never seen'. Was it, as O'Grady thinks, a huge trout, or was it, as I believe, a big Mask pike?

Des Elliott's 13½-pounder

is to them.' Then he most interestingly counters this observation with this little story of the capture of a 15-pounder:

A friend and I went one winter morning to fish the moat of a certain castle. One of the first things we saw on arrival was this pike lying in about a foot of water close to the bank. My friend promptly put a bait beautifully over him, but he never so much as wagged his tail. After trying every bait he had with a like result, he gave it up in disgust, saying that the pike must be blind, and threatening to try to snatch him. Meanwhile I'd visited the stable yard, where I'd noticed a box mouse-trap with a live mouse in it. With this I returned, and then with loving care extracted the mouse, fastening him to a large single hook with the aid of an elastic band round his middle. This I swung out just outside the pike. As soon as the mouse struck the water, he naturally started to swim ashore, but before he had gone a yard the pike had him, and I had the pike. My friend was quite annoyed!

26 Fly-fishing

With such a fly, scarlet bodied, two big bright beads for eyes, wings of flaunting peacock's feathers, and carrying at its tail sauce piquante, in the shape of enormous hooks, you will, on auspicious days and in good pike water, have rare sport.

This account, and the one that follows were part of a letter published in the *Fishing Gazette* (28 February 1891).

I was fishing one day from a small skiff in the lake on Lord Rosse's estate [near Parsonstown] with a pike fly of enormous size, the day being very rough and the waters high; when just as I had worked the fly up close to the boat, and was making ready to cast it again, I beheld a vast pair of green-hued cavernous jaws issuing from the water near the boat close to the fly, and with a rush that made the big salmon

The pike fly

wheel scream, away went the great fish to the water depths, carrying out without a check fifty yards of line. Nor did he stop then, for, having no more line to give him, he actually commenced towing my little skiff, which was just large enough for one person; and so strong was the fish that I was quite unable, for upwards of half an hour, to recover a yard of line, and when at length I succeeded in bringing him to a pause, he repeatedly manifested his disinclination to make my acquaintance by tremendous rushes, comparable only to those made by a large first-run salmon or white trout when they carry out all the line. It was well that this and my rod were very strong, otherwise the pike would soon have effected a divorce with the tempting fly; but as it was I had no apprehension of a rupture of the tackle as long as I could keep clear of weeds near the shore. This, however, was difficult; for when the pike took a fancy to make a rush I was obliged to hold the rod with both my hands, which were thus unable to

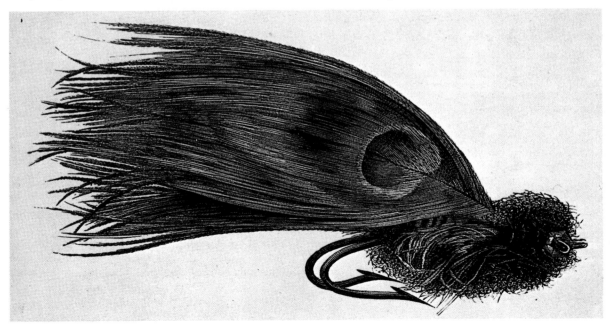

214

This pike weighed 28 lb and was caught on a fly. I learned this much from the pike's captor Frank Childs when we were both fishing the River Tay for salmon. Frank Childs was astonished when, from the same spot on the River Dee, I helped him to catch eleven pike on a modern bait – the tail end of a mackerel

control the boat by the use of the oars. It was only when my captive remained quiet that I was at all able to manage the boat, an operation rendered additionally difficult by the high wind which was blowing. In this manner upwards of an hour passed, and I began to despair of getting my pike. My only chance was in landing in a locality free from weeds; but even then I knew that I could not kill the pike unassisted. At length I saw a labourer approaching the lake, and by shouting made him hear that I wanted a gaff. While he was absent procuring this, I succeeded in rowing the boat close to a favourable part of the shore, retaining the butt end of the rod between my knees, and allowing the line to run out so as not to disturb the pike, which had gone to the bottom. On the arrival of the man with the gaff I leaped on shore, and now, having solid ground under me, and great faith in the strength of my tackle, I commenced a new series of operations, which terminated by the pike becoming my prize about two hours after I had hooked him. He weighed twenty-seven pounds, and was in admirable condition.

This colourful account of the landing of an Irish pike, which had taken a *pike* fly, gives credence to a method of fishing so often mentioned in angling books but rarely practised by anglers.

Sir Herbert Maxwell, who edited the *Chronicles of the Houghton Fishing Club, 1822–1907*, recorded in his book from notes extant what is probably the finest bag of pike taken on the artificial fly: 'On 15 March, 1848, Lord Gage came down to fish the Peat Pits, and on 16th 17th caught 14 jack weighing 83 lb 9 oz with a small red fly, ribbed yellow and gold.'

From this it is quite clear that we have to differentiate between pike caught on a trout or a salmon fly, since most of these would have been caught by accident, and pike that have been taken by anglers who set out to catch a pike on a pike fly.

There is a difficulty with the former since we simply cannot always be sure, just because a fisherman was wielding a fly-rod and retrieving a confection of feathers, or tinsel and feathers, that the pike attacked the fly on which it was subsequently hooked, played and killed. I suspect that in many cases the pike had taken a small fish that had previously become attached to the fly without the angler's knowledge.

This delightful branch of the sport must have had a following in the eighteenth century, for in those days tackle shops stocked suitable flies.

Daniel's classic book, *Rural Sports* (1801), gives readers careful instructions for tying their own flies.

The *Pike* fly must be made upon a double hook, fastened to a good link of *gimp*, and composed of very gaudy materials; such as *Pheasant's*, *Peacock's*, or *Mallard's* feathers; the brown and softest part of *Bear's* fur; the reddish part of that of a Squirrel, with some yellow Mohair for the body. The head is formed of a little fur, some gold twist, and two small black or blue beads for the eye; the body must be framed rough, full, and round; the wings *not parted*, but to stand upright on the back, and some smaller feathers continued thence all down the back, to the end of the tail; so that when finished, they may be left a little *longer* than the hook, and the whole to be about the size of a *Wren*. A *fly* thus made will often take *Pike*, when other baits are of no avail, especially in *dark, windy* days; the fly must be moved quick when in the water, and kept on the surface if possible. Several sorts of these *flies* are to be had at all the fishing-tackle shops.

Even in Daniel's day, we can see that some anglers were sceptical of the claims made for the fly-fishing method, for we read – again in *Rural Sports* – 'Another way of taking the pike is with an artificial fly: many have asserted that they are not to be caught at all with the fly.'

Nevertheless, Daniel proceeds to prove the method to his own satisfaction, by referring to the capture in Loch Ken of a 72 lb monster pike '. . . with a common fly made of peacock's feather'.

Later, in the nineteenth century, John Bickerdyke tells us in his *Book of the All-Round Angler* that Ireland is the place where pike of respectable dimensions are caught on the fly. He is more specific:

In Lough Derg, on hot days, when the pike lay near the surface, I have known them take a fly well, even when the water was very deep. An old Irish fisherman of Banagher told me that a fly made out of the tail of a brown calf was very killing, and that he had taken many fish on such a one in a weedy backwater of the Shannon. Only the tip of the tail is used. It no doubt represents a rat. Pike probably take the usual pike-fly for a bird.

Stoddart, writing of Scotland's pike fishing in *Stoddart's Angler's Companion* (1853), gives evidence of catching pike on the fly. 'With regard to fly-fishing for pike, I used to practise it, many years ago, with tolerable success, in a shallow loch in Fife.'

Stoddart found that pike would only take the fly in shallow or shoal waters, and then only on dull and windy days. Of flies, Stoddart had this to say: 'Pike flies ought to be big and gaudy, the wings formed each of the eye of a peacock's tail-feather – the body plentifully

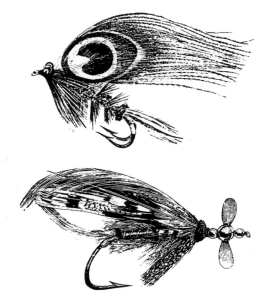

The pike fly on page 214 and the one above (*top*) are eighteenth-century dressings, while the 3 in. long Carter Halcyon (*bottom*) with its revolving head, is late nineteenth-century

bedizened with dyed wool, bright hackles, and tinsels. Bead-eyes, also, are held in estimation, and gimp or wire arming is of course essential.'

Major G. L. Ashley Dodd gave a dressing for a pike fly in *A Fisherman's Log* (1929):

I have a wonderful creature I once tied by the waterside, and on which I have caught a good many pike at one time or another. Its body is half a claret cork whipped round with red and yellow wool (taken from a rug in a farmhouse); hackle a piece of emu feather which came out of the guid wife's hat, and two peacock 'eyes' as wings, reluctantly given up by a peacock after a stern chase. The tying silk used was a bit of unravelled string off my packet of sandwiches, which string I had waxed with the cobbler's wax I always carry.

It is interesting to note that William Blacker, the first author to have attached real specimen trout flies to the pages of a book, *Blacker's Art of Fly Making* (1855) was recommended by Ephemera in the *Handbook of Angling* (1847):

I have seen nondescript large gaudy flies kill pike well, and Mr. Blacker, of Dean Street, Soho, is the best dresser of them I know. An imitation of the

This 14 in. pike fly comes from Hutchinson's *Fly-Fishing in Salt and Freshwater* (1851). The fly was illustrated in colour and instructions were given to load the fly with lead to give it 'casting weight'

sandmartin or swallow, dressed by means of feathers on a large hook, will prove an attractive bait for pike in the seasons last mentioned.

The fourth largest British pike taken on fly, known to the author, was taken by ex-prime minister Sir Alec Douglas Home, now the Rt Hon. Lord Home of the Hirsel, Kt.

This lake, at the Hirsel by Coldstream in Roxburghshire, was formed in the middle of the nineteenth century by damming a stream so as to flood a moss (bog). Hirsel House is seen in the background. The Homes have lived at the Hirsel since the early 1600s. The word 'Hirsel' is derived from the more ancient word 'Hirishille', meaning an area managed by one shepherd

One late November afternoon as he was walking home, rod in hand, after a day's salmon fishing on the River Tweed, he cast his fly, the largest Wilkinson, into the lake at the Hirsel. The fly was seized by a large pike.

Fortunately for the angler the hook was imbedded in the 'scissors', where the lure was safe from the pike's teeth, and he was able to kill the fish with his huge 17 ft double-handed salmon rod in about ten minutes. Sir Alec told me that the 27½ lb pike made two long runs before it capitulated.

The fly-fishing propensities of one British pike-fishing prime minister lead not unnatur-

The moat at Salisbury Hall where the young Winston Churchill shot his pike. The stuffed pike hung in the gentlemen's cloakroom on a wall gratuitously decorated in 1940 with sketches and calculations for the proposed design of an aircraft fuselage. The moat now contains fine rudd, carp and gudgeon but, alas, no pike

ally to the pike-shooting proclivity of another and may demonstrate *en passant* the essential differences in their approach to sport and, possibly, even to life.

After the last war Walter and Audrey Goldsmith secured and renovated Salisbury Hall, near St Albans, when it was near derelict. This famous mansion, which has figured for over 1000 years in the nation's history, was once the home of Winston Churchill. He came to the house with his mother, Jennie Churchill, after she married her second husband. Two years later Churchill shot a pike that was subsequently set up in a case. The brass plaque was engraved, 'This pike was shot by Winston Churchill in the moat in 1907.'

Churchill did nothing by halves. In 1939 when Salisbury Hall became an aircraft design centre his stuffed pike played a vital role: its streamlined shape became the inspiration for the design of the Mosquito's fuselage, the hit-and-run bomber of the second world war.

I must sadly report that when I contacted the owners with a view to photographing the pike I was told that the vandals had preceded me.

The revival of fly-fishing for pike

In spite of a long history, the sport of fly-fishing for pike has been in the doldrums for nearly half a century. Now there are indications of a revival.

Fred J. Taylor, one of the few moderns with experience of catching pike on the fly, describes his methods thus:

It was my pleasure in 1967, to visit and talk with Leon Martuche, of Scientific Anglers Incorporated,

Ted Trueblood's bucktail pike fly (*top*). Ted Trueblood, associate editor of *Field & Stream*, ties his own pattern of pike fly which is approximately 6 in. long with black and white bucktail. The No. 1 hook is dressed with silver tinsel. Ted caught a 21 lb pike with one of these flies. Although the art of fishing with pike flies has been neglected in Great Britain for a long time, Fred J. Taylor, Ken Taylor and a small band of enthusiasts are rediscovering the sport. The two brothers have had as many as twelve pike up to 9 lb in a day on fly. The middle and lower flies (one white and one yellow) are based on the Keys tarpon streamer flies. But instead of being tied with bucktail, as are the Keys flies, they are dressed on a long-shank hook with a 'Palmer style' neck hackle and a streamer of six cock hackles. Both flies are about 5 in. long

in Michigan, USA. Leon makes fly lines and, because he is also a dedicated fly-fisherman, believes that almost *any* fish can be taken on fly tackle provided the lure and the presentation are correct.

It was he who first convinced me that fly-fishing for pike was a workable proposition. 'It is *not* the most efficient method,' he wrote later, 'but it sure is fun.'

At one stage of my stay in the USA, I met and fished with Ted Trueblood who told me he had

taken a pike of over 20 lb on a fly. He gave me one of his pike flies, a black and white bucktail creation, and described many others, some of which are illustrated in this book.

My experience of fly-fishing for pike is limited to the capture of nearly two hundred fish up to 9 lb, and although I admit that there are many more efficient ways of catching pike, I have to agree with Leon, that it 'sure is fun'.

The best fish I have taken weighed just over 9 lb. Oddly enough my brother Ken has taken a similar number of fish and his top weight is about the same.

Pike fly-fishing, to me, is a completely new and exciting venture which opens up a hitherto unexplored field. So far, I have fished only from a boat and used a single-handed reservoir fly rod with reservoir trout techniques: with lure stripping with big streamers, bucktails, coho-salmon flies and big polystickles. The retrieve is varied from time to time but I have found a slow, jerky (about a foot at a time) retrieve to be the most profitable. For this reason, and because I fish shallow, weedy water, I have done best with a floating line and a sinking leader; although I can foresee the possible use of

Left This composite picture shows a number of pike fly patterns dreamed up by two of the modern exponents of pike fly fishing, Fred J. Taylor and Ken Taylor

Right Just after dawn on a December morning, lured by the charisma of the legendary home of big pike – Loch Ken – I cast hopefully from the spot where John Murray might have stood on that day in 1774 when he hooked, played and eventually dragged ashore Britain's biggest pike – the celebrated 72 lb Kenmure monster. There is a most interesting account in the *Field* (January 1890) of two fishermen, one of whom used a Stoddart pattern pike fly, fishing in Loch Chon or Con in the Grampians, who amassed about half the bag of pike aggregating 236 lb

fast-sinking or high density lines for deep water in mid-winter.

The weight of the fly is usually sufficient to sink the whole of the leader. The fly line itself is the usual 10 or 12 yards of double-tapered floater, spliced to 100 yards of 25-lb test monofilament with the simple nail knot used by reservoir trout anglers. The leader is knotless and only 7 ft long. It tapers to a point of about 9-lb test. To this is attached a tippet of about a foot of 25-lb test monofilament to withstand the attentions of the pike's teeth. Frankly, I would be happier with wire but I have not yet found a means of incorporating a wire leader or tippet which did not adversely affect the casting.*

Some of my pike were taken while the fly was trailing behind the boat and this is very exciting. There are situations which demand the use of a sinking line when trailing is practised and I believe it would be better to have two outfits made up, just as the experienced reservoir trout angler has.

I have ideas of using surface lures, American popping bugs, goat hair 'mice' and other feathered 'flies' where it is allowed during the summer months, and I have ideas for tube dressings and other creations for later on in deep water.

I do not forsee pike fishing with flies ever becoming a standard method, but I do regard it as a method which will give fly anglers a somewhat extended fly-fishing season. When trout fishing is

* A new wire, called Thin-Troll, marketed by the Shakespeare Company, does not affect casting and should be used in place of the nylon tippet. *F.B.*

over for the year, October and November could well be spent in search of pike, and with a very good chance of success.

There is probably nothing new about fly-fishing for pike. I understand that, occasionally, salmon anglers and river keepers have caught pike on big double-handed fly rods. This is a somewhat different approach, however, and I believe that the new reservoir techniques will prove to be much more enjoyable and this, as far as I am concerned, should be the attitude towards pike fly-fishing. It is there to be enjoyed. If you want to catch big pike or a lot of pike and it is important to you that you do so, you would do better to stick to spinning, deadbaiting or livebaiting. If, however, you are interested in obtaining the maximum pleasure from your pike fishing, it is possible that you will find it in the use of fly tackle.

27 Trolling and trailing

Trolling

Since many anglers still confuse 'trolling' with 'trailing' it is necessary to define these terms.

The best definitions are given by John Bickerdyke in *The Book of the All Round Angler* (1888):

Deadbaits, when used in pike-fishing, are either arranged so that they spin when drawn through the water, or are placed on trolling-tackle, in which case they do not spin. Spinning baits are either cast out some distance, and drawn back through the water to the angler, or are trailed at the back of a boat. This trailing is often called trolling in Scotland and Ireland, a misnomer which has doubtless caused some little confusion in the minds of anglers. Trolling proper is the use of a deadbait which does not spin, and is worked with a *sink-and-draw* motion in the water [my italics].

Trolling is described by Alfred Jardine in *Pike and Perch*:

When trolling it is best to fish up stream, and to work the bait down with the current through the weeds. If the contrary way is attempted it will result in many a hang-up in the weeds; besides, there is this advantage in fishing up and bringing the bait down with the stream: it approaches the pike more naturally, and is better seen by them, as (except in gentle currents) they always lie, whether in ambush or not, with their heads up stream, on the look-out for small fish swimming past. It is not necessary to make long casts; in fact, it is better not to do so, for the bait being lifted and dropped almost perpendicularly in the openings between weeds, trolls, or gyrates in a much more tempting way than when drawn slantwise through the water; and as the pike are usually among the weeds or in deep weedy holes, from whence they cannot readily see the angler, it is better to carefully fish all the nearest water than to make long shots with the bait. Raise the bait to the

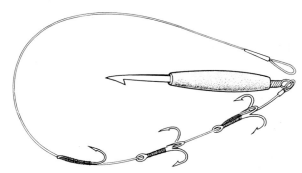

Figure 47 Hardy's drop-tackle. This is a simplified version of R. B. Marston's deadbait flight and was produced until quite recently. The spiked lead is pushed down the bait's throat and the single hook pulled right through the narrow fleshy part of the deadbait's tail. A twist of copper wire secures the bait

surface every two or three seconds and let it sink head foremost, giving a foot or so of slack line, and then it will have a darting rolling movement as it drops to the bottom. Keep continuing this, and if a check is felt, slacken the line by paying off a few yards from the reel (if none is already unwound), and see that all is clear for a run, in case a fish has taken the bait, which will soon be known by the fish moving off or by a few fierce little drags at the line; then allow the few minutes that are usually given the fish to pouch, wind up the slack line, give a firm draw with the rod, and play the fish on and off the reel, in preference to dropping the line in coils on the ground.

Trailing

That very fine angling writer, Hugh Tempest Sheringham, wrote the following note on trailing in *Elements of Angling* (1908):

There is what may by courtesy be termed spinning, the practice of trailing (it is often erroneously called

This fine old print, captioned 'Trolling with the Gorge', was taken from T. F. Salter's *The Angler's Guide* (1833). It depicts two pike anglers trolling with gorge-tackle. Nowadays we call the method sink-and-draw and we substitute a drop-tackle (Figure 47) for the gorge. Call it what you will it is surprising that the whole art has fallen into desuetude when we remember that it was the foremost method used to catch pike for over 450 years. Many modern anglers, when deadbaiting – or livebaiting for that matter – use a very slow or twitched retrieve before recasting while others like to use deadbait wobbling methods, both of which practices are somewhat akin to trolling

'trolling') for big lake trout in Ireland and Scotland. The angler simply sits in the stern of a boat and lets his spinning bait trail thirty yards or more behind while somebody else rows. The tackle and rod must be strong, as a big pike or a salmon is sometimes a possibility. No overwhelming display of skill is demanded of the angler, but the oarsman must know something about the geography of the lake and the nature of the bottom. Trailing may, however, be made something like an art if the angler does his own rowing, and is alone; in fact, *there are few kinds of fishing which demand more promptitude and resource.*

Deep-water trailing

As an angling method, trailing is often considered boring and lacking in finesse. But the fisherman who consistently takes good fish from the depths of what appears to be a featureless expanse of water is not, as many people seem to think, haphazardly dragging a bait about. On the contrary, he is being as calculating as the angler who fishes streamy water. His fish are caught by *design*, not accident. A skilful and imaginative angler who uses an echo sounder, and tackle which fishes at a specified depth, gradually builds up a complex and fascinating picture of the loch bottom and the best 'taking' depths. As a result he will, in the long term, catch far bigger fish than the less imaginative angler who moves aimlessly about, never certain of the depth of water or the depth at which his lure is fishing.

The disadvantage of the traditional trailing rig commonly used on the big lochs of Scotland and Ireland is that it is hard to make any bait swim deeper than about five feet below the surface. Adding more lead, as you would think,

223

is not the answer, since the extra lead required to sink the bait to the desired depth makes the bait swim 'head-up' thereby inhibiting or even stopping its action.

The plumb-line rig

One rig that can be used to get the bait down while at the same time allowing the bait to be properly orientated is the plumb-line rig.

The plumb-line rig was first used by the early professional mackerel fishermen before it was adopted and then adapted by the nineteenth-century professional Windermere char fishermen (see Figure 48).

A simplified one-bait version of the rig can be used for deep-water pike trailing and although the rig being held up by the angler in the photograph opposite was being used for a casting style of angling, the same rig can be used for pike trailing in deep lochs.

In Denmark, as in a number of other West European countries, where groups of specialist big fish catchers, especially big pike catchers, are on the increase, the pike specialists are adapting the plumb-line rig to trail large leaded plugs, or wobblers as they call them – behind a boat.

Figure 48 The shackle shown here (the Windermere char fisherman's shackle) is suitable for plumb-line fishing. A simpler device can be made using two swivels in the manner illustrated in the layout of the standing pike paternoster (Figure 32, page 187) but with the role of the element parts reversed – that is, the mainline supports the lead and the link supports the bait

Five rods are put up in the manner shown in Figure 49. Each rod is secured in an American quick-release rod-holder or rest. The most popular rod used for this kind of fishing – much to my delight – is the one I designed for Hardy's and which they distribute throughout Europe.

The downrigger (Figure 49)

A disadvantage of the plumb-line trailing rig is the heavy lead that forms part of the mainline tackle. This is most cleverly avoided in the downrigger – an American method of deep-water trailing that will get a bait (or baits) down to a considerable depth *without the use of lead on the mainline.*

Figure 49 shows the working principles of the rig with one or two homespun variations. To prepare the downrigger, a Nottingham reel of large diameter (A), holding about 50 yards of 60 lb BS terylene line, is secured with the usual winch fittings to the back of the rodrest. The last 12 yards are marked at intervals of three feet with tags of wool (B). (Two-inch tags of wool are passed through the braid of the terylene with the help of a coarse needle and then tied with a double knot, leaving an overhang of wool on each side. A colour code of wools is used so that an angler can tell precisely how much line is out at any time.)

The line is fed through the rodrest and a 1 lb or $1\frac{1}{2}$ lb lead (C) tied to the end.

Three feet above the lead a swivel (D) is tied into the line.

When the downrigger is ready, sufficient line is pulled off to allow the lead to rest on the back seat of the boat.

The rod, reel and line are now assembled and the appropriate bait (E) attached.

The difference between this tackle and tackle normally used for trailing or bait casting, is that the former carries no lead and includes a

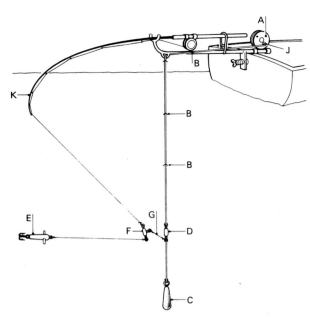

Figure 49 The downrigger

three-way swivel (F) in lieu of the usual two-way swivel.

Finally, a link (G) of cotton, elastic or lead wire joins the third eye of the three-way swivel to the swivel of the downrigger.

The tackle is now ready for use and the rod is placed in the rest with the *reel-check on*.

If two anglers are fishing together, one watches the rod, or rods, while the other rows the boat. The angler who fishes by himself will find it convenient to use one of the specially designed American trailing electric outboard motors, otherwise he will need to clamp the downrigger rodrest on to the gunwale within reach of the oars. I prefer the use of oars at all times owing to the greater variation of speed which rowing affords, but most anglers prefer to trail with the aid of a motor.

As soon as the boat is in motion the leadline is slowly released from the downrigger reel (A). Each coloured wool tag that passes the end of the rodrest indicates that the lead is fishing three feet deeper. While line is being released from the downrigger reel the corresponding amount of line is being pulled off the rod reel – which is under the tension of its check.

When the required depth has been reached, the lead line is looped round the handle of the downrigger reel (J).

The angler now knows the exact depth at which his bait is fishing. An echo sounder enables him to make any necessary adjustment to the depth of the downrigger lead to accommodate changes in depth of water, or any shoals of food-fish which the sounder may locate.

Some anglers make a point of tensioning the line until the rod dips slightly (K). Thus as soon as a fish takes the bait and breaks the cotton or lead connecting link (G), the rod straightens, giving immediate bite indication.

The nose-cone trailing tackle (Figure 50)

Some time ago, while admiring the action of a plug as it burrowed its way into the water, I considered the question of making a natural bait behave likewise. It occurred to me that hitherto any lifelike movement given to a non-revolving deadbait had always been imparted by the angler – by means of rod-tip movement, or an irregular retrieve. The well-known 'sink-and-draw' retrieve is an example.

The deadbait trailer is always hard put to get any sort of special action into his bait simply because so much of his time is taken up with the handling of his boat. With the intention of achieving a true *plug-action* on a deadbait trailing rig I set about designing a fibre-glass nose-cone that would (a) fit over the head of a herring, (b) incorporate a plastic diving vane of the type fitted to the majority of plugs.

After experimenting with numerous pat-

Figure 50 The Herring Magic nose-cone

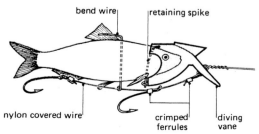

terns, I became even more convinced that the nose-cone was a practical proposition worthy of further development.

A chance conversation with a Canadian salmon angler, however, ended my quest for the perfect nose-cone. An American manufacturer with similar notions had anticipated my experiment. After trying out hundreds of different cones, involving thousands of comparative tests, his firm had finally developed a nose-cone that would give a herring deadbait the true plug-action.

This nose-cone is called the *Herring Magic, The Frantic Swimming Actionizer*! Purchasers are exhorted to: 'Fish it fast. Remember, you are simulating real, live, freshly-injured minnows trying to escape (herring, anchovy, sardine, mullet and freshwater shiners)!'

According to my Canadian informant, the Herring Magic nose-cone is used extensively and with great success in the famous 'Salmon Derby' – an annual competition for the biggest salmon, held off the west coast of Canada.

Since angling for salmon in British coastal waters with a trailed herring (or anything else, for that matter) is a waste of time, I suggest that the nose-cone should be used to catch pike. The large lochs of Scotland and Ireland are particularly suited to the trailing method, and I feel confident that if this new rig is used

intelligently it will open up new opportunities for pike fishermen. As a result, more big loch pike will be caught than ever before.

Hold the herring in the left hand. Push the retaining spike into the back of the herring's head. Swing the herring's nose into the cone. Clip the end of the spike (which has penetrated right through the neck of the bait) into its retaining clip. Push the 'bend-over' wire clamp up through the belly of the herring to just behind the gills, and bend the emergent wire back towards the dorsal fin. The bend-over wire supports the hooks and hook trace.

The skid trailing rig (Figures 51 and 52)

This is an improved trailing rig which was devised in 1965 by pike angler Colin Kinnear. It represents an advance in an area of fishing which during the present century has been both despised and neglected; indeed, in Britain there have been no significant improvements in trailing techniques since the semi-professional char fishermen of Windermere developed their unique but killing char-trailing rig during the nineteenth century.

The major problem with trailing in lakes, particularly in the large lakes that occur in the mountainous districts of Britain, is to overcome the difficulty of fishing a measured distance from the bottom where there are so many unseen variations in depth. As Kinnear puts it: 'I have done a great deal of trailing and

Figure 51 The skid trailing rig

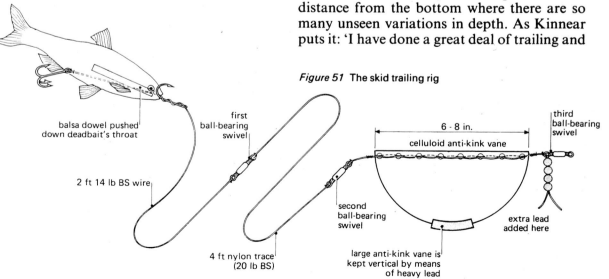

balsa dowel pushed down deadbait's throat

first ball-bearing swivel

2 ft 14 lb BS wire

4 ft nylon trace (20 lb BS)

second ball-bearing swivel

6 - 8 in.

celluloid anti-kink vane

large anti-kink vane is kept vertical by means of heavy lead

third ball-bearing swivel

extra lead added here

227

used to be continually worrying how far off the bottom the bait was. Now I know it is never more than six feet. With this rig, the bait must be faithfully following the contours of the lake bed, regardless of any variation in depth.'

Kinnear uses his new trailing rig not as an end in itself but as a means of finding the 'hot-spots' that are known to exist somewhere in a vast and bewildering expanse of water. Having found a 'hot-spot' with this rig, a pike angler can then fish it with more conventional methods.

The basis of the rig is a very large anti-kink vane made up from one half of a circle of celluloid 6 in. or 8 in. in diameter. As can be seen in the diagram, the line runs along the top of the vane, while the lead is located at the base in the form of a keel. This keeps the vane in an upright position, so that when drawn along the bed of the lake it acts as a skid.

If required, extra lead can be added in the form of swanshots pinched over a loop of nylon and hung from either swivel.

The deadbait is 'loaded' with a suitable piece of varnished balsa dowel which is pushed down the bait's throat. Once the dowel is fitted, an appropriate treble is wired up with 14 lb cabled wire. A small celluloid disc is then slipped on to the wire. This prevents the treble from pulling into and damaging the body of the bait (see Figure 51). The wire is then threaded through the bait with the aid of a baiting needle. A large single hook is slipped on to the emergent wire. Once the hook is positioned to suit the length of

Figure 52 The skid trailing rig in operation. When the boat is in motion the bait moves close to the ground; as soon as the motion stops the bait rises nose first due to the buoyancy of the balsa dowel

the bait it is secured with a few turns of wire. The hook is then pulled through both lips of the deadbait.

Use of the rig is simple and straightforward. The baited tackle is put over the stern of the boat and some 30 yards of line released from the reel. The leaded skid sinks to the bed of the lake and takes the buoyant deadbait to within six feet of the bottom. The first pull of the oars brings the bait wobbling down towards the bottom and, as the momentum of the boat gradually fades, the bait rises again due to the buoyancy of its balsa content. Another pull at the oars repeats the action, and so on.

Kinnear uses mackerel as bait, although he concedes that other baits such as roach or dace are perfectly suitable. He has found that it pays him to dress a number of baits with balsa and hooks prior to a fishing trip. This advance preparation of baits gives him the opportunity to test and, if necessary to correct their buoyancy. This is done in the bath. After which, the baits are wrapped in damp newspaper.

Livebait trailing (Figure 53)

The most persistent problem facing pike anglers when they ply their art on large lochs and lakes is the problem of locating the pike. Any reader who recalls the first time he excitedly slipped a livebait over the side of a boat into one of these seemingly endless acres of fresh water, will remember the sickening feeling of anti-climax that followed when a dozen lusty foragings of the livebait brought no response whatever from the pike. Many pike anglers reject the traditional trailing method

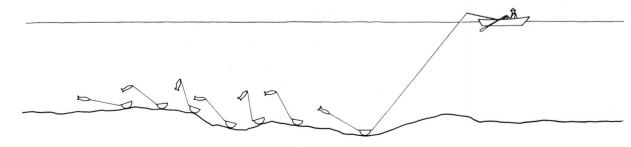

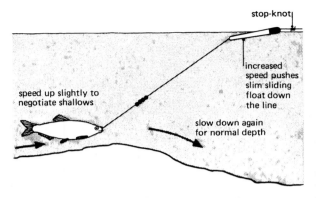

speed up slightly to negotiate shallows

stop-knot

increased speed pushes slim sliding float down the line

slow down again for normal depth

Figure 53 Livebait trailing (Peter Butler method)

with deadbait or spoon because, for them, the occasional reward of a 'take' does not seem to justify long hours spent travelling backwards bent over plodding oars. Nevertheless, those who remain wedded to loch fishing find through inquiry and experience more likely times to pursue their physical art. A few persistent loch anglers are able to give the oars a rest once they discover special locations which are amenable to livebait or deadbait methods – fished with normal float or ledger rigs.

For some years I have endured the frustrations of loch fishing in the pious hope that one day an essential clue would be revealed that would illuminate the dark mysteries of loch pike behaviour, and open the door to a new and richer vein of pike fishing. The prospect of such a find dwindled until I read a piece written by Peter Butler, which describes the method he uses to improve his catches of pike from Blenheim Palace Lake.

Essentially his method is to trail a lip-hooked *livebait* very slowly, just off the bottom, utilizing a streamlined float. The float is an important element of the rig because it prevents the bait fouling the bottom as it is being trailed some 40 to 60 yards behind a boat. Peter lays his rod over the back of the boat with the reel set on a light clutch or check; this way the reel gives line to a taking fish. The Butler style of livebait trailing allows the angler to cover a lot of ground but with a slowness that gives the pike much more time to attack the bait. Those

of us who have witnessed a pike making a stealthy approach to a livebait will realize what a difference this extra time means to our prospects of a run. With Butler's trailing method we can hope to interest any feeding pike within sight of the bait – not just the hungry athletic ones, as we do with normal trailing methods. Great care must be taken to ensure that the bait is trailed over water of fairly constant depth. To this end, anglers must either refer to a map giving depth contours or make a prior survey of the water with a plumb-bob.

As far as I know, this style of livebait trailing has not been practised in Scotland or Ireland (in fact livebaiting is now prohibited in Ireland), but I am quite sure it will develop into the deadliest style yet devised for loch fishing.

When I wrote to Peter Butler for permission to include the aforementioned account of his method, he replied giving the following extra details which I now include.

One point I would raise in that section concerning depth. The method I described entails using a slider float so that difficulty is not experienced with the float hitting the rod tip when a fish is played out to the boat. However, there is another reason for using a slider and that is for negotiating shallower banks during a trail. By increasing one's boat speed as a shallow bank is approached, the float can be made to run down the line a little as the bait rises in the water due to the increased speed. Therefore, it is possible to fish waters of variable depth with this method, provided of course that you know the contours of the bottom and change the boat trailing speed to negotiate shallower areas than the average depth being fished.

Thermal stratification (Figure 54)

Having described five different aspects of the pike trailing method, I conclude that trailing is at last being looked at again by a number of innovative anglers.

The method still requires considerable development and I hope that British pike fishermen will be the ones to break new ground. So far the pace has been set on the equipment side by the

North Americans with downrigger systems, echo-sounders, deep-water thermometers and electric outboard motors. But the prospect of improvement lies not only with improved gadgetry but with a much better understanding of what is happening below the surface.

Before attempting to fish large deep lochs, loughs and lakes every pike angler should have a thorough understanding of lake temperature gradients as these affect the behaviour of all the inmates – pike included. When the coldest part of the winter has passed, deep lakes in cold and temperate regions develop a uniform temperature from top to bottom (approximately 39–42 °F – that is 4–6 °C).

As the summer advances, the surface layer – unlike the lower layer which has no source of heat – absorbs heat from the sun's rays. This upper layer of warmed water is known as the *epilimnion*.

The lower layer of cold water is known as the *hypolimnion*.

The 'sandwich' in between these two layers – a region of rapidly dropping temperature – is known as the *thermocline*.

Since warm water is lighter than cold water it floats on top; so that during windy spells, when surface water is blown across a lake, the warm water of the epilimnion circulates independently (see Figure 54).

Most living organisms in a temperature-stratified lake live in the warm epilimnion where the oxygen supply is constantly replenished from contact with the surface. All

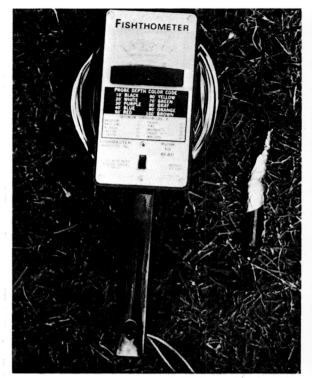

Above A deep-water thermometer. The temperature 'dolly', on the right of the photograph, is lowered into the water on a colour-coded cable and the temperature is shown on the dial when a switch is pressed

Below An echo-sounder, an essential piece of equipment for recording depth and the underwater contours of a lake. Each lake has its own particular characteristics and the readings given by deep-water instruments need careful interpretation. Their true value can only be determined from a series of experiments, with data recorded, on each individual lake

Figure 54 Thermal stratification

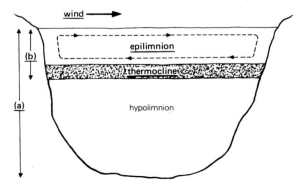

dead organisms, however, sink into the hypolimnion where the process of decay uses up the oxygen. Since there is no source from which this oxygen can be replenished, the hypolimnion gradually becomes more deoxygenated as the summer advances.

In *Life in Lakes and Rivers* (1961), Worthington and Macan record a typical example of summer depth of epilimnion and thermocline, in Windermere, July 1948:

Epilimnion: 0–30 feet.
Thermocline: 33–50 feet.

From this it can be seen that thermal stratification has a considerable effect on the activities of fish. American anglers have long been aware of this. As a result, echo-sounders and deepwater thermometers form a standard part of their fishing equipment.

An angler fishing a lake or loch from the bank might think that since he is casting into relatively shallow water (say, 20 feet deep), he will always be casting into the fish-holding epilimnion. He would be wrong. Although water stratifies horizontally, prolonged spells of wind from one direction can tilt the layers into the shape of a wedge. When this happens, the warm, oxygenated epilimnion is extra-deep on the lee shore of the lake, and the cold oxygen-starved hypolimnion reaches up towards the surface on the windward shore. It is mainly for this reason that, in summer, anglers should fish on the lee shore on all lakes that are subject to the formation of a thermocline.

In winter months the lee shore offers no such advantage. In autumn, as soon as the air temperature begins to fall, the epilimnion starts to cool down and with the advent of a gale is obliterated.

28 Trimmering

Nowadays, trimmer fishing is rarely described in pike-fishing books, for it stands condemned as an unsporting method! Nevertheless, trimmer fishing, or trimmering as it is sometimes called, is still a favourite method with river keepers whose job it is to rid trout waters of pike.

The trimmer, not unlike a very large pike float, supports a livebait in mid water. If a pike runs, after taking the bait, the trimmer is designed to release a further 12 yards of line. This extra line ensures that the trimmer remains in full view of the angler. (Although in very deep waters the trimmer would need to carry a bigger reserve of line.)

It is evident from *Thornton's Sporting Tour*, published in 1804, that its author put great store on the killing properties of trimmers, and fished with them wherever he went. No doubt, his success gave him a great affection for trimmers, for he always referred to them as his 'fox hounds'. (Presumably because he released not one, but a pack of them, to 'hunt the pike'.)

According to Yarrell in *British Fishes*, a gentleman of acknowledged celebrity in field sports caught in four days, 256 pike weighing altogether 1135 lb, with trimmers – or liggers, as they were provincially called. These pike averaged about 4½ lb apiece and were taken during March 1834 from Horsey Mere and Heigham Sounds in Norfolk. In Norfolk the trimmer float was made out of a bundle of reeds tied together at each end. Yarrell tells us that, 'Floats of rushes are preferred to others, as least calculated to excite suspicion in the fish.'

In the old days a very cruel sport of 'huxing pike' was practised. Huxing was a form of trimmering but with this difference: the trimmer was personated by a goose. The Rev. W. B. Daniel described this fiendish 'amusement' in his *Rural Sports* (1801).

Huxing Pike is also done by fixing an armed hook, baited at such a length as to swim about mid-water, to the leg of a Goose or Duck, and then driving the birds into the water. It was thus formerly practised in the Loch of Monteith, in Scotland, which abounds with very large Perch and Pike. Upon the Islands a number of geese were collected by the Farmers, who occupied the surrounding banks of the Loch, after baited lines of two or three feet long had been tied to the legs of their geese, they were driven into the water; steering naturally homewards, in different directions, the baits were soon swallowed; a violent and often tedious struggle ensued; in which, however, the geese at length prevailed, though they were frequently much exhausted before they reached the shore. This method has not been so long relinquished, but there are old persons upon the spot, who were active promoters of the amusement.

There is a much earlier record of Irish huxing, namely 1698. It occurs in one of the letters written by John Dunton published in *Maclysaght* as an appendix depicting *Irish Life in the 17th Century*. After identifying the lough at Mullingar in the County of Westmeath, Dunton wrote:

I cannot well omit acquainting you with one manner of fishing used for diversion on this Lough, they take into their boat or cott a goose, and about his body, under his wings, they tie one end of their fishing line, the hook being covered with some bait at the other, thus they throw the fishing-goose into the water, who sports and preens himself with seeming pleasure enough, until some unmannerly fish seizes the baited hook and interrupts her diversions by giving her a tug which douces her almost under water, this commonly frightens her so as to put her to the wing, but if the fish be heavy she

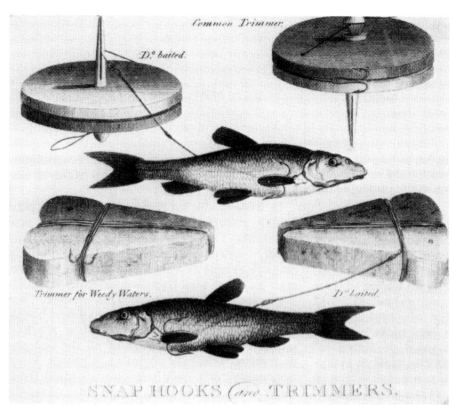

An eighteenth-century
engraving of trimmers

is forced to float upon the water, and though in romance the knight generally slays the giant, yet if the pike be of the larger sort Mrs Goose without the assistance of the spectators is sometimes like to go down to the pike instead of the pike coming up to her.

Mr Sturgnell's pike

A friend of mine, Brian Crawford, during the course of studying eighteenth-century Leicester newspapers for a Ph.D on the effects on labour relations in the City of Leicester during the industrial revolution, came across an entry which he knew would interest me.

In the *Leicester Journal* of 7 October 1796 a Mr Sturgnell was reported to have 'fished' Charlvey Pond near Windsor.

On this occasion he put a live perch on a double-hook tackle and tied the end of the line to a duck. The duck swam out to where a large pike had been seen disturbing the water.

The pike took the perch and a thirty-minute fight ensued during which time the duck was sometimes pulled beneath the surface. Eventually the duck reached the shore and the angler was able to take up the line, but even then he needed the assistance of a boy who put boards across an intervening mudflat in order to reach the pike.

We are told that this grand pike was purchased by Mr Puper, the fish purveyor to His Majesty, but that a Mr Wilmott kept possession of the head.

This 36¼ lb pike is probably the biggest ever taken by the ancient sport of huxing, where it was usual to tie the line to the leg of a goose rather than a duck.

233

29 Rods and reels

You must forcast to turn the fish as you do a wild horse, either upon the right or left hand, and *wind up your line* as you finde occasion in the guiding of the fish to shore.

This is how Thomas Barker advised his readers in *The Art of Angling* (1651) to play a fish on rod and reel when the last-mentioned half of the combination was still a novelty. Nowadays, of course, it is no use telling an angler that he must 'forcast to turn a big pike as he does a wild horse,' for his knowledge of handling this quadruped is likely to be even more wanting. Just the same, my experience of seeing all manner of unsuitable rods and reels in every-day use convinces me that some instruction in their choice is necessary. (Though judging by

some of the rods I see being used, I sometimes wonder if any notice is ever taken of the advice given in fishing books.)

In Britain, during the period 1965–78, pike fishing attracted a lot of converts and new adherents. During this period the sport was widely written about in all the fishing magazines and as a result it is true to say that pike angling was transformed into a much more sophisticated sport. This change, hastened by the advent of a number of new books on the subject, brought about a marked improvement in the design of all the component parts of the pike angler's equipment. Most noticeably rods have been transformed from short stiff rods into long supple ones of subtle

W. Hollar did this etching after a drawing by Francis Barlow (1626–1703?). A close inspection reveals that none of the anglers was using a reel, although reels were available during the seventeenth century (Print by courtesy of Prof. Selwyn Image)

design; materials like greenheart and tonkin cane and solid glass fibre have given way to tubular fibre-glass and carbon fibre.

Most British pike rods suitable for livebait and deadbait fishing are between 10 ft and 11 ft long and have to be capable of handling – while retaining their suppleness – bait-weights of up to 6 oz. A number of British rod-makers have a suitable rod in their range, a model that is probably endorsed with the name of one of the better known specialist pike anglers, indeed the author admits with no small measure of pride that Britain's most famous rod-makers, Messrs Hardy Bros., market a rod incorporating his own design requirements.

Since the fixed-spool reel, although not as good as the multiplier at coping with big fish, is the most popular choice of British pike anglers, rods still have to be designed to accommodate both types of reels. This is something that designers have to live with because it is unlikely that many of the fixed-spool-reel users will become converted to the multiplier although the latter is far superior for heavy work. The Mitchell 300 reel is probably the most popular fixed-spool reel, and deservedly so, but if lines

of more than 12 lb BS are to be used then the Abu Cardinal 77 is a far better bet.

I much prefer to use multiplier reels for nearly all my pike fishing. The three that I possess (two Quick 800 and one Ambassadeur 6000) are made up with three line strengths – 14 lb BS, 18 lb BS and 22 lb BS. I still have a Hardy Silex reel and, while I admit that there is nothing it can do that the multipliers cannot do better, I retain it for one reason, pleasure: the pleasure I get when casting with it and the pleasure I obtain when I find myself playing a fish on this, the most beautiful single-action reel of all time – is past wonder.

Unlike spinning, because livebait and deadbait fishing often become waiting games, many anglers have been in the habit of setting up a considerable number of rods. This ploy has received a growing amount of criticism in a growing number of countries, and rightly so in my opinion. It now seems likely, mainly due to the pressure of the number of people who want to fish for pike, that we shall all end up being restricted to the use of only two rods; meantime such a self-imposed restriction will be observed by a good sportsman.

30 Keeping livebaits

Baits can be kept at home using the Efgeeco large fish bucket illustrated in the photograph.

Transporting baits is a bigger problem. The same bucket or buckets can be used successfully for transporting fish providing the water depth inside them is kept to no more than 3 in. and providing not more than six baits up to 8 in. in length are kept in each bucket. The low water level ensures re-oxygenation, because of the favourable ratio between the air/water contact area and the relatively small volume of water.

A good bait kettle (see Figure 55) is a useful container as long as it possesses an inner liner. Such kettles are hard to find now as they are no longer manufactured in Britain (I bought mine in Poland). A bait-kettle liner is absolutely essential – as will be seen from these listed advantages.

1   Baits are selected by means of lifting the inner container and draining it momentarily; thus we can pick up a bait without getting wet cuffs!
2   When bait fishing we can use the inner container or liner in lieu of a keepnet, with the result that our baits will not sustain the usual damage that we associate with keepnets (keepnet tails, etc.). The liner can be submerged on a rope, or it can stand in the shallows during the bait-fishing operations, so that changes of water are unnecessary.
3   Where pike fishing is carried out from a boat, the liner can be hooked on to the gunwale so that the baits are maintained in good order without needing changes of water. It should be noted that when pike-fishing operations involve moving the boat, the can may be dragged along in the fixed

Keeping livebaits prior to a fishing trip can be a problem, especially when other members of the family object to the household sink or bath being used for the purpose. I find that fish keep really well in an Efgeeco fish bucket suspended between two bath taps. A continuous trickle of water from the cold tap keeps the water in the bucket well oxygenated. With this system there is no problem with water overflow, such as there might be from an outside tap. Additionally, the problem associated with a freezing water supply is entirely eliminated

position by the boat without causing damage to the baits, whereas baits dragged behind a boat in a keepnet soon die. Of course for extended trips in the boat the liner should be lifted out and put back into the outer can on board the boat. This will involve changing the water from time to time unless an oxygen cylinder is carried, in which case a steady trickle of oxygen bubbles will keep the fish quite happy.

If a good haul of baits is made, the surplus ones can be maintained in good order for days if they are placed six at a time in large oxygen-filled polythene bags into which only just enough water is put to cover them. Once the fish are in, grip the bag at the water level, squeeze out the air and refill with oxygen from the cylinder. The bags should be tied up well to prevent the escape of oxygen, before being floated and anchored somewhere in the shallows out of sight.

Outer can

Inner can

Figure 55 Extra large bait kettle (from an old illustration)

31 Pike gagging

The Buller pike gag (Figure 56)

Giving quarter to a pike is rather a novel idea. Traditionally, pike have been treated brutally simply because of their reputation and brutish appearance. But times have changed. Nowadays the pike fisherman seldom wants to kill all the fish he catches. He keeps one for the table, perhaps, and tries to return the others unharmed.

I write 'tries to' advisedly, because to return a pike to the water unharmed is not as easy as it sounds. The hook is usually embedded behind rows of razor-sharp teeth and the angler is faced with the problem of removing it.

Almost invariably this unhooking operation is performed with the aid of the conventional gag and disgorger, both of which should long ago have been confined to some angling museum. The gag has to be pushed sideways into the pike's mouth and then screwed round a full ninety degrees before it can function properly as a gag. Inevitably, the forked ends – *set nearly 2 in. apart in the closed position* – tear through the skin and bone of the pike's jaw. It is extremely difficult to use on a live fish reluctant to open its mouth. Even after a pike has been knocked on the head, the forcing open of its jaws with such a tool can be a hazardous operation, and many an angler has the scars to prove it.

The disgorger (like the gag, of Victorian origin) offers an angler the opportunity to inflict the maximum injury, for with it he can hack, stab, slice, wrench and slash – and indeed it is very difficult to avoid doing so. It is just possible for an expert to gag a pike and disgorge a hook with these infamous tools, but the majority of anglers use them at the risk of injury both to the pike and to themselves.

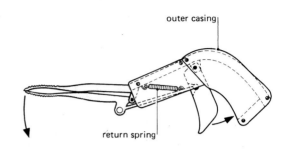

Figure 56 The Buller pike gag

Figure 57 The 'Hookout' disgorger

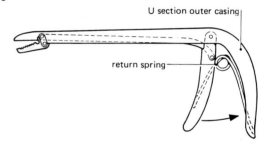

The Buller gag (drawn to shown the working principles for anglers who wish to make one for themselves) changes the whole picture. This gag can be slipped between a pike's clenched jaws and open them instantly to the required extent. While pressure is maintained on the trigger of the gag with one hand, the other hand is free to handle the disgorger. This disgorger, the 'Hookout' (Figure 57), is produced by an American company. It is both efficient and humane, and will remove a hook from a pike's mouth in a few seconds.

This sequence of photographs shows a treble hook being extracted from the back of a pike's mouth. If you are unaccompanied kneel down to do the extraction and have the pike lying on the ground or on the floorboards of the boat. Otherwise get your companion to hold and present the pike to you head forward and at elbow height

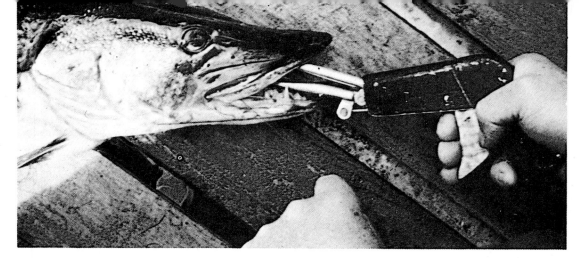

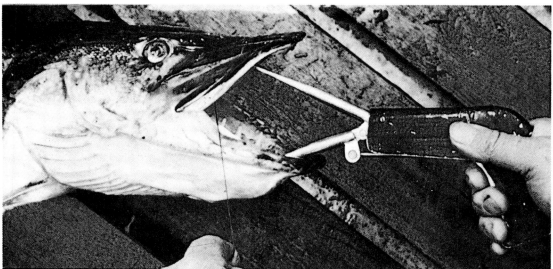

32 Knots

For centuries angling authors have been stuffing their books with diagrams of knots together with the appropriate directions for tying them. For centuries anglers have been ignoring this output with a heroic stubbornness.

With an equal stubbornness I have selected a few 'best' knots which I have illustrated with the appropriate directions for tying them.

The Cove or water knot (Figure 58)

From time to time, like all other anglers, pike anglers need to join two pieces of nylon together. Whenever one of the pieces to be joined is conveniently short (a few yards), then a knot developed by that indefatigable reservoir fly-fisher, Arthur Cove, fills the bill.

So far as I know the knot has not been previously described, other than by myself, but in all truth it would appear to be a development of an old gut knot first described by Lt-Col. T. V. Sheppard-Graham.

The following instructions when followed will make a join between two pieces of nylon and produce two droppers at the same time, so when the intention is simply to tie the pieces together, the droppers must be trimmed off.

Overlap two pieces of nylon some 10 in. (4 in. if droppers not required) as shown in Figure 58. Hold the overlap together with thumbs and index fingers, as shown in (a). Move the paired thumbs and index fingers closer together as shown in (b), until a loop springs into place as in (c). (*Note:* the right hand should be a bit closer to the body as both hands close.) Grip

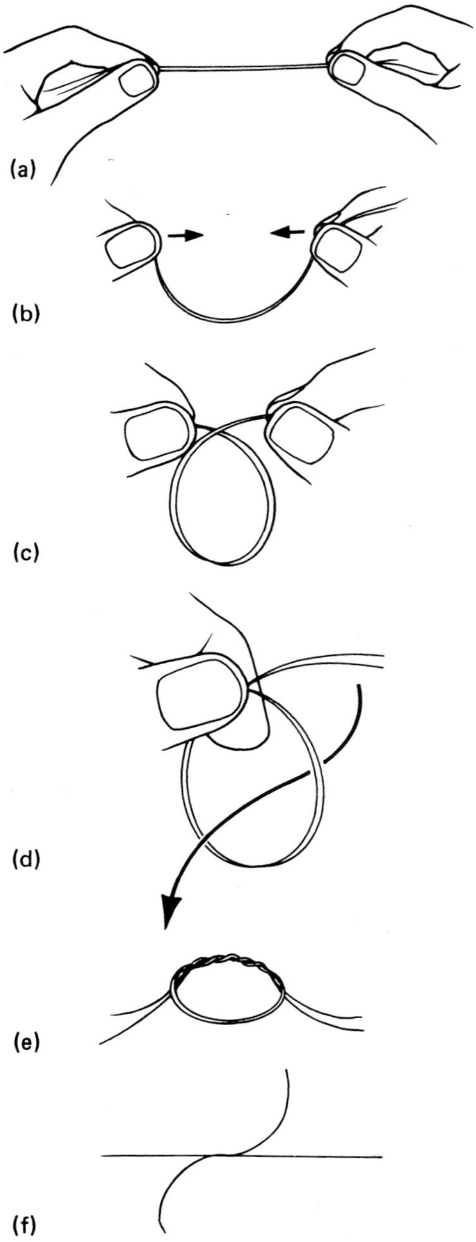

Figure 58 The Cove or water knot

240

the loop with a peck of the left thumb and forefinger as shown in (d).

Free the pieces of nylon held in the right hand and pull the ends through the loop from behind (see arrow in (d)). Repeat the last movement three more times until the picture in (e) emerges. Take the ends of the nylon between the thumbs and index fingers once more and pull tight. The resultant knot will then form as in (f).

I am not able to describe the efficiency of the knot in terms of a percentage, but I have tied the knot along with other popular knots on the same piece of nylon, and pulled the nylon to breaking point. In every case the Cove knot has survived.

As I found out after *Pike* was first published in 1971, a whole string of early writers had described this knot before Sheppard-Graham did in 1929; indeed the knot was described in 'A Treatyse of Fysshynge wyth an Angle' published in 1496. All of these old works described knots tied with two turns and the knot was called the 'water knot'. Arthur Cove's knot has three turns, in keeping with the need for tying nylon, a more slippery material. So it would seem that a two-turn knot is properly called a water knot and a three-turn knot a Cove knot.

Variants of the half-blood knot

The half-blood tuck knot (Figure 59)

The half-blood tuck knot used to tie nylon to the swivel on an Arlèsey bomb is the latest variation of that famous knot. The newest researches made by the Dupont Company indicate that five turns are needed to be made round the main line before the tuck is made. These extra turns ensure a much higher knot strength than would otherwise be obtained with the more usual three turns.

This is probably the best knot to use when connecting up the main line to a pike deadbait, or livebait trace, or for that matter to a spinning trace.

It is essential to snug this knot down neatly

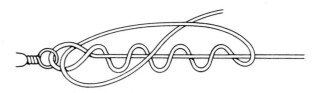

Figure 59 The half-blood tuck knot

and carefully in order to make full use of the actual line strength. If anybody doubts the truth of this statement, let them tie the knot in the way described and then tie a similar knot quickly without taking the same care to snug it down neatly. Pull both knots to destruction on a spring balance. The breaking-point differential is sometimes quite dramatic and I for one have made a promise to myself – never to tie a knot hurriedly. I have done so in the past – and paid the penalty. The half-blood tuck knot is not suitable for tying braided Terylene or braided nylon. For these materials use a hangman's jamb knot.

The half-blood stop knot (Figure 60)

To make this knot, pass the nylon through the eye of the swivel, then put a simple overhand knot in the end of the nylon before tying the half-blood as in (c). Hold the stop-knot against the eye of the swivel before tightening in direction of arrow. The knot tightens as shown in (d). Des Brennan, Ireland's famous sea angler, prefers this type of knot to any other. (His own version requires the nylon to be passed *twice* through the eye of the swivel.)

Figure 60 The half-blood stop knot

The grinner knots

Hugh Falkus, in the most recent edition (1981) of his book *Sea Trout Fishing*, introduces the

241

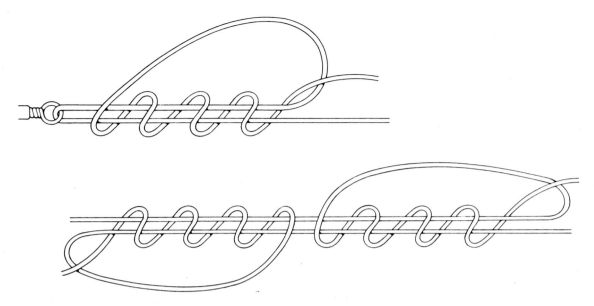

Figure 61 The grinner knot

Figure 62 The double-grinner knot

grinner knot (Figure 61) and the double-grinner knot (Figure 62) with these words: 'Good knots, to paraphrase Brutus, "must of force, give way to better"'!' He of course acknowledges Richard Walker's efforts in establishing that the grinner is the strongest knot that can be used for attaching a swivel or eyed hook to a leader, and that the double-grinner is the strongest for joining two pieces of nylon together.

The reel-line attachment knot

(Figure 63)

Figure 63 shows a safe method of attaching a nylon line or backing to a reel. Pull both parts of the knot tight and trim at A. Wet the tightened knot before sliding it back towards the reel. Finally, tighten the line firmly round the drum of the reel by holding the reel handles firmly with left hand and pulling the nylon in the direction of B.

Figure 63 The reel-line attachment knot

The figure-of-eight knot (Figure 64)

For joining a line (arrow A) to a loop in a leader (arrow B) the figure-of-eight knot is better than any other: simple both to tie and untie. *Note:* the stalk of the line does not stick out at an angle but lies in the same plane as the leader, thus reducing drag.

Figure 64 The figure-of-eight knot

33 Striking

I once wrote, with reference to general coarse fishing: 'Anglers of long experience usually concede that the most difficult part of the art is getting the fish to take the bait.' I still believe in this maxim. Even so, on reflection, I might have added: 'But with pike fishing (excluding spinning) the task of setting the hooks is jolly nearly as difficult.'

With pike we have many hooking problems, not the least being the very nature of a pike's mouth, since there are many parts including practically the whole of the inside upper jaw which do not provide a reliable hook hold. Secondly, even where the hooks *can* take hold there is a problem of hook penetration.

Most of us realize that a pike livebait or deadbait tackle has two functions: the first is to support the bait, the second is to secure the pike. But how many of us understand that, as a direct consequence of this requirement, the ensuing strike must have the corresponding power and function of pulling the hooks out of the bait before pulling the hooks into the pike? This problem looms large when the skilled pike angler starts to use very large baits in an attempt to fish selectively for really big pike, but although (without resort to gorge fishing) the problem is difficult to solve, it is not impossible.

First, let us try to arrive at some practical meaning of the word. By 'striking' do we believe in a fierce forearm movement which jerks the rod back? Pennell obviously did, for he observed: 'The strike should be as hard as the tackle can bear with safety', and 'Strike, and strike hard; and repeat the stroke until a violent tearing is felt.' He also observed that in his time one pike for every two struck was the average measure of success. He was of the opinion that better success could be obtained if his contemporaries would use fewer trebles on their baits.

Bickerdyke was sensibly of the opinion that no rule could be laid down. He saw some value in Pennell's method if the bait was 50 yards away, but saw the folly of the same proceeding when the bait was but 5 yards away. With great wisdom, Bickerdyke said: 'I can say only one thing for certain – that great judgement is necessary, and that it is particularly in the strike that the novice can be distinguished from the practised angler.'

Alfred Jardine, perhaps the greatest of all pike anglers, said '. . . give a firm draw (not jerk) with the rod'.

Francis Francis, writing in 1867, declared: 'I am bound to say that sometimes when using a tackle with many triangles I certainly do lose a good many fish, and the more triangles the angler employs the harder he must strike to be on the safe side.' Francis made another remark with that genuine ring of truth: 'As he holds it crosswise in his jaws, he has as much of the bait in his mouth the instant he is felt as he will have until he pouches.'

We can infer that there is no point in delaying the strike at all – unless we wait until a pike turns his capture to swallow it. We must either design our tackle and time our strike for the instant in which the pike takes the bait, or we must design our tackle and time our strike for the moment when we judge that the pike has turned the bait for a swallow.

There is a third stage in the proceedings, of course, and for that matter a valid tackle to go with it – the gorge tackle – but this is not to be considered except as a method to rid pike from a trout fishery. Walker's grandfather had the

During the afternoon of 8 February 1931, Mr P. H. Canova caught six pike over 20 lb. This photograph shows four of them (two were missed by the photographer). Mr Canova was fishing a private lake at Lound near Lowestoft. This bag of huge pike must surely be the best bag of 20-pounders on record. Mr Canova, besides being a good pike angler, must have been one of the last of the innocents for his person is closer to the camera than are his pike – a good many photo-conscious modern anglers would be pressed against the wall! (By courtesy of E. W. F. Siddell)

gorge timing worked out quite beautifully when he spoke these grave words to the young Richard: 'You don't want to be too previous! Never you offer to strike a pike my boy until that's had it for ten minutes – *by your watch*!'

From all this different advice readers may well think that there is a case for 'Who shall decide when doctors disagree?' I must say that I am inclined to follow the Jardine line '. . . with a firm determined draw of the rod point, to either the right or left'.

I will qualify this slightly, and describe my own method. I draw up all the slack until I feel the fish, then I tighten on the fish slightly which invariably induces him to move forward, and as soon as his move is felt I resist his pull by pulling the rod back and across the line of his movement. The resistance usually provokes a flurry from the pike which helps to pull the hook home, and in the next second the pike makes off against the maximum pressure that I dare to put on him. This way I avoid the dynamic blow of the hook which often breaks the line, since calculations just within the breaking strain of the line are not possible without knowing the size of the quarry. The fact that this latter type of strike works occasionally is due to a providential pattern of mechanical forces.

Apart from limiting the number of trebles

Dieter Ladwig's near-record Austrian pike, weight 51 lb 2¼oz

used on any tackle – a point that has been well argued in the forgoing – there is perhaps a point every bit as important – namely the size of the treble. In my Loch Lomond rig readers may have noticed that I chose a large treble – size 1 – but of course my tackle was dressed with only one treble. I gather from my reading of fishing journals and other pike-angling books that there is a general trend to use quite small trebles in tandem. It makes good sense.

34 Pike for the table

The rationale for killing a pike

Because fishing for pike is now the second most popular kind of fishing in Britain, responsible pike anglers, especially those who belong to the Pike Anglers' Club, have been conducting a 'put your pike back unharmed' campaign. Their seemingly altruistic behaviour is nevertheless based on common self-interest, which is best expressed in simple arithmetic:

MORE PIKE ANGLERS SEEKING FEWER FISH = BAD PIKE FISHING

The senseless killing of pike that had gone on for hundreds of years had to be stopped, and the pike anglers' campaign has managed to educate pike fishermen in Britain and Ireland to a remarkable degree. They still have a long way to go, however, before those who dislike the pike, or who kill it just for the sake of killing, cease their slaughter.

Inevitably, a campaign of this nature arouses in some individuals an extreme response that can only be likened to religious fervour. They would make the life of every single pike sacrosanct. *This is a nonsense.* The best reason that a human can ever have to hunt another animal – be it with rod, gun, dog, ferret or hawk – is to obtain or secure a meal. Sport is secondary; at its best it is merely a displacement activity, ritualized by 8000 years of experience since farming released some, and then more, of us from the hunting and gathering mode of life.

The pike meal in history

Throughout the centuries according to fashion, pike (as food) have either been despised or greatly esteemed. When esteemed they have commanded high prices, as evidenced by Yarrell, who tells us that during the reign of Edward I few people could afford them. At that time the price was: 'Double that of salmon and ten times higher than either turbot or cod.' And later, in the sixteenth century, pike '. . . fetched as much again as house lamb in February, and a very small pickerel was dearer than a fat capon'.

Although the Victorians were not great eaters of pike some of them wrote eloquently, and sometimes in favour, of eating them – as did H. R. Francis:

His goodness for food will in my view depend on three things; first, on clear water; secondly, on abundant food; and lastly, on the season when he is killed. When these three conditions are favourable, he is simply an excellent fish for the table, better than many sea fish for which we pay heavy prices. As regards the first requisite, a pike from a clear chalkstream, which is rarely even clouded, and that only for a few hours, has a great advantage. The late Sir Tatton Sykes, to whom the formation of the celebrated Driffield Anglers' Club was in great measure due, used to say to his fishing friends, 'Don't send me any of your trout, but if you can get me a pike from the Wansford Broad Water, I'll thank you heartily.' In this case it will be observed that the second requisite – a liberal dietary – was also fully supplied. And there are plenty of clear waters in England – or at least of waters generally clear – where food is abundant. It is the neglect of the third condition which causes the pike to be under-valued for the table. As a general rule, the pike is not in good condition before September, and will be found at his best about mid-winter. Even in the Thames, where food is so abundant, the hundreds of jack that are taken by trailing or live-bait in June, July and August are from a culinary point of view merely wasted; yet it is from the flabby, bony specimens caught by holiday-makers in the 'long summer's day,' that most people form their judgment of a pike's fitness for the table. Were our supply of freshwater fish better regulated, this misconception would not prevail.

Given, then, a well-fed, sizeable pike – for choice I would take one between 6 lb. and 12 lb. in weight – taken from a clear water between September and March, and we have the 'potentiality' of a capital dish. But, how is he to be cooked? Such a fish, I quite agree with Mr Dewy, should be plainly boiled. But I would go further, and say he should be treated like a cod, whom he closely resembles. He should be crimped, very deeply, the instant he is killed; should be boiled in water liberally salted, and should be served up with oyster sauce. I have no quarrel with Mr Lewis's stuffed and baked pike; indeed, I have often relished one so dressed. Walton's plan of roasting and basting, &c., also produces a savoury dish. But these modes of cookery, while they distinctly improve a second-rate specimen, are but attempts to 'gild refined gold' when applied to such a fish as I have endeavoured to describe above.

Dr J. J. Manley was one who wrote eloquently, but hardly in favour, of pike meat. Having caught a pike from a friend's goldfish pond, thereby ending its reign of terror, he wrote in *Fish and Fishing*:

I received the congratulations of the assembled family. With one voice it was determined that he should be cooked for dinner, and of course everyone was obliged to eat a bit and pretend he liked it. But oh! the taste of that jack! I have never forgotten it. 'The touch of a vanished hand and the sound of a voice that is still', are mere trifles in the way of memory to the reminiscence of the flavour of that jack which clings to me now, though nearly twenty years have passed since the day he was served. He was supremely 'fishy', and tasted of the quintessence of the dirty green stagnant water which had been his home, and, to use a grammatical form which may be questionable, he smelt as bad as he tasted.

Let us discount Manley's dreadful experience by reminding ourselves of a more common one – of having to endure, in the course of our day to day travels, all manner of frightful meals, even when these have been conjured from items of indisputable culinary value.

In the year 1845, the records of the famous Houghton Fishing Club reveal a letter written by Henry Warburton to a founder member, Canon Beadon. It concerns the gift of a pike, and says:

Do you know how to dress it? Roast or bake it of course, but the pudding what of that? The ancients had a celebrated dish called the Trojan Horse. The horse was personated by a pig, and the Greeks in the inside by small poultry and delicacies of every imaginable kind, animal and vegetable. At the first gash of the carver, out rushed the thrushes and larks and truffles, etc. Your Trojan Horse is the jack, and the Greeks are to be personated by some oysters and some full brown mushrooms, chopped small, and perhaps a little bacon, together with the other ordinary ingredients of a pudding. . . .

To me Warburton's delightful description of the recipe is as near irresistible as the prospect of the food itself.

I am indebted to W. Shaw Sparrow for bringing this gem to light in his absorbing book, *Angling in British Art*.

In matters of cooking, Mrs Beeton should always be consulted. In her *Dictionary of Cookery* (1872) she gives the following recipe:

Pike (à la Genevese). Divide a 4 or 5 lb pike into slices or cutlets one-and-a-half-inch thick; two chopped shalots, a little parsley, a small bunch of herbs, two bay leaves, two carrots, pounded mace, pepper and salt to taste, four tablespoonfuls of madeira or sherry, half-a-pint of white stock, thickening of flour and butter, one teaspoonful of essence of anchovies, the juice of one lemon, cayenne and salt to taste: Mode – Rub the bottom of a stewpan over with butter, and put in the shalots, herbs, bay leaves, carrots, mace, and seasoning; stir them for ten minutes over a clear fire, and add the madeira or sherry; simmer gently half an hour, and strain through a sieve over the fish, which stew in this gravy. As soon as the fish is sufficiently cooked take away all the liquor, except a little to keep the pike moist, and put it into another stewpan; add the stock, thicken with butter and flour, and put lemon-juice, cayenne and salt; lay the pike on a hot dish, pour over it part of the sauce, and serve the remainder in a tureen. Time, 1¼ hour. Cost, averaging 3s. Sufficient for six or eight persons.

With due respect to Mrs Beeton, the enervating task of cooking her pike appals me, and I should not be in the least surprised if certain Victorian ladies felt the same way. Fancy being married to a man whose pike-catching prowess was matched only by an abiding passion for pike à la Genevese!

There can be no pleasure in dining off a pike if the diner needs to dispossess himself of mouthfuls of small bones before he can sample the fish. Most of those who prepare pike for the table have a notion, seemingly, that a pike should be treated like a cod and cut up crosswise into a number of steaks. This is quite wrong. Pike should be boned right out before any attempt is made to cook them. Once the boning is done, any plain or fancy method of cooking can be attempted.

Fish-cakes

Izaak Walton, in *The Compleat Angler*, said of pike: 'This dish of meat is too good for any but Anglers, or very honest men.' Had it been my good fortune to coin this classic phrase, it would have referred specifically to pike fish-cakes – for these are really delicious. I don't propose to write a 'How to cook 'em' chapter, but a few words about my wife's way with pike fish-cakes will confer a great favour on my readers!

Preparation (see sequence of photographs opposite)

Two knives are required; one pointed and sharp (fish-gutting knife) and another broad and less sharp. Place the pike belly down on a table; press the point of the gutting knife into the pike's back at the rear of the skull and make a cut about an inch deep along one side of the backbone until the cut passes alongside and

beyond the dorsal fin (a). Repeat the same stroke on the other side of the backbone (the cuts should be about ⅛ in. apart), which will bring the blade past and beyond the other side of the dorsal fin. In photograph (b) we can see the backbone just revealed. Lay the pike on its side and with the same knife make a cut down the side of the body immediately behind the gill-cover, and another, a few inches forward of the caudal or tail fin (c). Still using the same knife slit open the belly from the vent until both cuts are reached (d).

Lay the pike on its side with its back towards you and place the broad flat knife in the uppermost cut (one of the two cuts made along the backbone); draw the knife gently from end to end in a flowing motion: the blade follows the ribs until the whole side falls away complete (e). Turn the pike over (still with its back towards you) and repeat the same operation until the other side falls away. Cut out the ventral fins with the fish-gutting knife as shown in photograph (e). Now grip the thin end of the fillet after laying it skin down on the table and proceed to cut through the flesh down to the skin, starting the cut as close to your fingers as you dare. Once down to the skin change the angle of the knife so as to make it run almost parallel to the skin and proceed with a sawing action (as in bread cutting), taking care not to cut through the skin (f). Notice that the unusable remains, except for the skin and ventrals, are left intact (g). Once the fillets are isolated and washed hold them up for a minute to drain; then place them on a large plate and sprinkle with a fine layer of salt. Two or three hours salting is sufficient if they are to be cooked the same day; otherwise place the salted fillets in a domestic refrigerator.

Cooking

Boil the fillets for ten minutes; drain off and mash. Mix the cooked fish with an equal amount of boiled, mashed potatoes; season with parsley. Shape the fish/potato mash into fish-cakes and dip these in breadcrumbs or flour. Fry until crisp and brown on the outside.

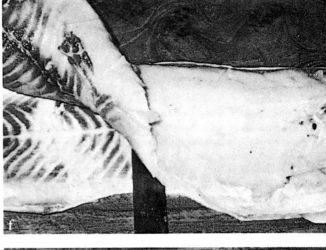

Serve with a small knob of butter on each fish-cake and when the butter melts add a fine sprinkling of salt and a dash of sauce according to palate.

After eating about five of these delicious fish-cakes retire to an armchair with a good cigar. Contemplate with a new-found reverence Izaak Walton's statement and consider whether even honest men should qualify for such a feast.

A recipe for pike

I suppose that the usual way to cook pike is to bake it. That is quite a job, but the result can be delicious. First of all you must scale the fish and then dry it carefully with a clean towel. Then you need a pound of beef suet and a pound of grated bread, and mix and season with salt, pepper and nutmeg; work into this some shredded lemon peel and some thyme and some chopped anchovies and the yolk of eggs (three eggs to an eight-pound fish), and then squeeze lemon juice over the whole, and place it in the stomach of the fish. Sew the fish up and bake in an oven until the skin cracks. And now you need a sauce. This sauce is the real secret of baked pike. And the best sauce is compounded thus: a pint of beef gravy, a pint of skinned shrimps, half a pint of stewed mushrooms, a quart of stewed oysters, a wineglass full of port; mix this into a pound of melted butter. Now take the thread out of your pike, pour the sauce over him, and enjoy yourself.

But the best way of all, in my opinion, to cook pike is this: Clean and scale your fish, and then boil or parboil it and then bone it: cut the white flakes of flesh into strips of an inch or so, and fry them in bread crumbs (if you have an egg so much the better). That served hot (with a lemon if possible) and thin bread and butter is a dish for a king.

BRIAN VESEY-FITZGERALD, *The Hampshire Avon*

Pike quenelles

In 1898, Georges Auguste Escoffier, sometime chef de cuisine at the Carlton Hotel and one of the best chefs of his time, began writing notes for a book which was to become the classic work on French cuisine: *A Guide to Modern Cookery*.

Since Escoffier is regarded as *the* master in matters of cuisine, anglers may be interested to know that he described a special dish (No. 1040) – *Quenelles de Brochet à la Lyonnaise* – the details of which I am happy to provide.

Pound separately 1 lb of the meat of pike, cleared of all skin and bones, and 1 lb of the fat of kidney of beef, very dry, cleaned, and cut into small pieces. If desired, half the weight of the fat of kidney of beef may be replaced by $\frac{1}{2}$ lb of beef marrow.

Put the pounded meat of the pike and the kidney fat on separate plates. Now pound 1 lb frangipane Panada (No. 192) and add thereto, little by little, the white of 4 little eggs. Put the pike meat and the fat back in the mortar, and finely pound the whole until a fine smooth paste is obtained. Rub the latter through a sieve; put the resulting puree in a basin, and work it well with a wooden spoon in order to smooth it.

With this forcemeat, mould some quenelles with a spoon and poach them in salted water.

If these quenelles are to be served with an ordinary fish sauce, put them into it as soon as they are poached and drained, and simmer them in it for 10 minutes that they may swell.

If the sauce intended for them is to be thickened with egg yolks and buttered at the last moment, put them into a saucepan with a few tablespoons of fumet, and simmer them as directed in the case of an ordinary fish sauce, taking care to keep the saucepan well covered that the concentrated steam may assist the swelling of the quenelles. In this case they are added to the sauce at the last moment.

N B – Slices of truffle may always be added to the sauce. The quenelles are dished either in a silver timbale, in a shallow timbale crust, or in a fine vol-au-vent crust, in accordance with the arrangement of the menu.

Frangipane panada

Put into a stewpan 4 oz sifted flour, the yolks of four eggs, a little salt, pepper and nutmeg. Now add by degrees 3 oz melted butter and dilute with $\frac{1}{2}$ pt boiled milk. Pass through a strainer, stir over the fire until the boil is reached; set to cook for five minutes whilst gently wielding the whisk. Lightly butter the surface of the panada in order to avoid its drying while it cools.

Choosing a pike for the table

In the first edition of *The Driffield Angler* (1806) Alexander Mackintosh, speaking of the ideal culinary weight for pike, said:

They are in season from the beginning of May till spawning time; the flesh is firm, dry and sweet; from seven to twelve pounds are the best fish, and under three they are watery and insipid.

At 50 lb 12 oz, Austrian Helmut Firzinger's biggest pike is big enough for a banquet!

43 lb 6¾ oz pike caught by the Finn Kyosti Kurimo – through an ice-hole

Appendices

Bill Giles with one of his big Norfolk pike

1 Notes on Norfolk pike fishing

Bill Giles

Norfolk and the counties which border it form the richest complex of fishing waters to be found in Britain. Certainly the Broads and rivers of Norfolk have a unique reputation for producing big pike. This being the case, it seemed to me that no book on pike fishing would be complete unless it contained a substantial account of the sport to be found in that area. Since my experience of broads-fishing is limited, I asked Bill Giles of Norwich to comment on all matters of interest to pike fishermen from the Norfolk angler's point of view.

Bill and his close friend Reg Sandys have a reputation for catching large pike. Indeed, few anglers alive or dead can have caught more 20 lb pike than these two. It is not for this reason that I asked for Bill's help; I asked him because he has kept meticulous records of data collected from observations made in the field. Bill constitutes a rare type of witness – he is expert, accurate and imaginative. *F.B.*

Food of big pike

I had my first 25½-pounder (1950) set up and the taxidermist took out of it the remains of a bream estimated at over 2 lb. Dennis Pye told me that he was once playing a bream of around 3½ lb in the summer when it was taken by a very big pike.

A few years back he was playing a rudd on Horsey Mere (also in the summer) when it was taken by a pike of about 3½ lb. This, in turn, was taken by a pike of 33 lb 2 oz. He was only using a 4 lb BS line and so steered the pike rather than played it and eventually steered it close enough to use his gaff. He told me that he

believes that the pike never realized that it was attached to the line; a very clever piece of angling and reasoning.

Jim Vincent used to watch out for the disturbed water caused by a shoal of large bream and then spin a dead roach, or the spoon he invented, round the shoal. The late Mr Piggin, head keeper of the Hickling area for a great many years, told me that Jim was the most indefatigable worker and would spin a deadbait all day. (His son Edwin uses the same methods.)

In case you don't know the story of the Jim Vincent spoon I will tell it to you in brief.

While in Canada Jim saw an Indian having some wonderful sport with pike and asked to see his lure. It was made of hard wood. Jim brought one back to England and had it copied in chromed copper.

About sixty were originally made and two of them came into the possession of Mr Hannant, late of the East Suffolk and Norfolk Fishery Board. He lost one of them in a fish and, not wanting to lose the other, kept it as a souvenir. This one he, very kindly, lent to me and I was able to make an exact copy, even to the thickness of the metal. I believe that Hardy Bros. made some but they are no longer on sale anywhere.

I don't think they are very effective in Norfolk now as many of the broads have silted up considerably, but I should think they would be very effective in deep waters like Loch Lomond. However, I am digressing!

I think that once bream reach a weight of 5 lb they are fairly safe. I know one land-locked Broad where bream over that size never show signs of having been attacked, though there are some very good pike in the water.

A bream of 5 lb is a difficult 'swallow' but not so a pike of similar weight. I have many times caught pike of up to 12 lb with fresh tooth marks on them, and on 24 February 1962, while fishing Heigham Sound's Duck Broad, I was playing a pike (which eventually turned the scale at $17\frac{1}{4}$ lb) when it was seized by a much bigger pike which hung on to it for nearly five minutes. Tony Goldstraw (my companion at the time) wondered what on earth had happened, when this spirited pike turned suddenly into a solid weight which cruised slowly and irresistibly around. Eventually it let go and we were able to land the 17-pounder, which was bleeding profusely from great gashes down both its flanks.

On 14 March 1965 Reg decided to use a $1\frac{1}{4}$ lb pike as bait, since we were running short of herrings. It had been out for about twenty-five minutes when the float dived under and Reg found himself fast into a very heavy pike. When it came into view in the clear shallow water (about 2 ft) Reg was so astounded at its size that he involuntarily gave the pike a little slack line. The small pike was completely out of sight in the big one's mouth, but with one movement it was able to eject the bait and sink slowly down to the bottom just out of gaffing range! That day and the day before we had landed three pike over 20 lb, including one of $26\frac{1}{4}$ lb. Both of us put the length of Reg's lost pike at about 6 in. longer than the 26-pounder.

There are days on which big pike will take a small bait just in the same way as large summer tench will become preoccupied with small baits but, by and large, 'big bait, big fish' is a very good maxim. They will bring you fewer pike but much bigger ones.

I believe that if more anglers used 5 lb pike as bait it would not be long before there would be more pike taken like the Knipton Reservoir 39 lb monster. The only snag is that the anglers would probably have to put in many patient days of effort.

Several years ago we used to spend many June nights fishing for tench in a lake where an extensive colony of terns was nesting. Their nests were on an island almost level with the water. At intervals all night long the enraged cries of the parent birds could be heard as pike levered themselves out of the water to engulf the nestlings which were too close to the edge. We returned there for two nights this summer, but there were no terns. I suppose they had learned their lesson!

So far only livebaits have been discussed. In our experience (Reg Sandys's and mine) deadbaits (herrings, mackerel and large roach) are far and away more deadly for really big pike than any livebait (possibly small pike excepted, as we have tried that only once).

Since using deadbaits, which we have now been doing for thirteen years, we have also discovered that the average size of pike taken on a deadbait lying on the bottom is much greater than for a similar bait suspended from a float (i.e., off the bottom). During the last two seasons, using herrings or mackerel suspended on float tackle about a foot above the bottom, we have taken eleven pike averaging 10 lb 9 oz, best $23\frac{1}{2}$ lb. In the same period, the same baits lying on the bottom on free ledger tackle have produced sixty-eight pike weighing 960 lb 3 oz, an average of 14 lb 2 oz (to the nearest ounce).

I think that herrings have one big advantage over large dead roach, in that the hooks tear out of them very easily on the strike. Most fish are hooked if a good firm strike is given.

Pike's hearing

When pike are ravenous they pay less heed to any warnings their hearing may give them. But it is not often that they are ravenous, and so most of the time it pays to make as little commotion as possible. Knocking a pipe out on a boat (as I have seen some anglers do) can be fatal, as can moving the oars noisily or dropping the weights overboard with too much of a clatter.

When we approach a broad from a river we only use the outboard as far as the entrance; then we use oars for the rest of the day.

Before Horsey Mere was 'discovered' we made good bags of big pike nearly every time, but this season especially we have been less than a quarter as successful. The first weekend in February fished well with several good fish up to 28¾ lb because the pike were not expecting the invasion.

Last Saturday there were eight boats out and not one run between the lot of them. Why? Because many anglers apparently have to start their engines to go 100 yards. We like to fish a known pike run which may be up to 200 yards long, dropping down wind in about 25- to 30-yard stages, but what is happening now is that, having dropped our weights in at the head of the run, someone comes charging through the swim with his engine running, and the 'run' is spoiled and the pike put down – often for the rest of the day. It is a great pity, because pike have very good hearing and are easily scared. No doubt many visiting anglers wonder why a Broad with such a good reputation is producing so few fish. If they read this I am sure we will all enjoy better sport. (Horsey can support ten boats at a time but only if they do not use their engines. Edwin Vincent tells me that there were twenty boats on there one day at the end of this season.)

A great pike angler

Jim Vincent – twenty-seven pike over 20 lb in his lifetime, best 29½ lb from a private landlocked broad – is held by many knowledgeable Norfolk anglers to be the greatest pike fisherman ever. The Heigham Sound–Hickling–Horsey area owes its present good pike fishing to him. When the sea broke through the Horsey Gap before the war (1938) it killed every pike in the area, but when, after several years, these broads were once more fresh, he spent all his spare time outside the area catching pike for restocking. I am told that he once caught and transferred over fifty pike in one day!

Voracity

It is very common in Norfolk to catch pike which at some time in their lives have been attacked by other pike. It is not uncommon for a pike to be attacked by another one when it is being played. Many anglers, including Reg Sandys, have seen ducklings and other water fowl pulled under, though I have never seen this myself.

Once, when spinning a dead roach on Wroxham Broad, I caught a pike with an eel sticking out of its mouth. The eel must have been very recently swallowed, as the foot or so outside the pike's mouth was perfectly fresh, yet the part in its stomach tapered away to bone, so strong are a pike's digestive juices.

Allowing time for pike to swallow bait

We do not follow the practice of waiting for the second run as we find that most pike do not stop to turn the bait, and so there rarely is a second run.

When livebaiting we just wait long enough to make sure that the fish is moving away from the line of strike and that the line is straight enough to hit the fish hard first time. It is not really a strike but a matter of holding the fish hard enough to set the hooks.

With a herring on the bottom we hit the pike immediately the line starts to move, so long as it is not actually running towards us, in which case we wait until it has swerved away to one side.

When spinning a dead roach, we hit pike immediately if they are taking well. If they are finicky we spin as slowly as possible with the rod at right angles to the line so that the sensitive rod tip will signal a take, then we swing the rod towards the fish to give slack line and wait until the pike moves off before striking.

When a pike has gorged a bait

This is more likely to happen with deadbaiting than livebaiting, since a pike, on finding a deadbait on the bottom, will sometimes swallow it before giving the angler any indication that it is there. Luckily, on the Broads the average pike which gorges a deadbait is well over 10 lb, has a very large mouth and can be dealt with quite easily and without harming the pike. This is not guesswork because I have done a lot of tagging for the river board and have re-caught the same pike sometimes months, sometimes a year or two later in good condition.

On opening the pike's mouth with the gag and finding a triangle out of sight, pull gently until you can see it, then insert long-nosed pliers via the gill-covers and turn it upside down. With luck it will come clear away, but sometimes there will be folds of skin over the bends of the hooks. If this is so, insert your hand via the other gill-cover and with the forefinger push each fold of skin over the bend of the hook until it is clear. If both triangles are out of sight, deal with each in the same manner. Due to the cushioning effect of the bait, itself well down the throat, the hooks will rarely be found to have penetrated and if you are careful in your 'operation' the pike will not be harmed. (Reg and I call it carrying out a pikelectomy!)

No doubt, many anglers are put off trying this operation by the hundreds of teeth inside a pike's mouth, and I must confess that I rarely get away without a bleeding hand; but one is working well away from the main teeth and the scratches are always only superficial and are a small price to pay for the pike's future well-being.

This fine 38 lb 9¼ oz pike, one of the biggest taken by a Dutchman, was caught on a home-made spinner by Ruud Van Dort in a lake near Utrecht. It is one of those rare examples of a pike that probably weighed more than the claimed weight. It may well have weighed some 42–44 lb

The usual practice seems to be to cut the wire as far down the throat as possible and hope that the digestive juices will get rid of the hooks before the pike dies. Pike are tough creatures but not all that tough and I well remember catching an 11-pounder which was so thin round the middle that I decided to kill it and investigate. (The only pike I have killed in many many years.) The trouble, as you have no doubt guessed, was a set of ragged-looking triangles and wire trace.

Build of pike

This varies considerably according to their type of feed. The Horsey pike have the biggest heads on Broadland, probably because they feed off the prolific bream shoals and other pike. When we have a day on one of the small landlocked broads we notice immediately how small their heads are in comparison. Some of the big Horsey pike look like crocodiles.

The very largest Norfolk pike do not have to exert themselves very much to catch a 3 lb bream when they want one, and so develop stomachs like that of a dowager countess. I should imagine that Scottish or Irish pike which have to catch salmon and trout must have much more athletic figures.

Gaffing versus the landing net

Gaffing is certainly quicker. When the pike are well on the feed you can sometimes be caught with a pike in the net and a flying triangle caught in the meshes, while at the same time the second angler is bringing another pike alongside. With a gaff this situation would never arise.

However, I am never happy about gaffs, and use a net whenever possible. The correct place to gaff a pike is just inside the chin; but often, a lively pike will jump and twist about before one is able to disengage the gaff point, and by this time its gills can be badly damaged. From time to time, Reg and I have caught pike terribly mutilated by the bad gaff work of other anglers.

I make my nets out of 52 lb BS Courlene, the only material I have found so far that will stand up to the tearing of a pike's teeth. I fit the net on to a 24 in. ring, which is the largest I can find, and bend it till it measures 28 in. across. With it I have so far landed pike up to 44 in. without any anxious moments. The largest Broads pike only go another 4 in. so I am sure the net will cope if I am ever fortunate enough to meet one of them.

Shop-bought nets, I always feel, are the wrong shape, tapering more or less to a point. I knit a large square of netting and then work all round the edges of it to a depth of about 1½ ft. When it is fitted on to the ring it bellies out, so that once a pike is past the ring it has no chance of rolling itself out as I have seen happen with a shop-bought net. A pike in the bottom of the net will lie a good 3 ft from the rim.

So long as you can get more than half the pike across the rim of the net it will all go in.

Keeping livebaits alive

In winter this is no problem if you are lucky enough to have a nearby lake, which we have. We have made a large box with a hinged lid on top for easy removal of baits. It is 2 ft × 4 ft × 1½ ft deep, liberally bored with holes. The bottom is close-mesh wire-netting. We rest it on the mud at the outlet to the lake so that a current is always going through it. Even when the lake has been several inches thick with ice we have found the baits still in good condition afterwards.

We find that early in the season, September and October, when the temperatures are still comparatively high, livebaits won't keep. It is not worth trying till November, or when the first frosts have cooled the water.

It is as well not to make a livebait box too large. After it becomes waterlogged it becomes twice as heavy, and then it sometimes needs more than one angler to pull it out of the lake.

Quality of hooks

It is advisable to test one hook out of a batch as some are tempered too highly and will snap; others under pressure will straighten out.

One other point that I think important. Under a high-powered magnifying glass I sharpen the point of every triangle before use until they are like needles, and I don't forget to examine them carefully after use. I am sure that this has been the means of landing many fish that might otherwise have thrown the hooks.

Pike lines

A line we like to use for float fishing is Courlene, which has the peculiar property of floating just beneath the surface. A bait can be cast across the wind and will remain there for a long time as there is nothing for the wind to get hold of except the float. For those who like float fishing, it is possible for two anglers in a boat to use two rods each and keep their tackles widely separated by using one Courlene and one fully floating line each.

For herring fishing, both Reg and I use Platil (ordinary) about 15 lb BS. We have from time to time used other makes; some are too springy, others tend to fly into birds' nests, especially when new. We have never had any of these troubles with Platil, even when using a new spool for the first time. I once used a famous and expensive American make, but I finally had to scrap it as it had all the faults mentioned above.

Power of pike in different locations

Since 90 per cent of my pike fishing has been done in Norfolk, I cannot comment. Most of my other pike were caught in Thames weir pools, where I believe they fought harder than Norfolk pike of the same size, often jumping clear of the water. However, the biggest of them weighed only 4 lb!

John Nixon, who has caught pike in salmon and trout waters, reckons that they are different fish altogether.

In brief, it seems to me that a 30 lb Norfolk pike has only to amble after a bream shoal to keep herself well fed and so never becomes very athletic, whereas I can imagine the effect of continuous exercise on a pike which has to rely on salmon and trout for its food.

Size of livebaits

If you use 2- to 3-oz livebaits you will catch large numbers of small to medium-sized pike with the odd big one now and then. Also, you will miss very few pike on the strike, if you hit them properly, as even a small pike will be able to get such a small bait well into its mouth.

When using 8- to 12-oz baits your average weight of pike landed will show a big increase, but you will fail to hook a much greater proportion as the small fish will still attack the baits but will not be hooked when you strike. It is not always easy to hook even a big pike with a 12 oz roach. Roach are quite hard, solid objects and it needs quite a hefty strike to pull the hooks out of them and into the pike.

I have mentioned the use of a $1\frac{1}{4}$ lb pike as bait. The following story shows how difficult it is to know when to strike when using a large bait.

A friend of mine, Noel Paul of Norwich, was fishing for pike in the lake where we keep our livebait. He hooked one of about $3\frac{1}{2}$ lb and was just drawing it towards the boat when a huge pike appeared and, seizing the small one across the middle, sank with it to the bottom. This lake is extremely clear at times, and was on this occasion, so that my friend was able to see this great pike clearly on the bottom. It lay there motionless for three-quarters of an hour before it suddenly ejected the small pike, took it again head first, and in three or four gulps swallowed most of it out of sight. Noel then tightened on the fish and played it until he had it lying tired out in front of him. Then, horror of horrors, no gaff! Since his landing net was too small, he

pulled up the poles, drifted in to the side and scooped the pike out on to the bank with his wellington boot. It lay there for a second or two. But before Noel could leap ashore it opened its jaws, flung the 3½-pounder and hooks clear, and flopped back into the lake. I saw this fish, or what I believe to have been this fish, a month or so later in the close season. It was all of 30 lb.

As regards livebait, roach are used more than any other species, probably because they are most easily procured. I often think that rudd work better, and for a longer time, on the hooks. Some anglers swear by dace and others bream. Fred Wagstaffe, I believe, uses chub and does well with them.

Size of deadbaits

When using herring on leadless ledger, our favourite method, we use the ordinary average-sized herring such as you find on any fishmonger's slab.

Bill Giles and his companion Reg Sandys joined forces with Richard Walker and myself on Loch Lomond. Bill's first Loch Lomond pike took a herring fished on his own patent drift tackle (Figure 25, page 175); it weighed 26½ lb!

Herrings have some big advantages over roach for deadbait fishing on the bottom. They are big, and so attract big pike. They are easier to see in thick water. An oily slick spreads away from them which, in itself, is attractive. Also, when a bait hits the water the small silvery scales burst away from it in a cloud and then, settling around it on the bottom, catch the eye of any marauding pike that comes close enough. A herring is much softer than any dead freshwater fish and so, when the time comes to strike, the hooks are torn out of it and into the pike without any resistance.

For float fishing we use both herrings and mackerel. Herrings are satisfactory when fresh but tend to droop unnaturally after a time, so we prefer to use mackerel which keep a straighter back and, we suspect, are taken for small pike by the big pike. The mackerel we use probably average an inch or so longer than the herrings. We occasionally use dead roach and sprats on the bottom. They are effective but we prefer herrings and mackerel.

Mona's scale and Norfolk pike

Forty inches for a 20 lb pike is not far out for an average Norfolk fish. Having said that, I thought I had better make sure and so drew a graph, with rather surprising results. All (except the one caught by Derek Hatcher) were taken, and very carefully measured, by me. I measured his, too. All were taken in the last three seasons, except the $25\frac{1}{2}$-pounder which I took in 1950. (This one had a girth of 23 in. and a skull measurement of $11\frac{1}{4}$ in.)

The fish marked 'A' was $16\frac{3}{4}$ lb and 39 in. when I caught it on 13 March 1965 and was so thin that I thought it was a large male. I caught it again on 5 March 1966 when it measured $40\frac{1}{8}$ in., weighed $21\frac{1}{4}$ lb and was an obvious female. On 13 March 1965 it must have either just spawned (most likely) or was not spawning that year, which I think sometimes happens.

The fish marked 'B' has had a very interesting history. I first caught it on 10 December 1966 when it measured $43\frac{1}{8}$ in. and weighed $26\frac{1}{2}$ lb. In February or March 1967 it was caught by Colin Dyson at the opposite end of the same broad (Horsey Mere). It then weighed 25 lb and was returned to the water at Stubbs Mill about $1\frac{1}{2}$ miles from where I had first taken it. On 11 November 1967 I once more caught it in the original spot exactly. Its length was still $43\frac{1}{8}$ in. but its weight had dropped to 24 lb. It fought well in spite of being very thin. It was easily recognizable because someone had gaffed it badly before either of us caught it, and had slit its throat, making it look a very ugly fish. I have a photograph of it and I think Colin Dyson has; anyway he recognized the fish from my photograph.

Fish 'C' was taken by me twice, at two swims several hundred yards apart, on the same broad; first, on 11 December 1965, and again on 19 February 1966. Peter Beck also caught the same fish in January 1966, and made it $27\frac{1}{2}$

Tom Stevenson's 31 lb pike, taken from Heigham Sound on 14 February 1937, from which water Mr A. Jackson took his $35\frac{1}{2}$-pounder in December 1948 (By courtesy of N. Weatherall)

lb on his spring balance. The length and weight were exactly the same on the two occasions when I caught it: 43 in. and 27 lb.

Another fish, which weighed $23\frac{1}{2}$ lb when I caught it, weighed 23 lb when caught by Reg

Sandys a year later and weighed in my presence; so fish do not always increase in weight with age. They appear to reach a maximum and then drop back.

A 44½ in. pike weighed 28 lb when caught by Arthur Smith of Norwich. He actually caught the same fish one week later when it weighed 26 lb! He said that it was beautifully fat the first time and thought that the shock of being caught put it off feeding for a week.

Now and again, short fat fish are caught. These are the ones that I think will turn into future record breakers.

One thing that this graph shows is that Mona's scale can only be taken as a rough guide. It steers an average course through all my thirty fish, but only one of them is actually on the line, the 43 in., 24¾ lb pike.

(*Note:* Bill Giles's pike are plotted along with other pike in Figure 18, page *63. F.B.*)

	lb	in.	
A	16¾	39	13/3/65
A	21¼	40⅛	5/3/66
	21¼	41½	
	21¼	41¾	
	21½	42	
	21¾	39	
B	24	43⅛	11/11/67
	24½	42¾	
	24¾	43	
	25	41½	
	25	39½	
	25¼	42½	(girth 23 in., skull 11¼ in.)
	26	43	
	26¼	40¼	
B	26½	43⅛	10/12/66
C	27	43	11/12/65
C	27	43	19/2/66
	31½	47	(Derek Hatcher's)

At least one fish, Peter Hancock's, has managed to survive the course without setbacks, so there are very likely to be others. I suspect that catching a fish, especially if it is badly hooked or gaffed, can cause a shock that will hinder, stop or even reverse the putting on of further weight. So it looks as though, if we want record pike, all of us will have to be extra careful and gentle in the way we treat them.

Spinning

I used to spin all day long, and there is no doubt that if you spin properly you will catch very many more fish than with either livebaiting or deadbaiting. But although you *will* catch some big fish (I have had some in the mid twenties), your average size will be much smaller.

I once took the trouble to work out the average size for all methods, and found that at the bottom of the list came plugs and small spoons with an average of under 4 lb; and at the other end came herrings, on leadless ledger, with an average weight of over 14 lb.

All artificials will take fish at times; but it pays to ring the changes, as I believe that the amount of colour in the water makes different baits successful on different days. Of all the artificials, I have found a 3 in. home-made copper spoon the best. The reason behind its success may be in the hammering to get the correct curve. When polished, this produces many facets of light. Norwich spoons come nearest to this, I believe, in the ones you can buy. Some of the Abu spoons, with similar markings and a 'Jim Vincent' curve to them, are also successful.

However, I must confess that I hardly ever use an artificial now, although I always take an assortment of plugs and spoons with me. I still spin, but use a dead roach about 90 per cent of the time, a sprat 8 per cent and a herring 2 per cent. When spinning these baits the best fish I have taken are as follows: sprat, 20¼ lb; roach, 25½ lb; and herring, 26¼ lb.

To avoid scaring big fish which are more wary than their smaller brethren, we do not as a rule spin until we have tried out the swim with livebait and deadbait.

I always spin as slowly as possible, commensurate with not catching the bottom, and 'work' my rod tip so that the bait dips, rises and lurches from side to side.

If the fish are taking well I keep the rod tip low and pointing not straight at them but slightly to one side, so that I can give a good solid sweep to set the hooks. I never strike upwards but more or less parallel to the water.

There are some days when pike will tooth-mark a bait and drop it, often so gently that you may not notice it until you examine the bait. On days like this you can sometimes hook these fish by keeping the rod at right angles to the line, and by watching the sensitive tip. Your eyesight will then be able to help you confirm the lightest of takes. When pike are in this mood I slacken off immediately I sense a take, and watch the line. After a few seconds the line may start to move, in which case you can tighten up and strike. If nothing has happened after about half a minute, I strike anyway – just in case. More often than not it is a weed, but now and then you get a pleasant surprise. For this type of fishing, a Mk IV Carp rod is an excellent weapon. (Thanks to Mr Walker for inventing it. I fully believe that it is the most versatile rod ever.)

I often wonder if the broads have silted up considerably since Jim Vincent's day. When using his famous spoon, except in the deepest water, I find I am into the bottom before I can start to retrieve it. The only place I have been able to use it without trouble is in the Ormesby group of broads.

One more small but important point: many anglers put a twist in the tail of a dead roach to make it spin. I think this is unnecessary, unnatural and makes a mess of the line. I put one triangle through both lips from under-neath and the other in the tough skin just abaft the pelvic fins. In this way both triangles act as a keel and keep the bait upright at all times. Just draw a bait through clear water hooked in this way and see how natural it looks.

True tall story

Some years ago, while Reg Sandys and a friend were fishing a private broad, the friend had a run and played what he thought was quite a heavy pike. The water was very clear, and when the fish was near the boat the two anglers were amazed to see that it was an enormous bream, which they estimated at around 10 lb. There was no doubt that it had the live roach well and truly inside its mouth. Unfortunately their amazement was their undoing because in a trice the bream was round the mooring pole and away.

We had not previously suspected the presence of really big bream in this water, but the following June we baited a swim and the first one to come to my landing net went 7 lb 7 oz. The following close season an angling friend of mine, Ron Yates, picked out from this lake two bream which had died in the act of spawning. They went $9\frac{3}{4}$ and $10\frac{1}{4}$ lb!

Night fishing for pike

Reg and I have occasionally experimented with pike fishing at night. We have not done a lot of it, but enough to know that it has possibilities.

The first contact I had with a pike at night was many years ago when I was bream fishing, at about two o'clock in the morning, near the entrance to Candle Dyke. It was very dark, very quiet and very still, when suddenly I had the shock of my life. Something took hold of my keepnet and shook it until I really believe I could see the froth in the water. Grabbing the end of the net, I pulled – and out on to the bank came a pike of about 15 lb with its teeth firmly caught in the meshes. Unfortunately, it jumped back into the water before I could weigh it, but it set me thinking.

In early summer, pike are very active all night because the nights are very short. One night I put into practice something which had been in my mind for a long time. I went to Haveringland Lake for a night's tench fishing, and on arrival found a daytime angler just packing up. He very kindly allowed me to transfer all his roach to my keepnet; and so all night long, a little way to the right of our tench swim, I had a live roach on a free weightless tackle. My buzzer outfits were in action with my tench tackle, so I stuck the butt of my pike rod in the soft mud and attached a small sea bell to the tip. It was ringing on and off all night and by dawn I had taken half a dozen pike up to 6½ lb, not big ones I know, but enough to show that it can be done.

Spinning, unlikely as it may seem, can also be done at night. Some years ago, after a good day on Ranworth Inner Broad, I was rowing Reg back down the river towards the staithe. It was already dark but Reg was spinning a copper spoon as an experiment. Suddenly, it was taken with a bang. I stopped the boat as soon as I could and back-pedalled furiously, but the fish broke him.

A friend of mine, Brian Betts, has been having some success casting a black plug on the Ouse and Cam at night. He tells me that casts made close to the bank are the most successful.

When I phoned Ken Latham of Potter Heigham for his records, he gave me some most interesting information which is quite new, all his own idea. In the summer he goes on all-night breaming expeditions on the sounds, very successfully, too.

He and his friends used to note the occasional very heavy splashes on the edges of the swim, so after a time he made a 6 in. unjointed plug, painted it with wavy slashes of luminous paint, and kept it handy on a set of tackle ready for the nightly swim-invaders. He says that when caught in the rays of his fishing lantern, it looks just like a shooting star as he makes his cast! But it catches pike, and on the darkest night.

I haven't had a chance yet to go and look at one of his plugs, but it sounds to me as though he has discovered something really new, which could take on and become very popular. Ken reckons that some of the biggest pike feed at night, judging by the weighty sound of their splashes.

Records

I do not know what started me keeping an angling diary way back in June 1932, but I do know that keeping it regularly over the years has been very rewarding and has doubled the enjoyment I have got out of angling. Without it I certainly would not have been able to write these notes. No one really needs telling how to keep a diary, but for what it is worth here is how I keep mine. After heading the page with the date and the name of the place fished, I follow with weather particulars, e.g.:

January 6th Ormesby Broad

Sky O [meaning overcast] rain for first half hour then dry. Wind W lt first hour then WNW mod for most of the day, lt for last hour. AT [air temperature] 38° most of the day dropping to 32° late p.m. WT [water temperature] 36°. Bar [barometer] 29.54 a.m. 19.63 p.m.

Sometimes I make a note of the weather preceding the day fished if I think it has affected the fishing in any way, such as a mild day following a cold spell. If I find that I had some good sport on a mild day and then find that it is followed by a cold spell I may, even a week or so later, add a note to that effect if I think it the reason why the fish fed well.

The weather records are followed by an account of the day's sport, the swims fished and methods used. I keep all the writing on the right-hand pages and use the left-hand ones for a record of the day's catch, e.g.:

10.43 start		
11.35 run (dropped)	HLL	
1.15	7 lb 0 oz	DR (drifting) (Reg)
1.40	2 lb 10 oz	DRLL
2.5	5 lb 7 oz	SDR
3.10	17 lb 4 oz	SDR
3.15	15 lb 4 oz	LB
3.25	7 lb 12 oz	SDR
4.0	17 lb 8 oz	LB (Reg)
4.20	13 lb 0 oz	HLL (Reg)
4.30	8 lb 0 oz	LB (Reg)
4.45	7 lb 0 oz	LB
10 fish 99 lb 13 oz		

Key to abbreviations:
LB = Livebait
SDR = Spinning dead roach
HLL = Herring on leadless ledger
HFT = Herring on float tackle
Spun H = Spun herring
MFT = Mackerel on float tackle
DRLL = Dead roach on leadless ledger
LRLL = Live roach on leadless ledger

At the end of each day's entry I record the number of fish taken, and the weight of best one, and keep a running total of the number of fish of each kind for the season.

After 15 March, I draw up a record of the weights and particulars of the best fish of each species.

I also keep a separate record of all pike of over 10 lb.

Biggest ones get away

I have mentioned two of them already. I can think of two more, both on the same private broad though not in the same season.

Reg was using an old sea rod which he thought was too heavy for pike fishing. I think he was using it because it was early in our herring-slinging days and we did not want to put a set in our best rods. We now have glass rods that will cast herring year in year out without flinching.

However, he had a slow run from what must have been a very heavy fish, because when he struck there was an ominous crack from the ferrule and, seconds later, the rod sailed off down the line to join the fish. I just managed to take a photograph of a very disgruntled Reg holding an inverted L-shaped rod before it went. For some minutes he gamely battled, with only the butt ring to guide the line, but it was a losing battle and we never saw the fish.

On the second occasion we had been having a wonderful day. The pike were mad on, and we had two 2 cwt sacks over the side full of pike.

At about 3 p.m. another angler rowing past asked how we had been doing. I turned round to tell him and had not taken my eyes off my livebait float for more than a minute when there was an almighty clatter and bang and I turned round to see the frayed end of my (I blush to say it) 50 lb Courlene line sailing up the broad. We could see the orange top of the float travelling at a rate of knots just below the surface about 50 yards away. Up came the weights and Reg struggled manfully with the oars, but what with rods and tackle trailing

over the side and the two sacks full of pike it seemed an age before we caught up with the frayed end , ran it down the rings and prepared to connect up again. Then just at the very last moment, when I was bracing myself for what must surely be the biggest pike ever – up bobbed the float!

The ones that didn't get away

This story in some respects is like the last one, but it has a happy ending. Reg and I wanted to fish a certain small bay on Horsey Mere. Since an east wind was blowing straight out of it, we decided to creep along quietly close in to the edge so as not to disturb the water we intended to fish. We were about half-way along, in no more than a foot of water when, as in the last story, there was an almighty clatter and bang and I turned round to see my Mk IV about to dive overboard. There were a lot of reed stalks sticking up and the thought flashed across my mind that my hooks must have fouled one of these, as I had left my dead roach trailing behind the boat on about a yard of line. However, there was my rod just about to dive overboard so I flung myself at it and found myself playing a 25½ lb pike on 3 ft of line in 1 ft of water. Could there be a more ludicrous situation! If that rod had been designed by anyone else but Richard Walker we would never have landed that fish. As it was, it won for me a *Sunday Express* prize rod for the best fish of the month. I certainly did not deserve it! Mr Walker did.

Pity for pike

There are some, otherwise sane, anglers who seem to go berserk at the sight of a pike. I can only suppose that it is some sense in man which goes back to prehistoric times, probably born out of fear. To an angler fairly new to the game, a pike with its mouthful of 700 teeth is certainly an ugly brute, and its baleful stare does not improve matters. However, he is a fish who

Above: Horsey Mere in Norfolk not only produced one of the biggest English pike taken on rod and line (40 lb 1 oz) since John Nudd caught his 42-pounder on Wroxham Broad in 1901, it also produced at least seven others that weighed 30 lb or more.

The eight plottings on this aerial photograph (courtesy of R. A. Jeeves) indicate the location of capture of the eight pike, their weights and the initials of the anglers who captured them.

EV – Edwin Vincent
FW – Frank Wright
PH – Peter Hancock
DH – David Hazard

Below:
An armful of unruly rods; the torture of an overloaded shoulder bag; the hand-severing weight of a water-filled bait kettle and the seemingly endless trudge along the sucking bog of an approach road: all are trials soon forgotten the moment the angler catches sight of the water. As he reaches its edge, the unimpeded fresh-smelling wind, now some few degrees cooler, presses against his frame and his pulse quickens. Wriggling out of the festooning gear he stands up, seemingly weightless. Now he can hear the lapping waves and the hiss of the bowing reed stems, but above all he can hear the welcoming knock and gurgle of the boat as it chafes the jetty. He is impatient to be afloat and trying for a big pike

improves with acquaintance, and with the passing of the years becomes an old friend, even one of beauty, whom one misses greatly in the summer months and without whom the winter would lose much of its magic and charm.

Ken Smith told me about an angler who, playing his first pike, wanted to gaff it himself. When Ken handed him the gaff the angler said: 'When do I bash it, now while it is still in the water or when I get it inside the boat?'

Fishing depth

On the Norfolk Broads we set our bait to swim a foot above the bottom in deep water, and so that it is just clear of the bottom in shallow water.

As we use weightless tackle the bait is then free to swim at any depth.

Where to locate pike

Some broads, like Hickling with its 460 acres, are quite a problem and can take many years to know properly, as pike in all broads have a distinctive pattern of movement, and even that can alter due to such factors as silting up, variations in weed growth, dredging, alterations in reed-beds because of attention from coypus, weather conditions, and even overfishing by anglers themselves.

Twenty years ago nearly every (I could almost say every) pike angler would be found fishing around the reedy fringes of the broads. There are still plenty of pike to be caught there. But I do not think in those days it was generally recognized that pike can be found in some of the deep central channels, often in quite large concentrations, particularly towards the end of the season. The difficulty is to find these concentrations.

The other day, Edwin Vincent told me that he has come to the same conclusion, independently, as that reached by Reg Sandys and myself. He looks for what he calls the 'attack' area in open water, by drifting often the full length of a broad spinning a dead roach as he goes. If he gets a fish, in goes the weight to hold the boat while he thoroughly searches to see if he has found the 'attack' area. He tells me that on the occasions that he has found it he has taken as many as twelve to fifteen pike without moving.

Reg and I, too, have found these attack areas, but count ourselves lucky if we catch half the number that Edwin Vincent does. This is because we do not spin nearly as much as we used to, fearing that the constant splash of the dead roach around the boat may scare a really big and wary fish. We may be missing something as Frank Wright, who spins all day, catches a lot of small ones but he gets the big ones too. Cutting out spinning we get a much higher average (well over 10 lb a fish for the last three seasons – in this period, using herring and mackerel only, I have had 68 fish weighing 960 lb 3 oz, an average of 14 lb 2 oz to the nearest ounce), but we do catch a very much smaller number of fish. So it boils down to what the angler wants as far as method goes, but I would say that spinning the dead roach is the best way to find the better pike areas. Having found them the angler can fish according to taste.

In the early days we used to describe a place as looking 'pikey' but fish do not think like we do and often we found that these places are sadly lacking!

Postscript

In March 1980 Bill Giles, in a personal letter to me, wrote:

With the advent of the end of the season I've been bringing my pike records up to date. Having kept records for 33 years I feel it would be a pity just to fade away without leaving them in your hands.

Bill's detailed records are fascinating and show a total catch of forty-five pike over 20 lb; and, taking the best fish of each season for the past thirty-three years, the average weight works out at just over 20 lb 1 oz. *F.B.*

2 Related forms of pike and their history

E. J. Crossman

Curator, Department of Ichthyology and Herpetology, Royal Ontario Museum, and Associate Professor, Department Zoology, University of Toronto

The pike is a member of a unique and interesting group of fishes called the suborder Esocoidei of the Order Clupeiformes. In order to learn more about the pike and its role in the aquatic environment it is important to know something of the other species in the same family and several interesting fishes with which they are closely related.

As a whole the group is composed of the pikes and pickerels, family Esocidae; the blackfish, *Dallia pectoralis*, of Siberia and Alaska; and the mudminnows of the genera *Umbra* and *Novumbra*. A single mudminnow, *Umbra umbra* or *U. krameri*, occurs in Europe in the basins of the Danube and Dniester rivers. In North America there are three mudminnows. The eastern mudminnow, *U. pygmaea*, lives in streams on the Atlantic seaboard east of the Appalachian Mountains. The central mudminnow, *U. limi*, occurs in the Mississippi – Great Lakes area of central North America and the olympic mudminnow, *Novumbra hubbsi*, is found in a small area in the north-west corner of the USA. The blackfish and the mudminnows are variously referred to two families, Dalliidae and Umbridae or to the single family Umbridae.

The blackfish is a small (8–10 in.) fish with a blunt, flat head, a dark, marbled body, very large, fan-shaped pectoral fins and a rounded tail. It lives in small tundra ponds and flooded areas of Alaska and Siberia. It survives under the most adverse conditions of oxygen and space. An exaggerated story often repeated, and attributable to a traveller in Alaska in the 1800s attests to this and reports that Eskimos chop blackfish out of the ponds in solid pieces of ice and throw them to their dogs for food.

The dogs swallow them whole, the warmth of the stomach melts the ice, the activity of the fish makes the dog regurgitate and the fish are brought up alive and well.

The mudminnows are smaller (2–6 in.), more laterally compressed fishes, usually mottled or speckled with brown, and with a dark spot at the base of the caudal fin or a row of spots on the dorsal fin. They, too, have large, fan-like pectoral fins and rounded tails. Mudminnows, as the name implies, live on the bottom of streams with thick silt or mud deposits, where they feed on the aquatic stages of various insects.

At one time the esocoid fishes were considered a separate order (Haplomi) and placed close to the eels above the minnows. More recent studies have shown that these fishes are only highly evolved members of the herring-salmon order Clupeiformes. Their unique shape and structure, which gave rise to their more elevated position in the past, are probably modifications resulting from adaptation to their extreme predatory habit. These more recent concepts place the pikes, blackfish and mudminnows farther down the evolutionary tree near the smelts, Osmeridae, and mooneyes, Hiodontidae.

The group is a moderately old one, probably differentiated in the late Cretaceous from some ancestral stock which gave rise as well to the salmon, trouts and chars. The earliest known fossil representative of the group is *Palaeoesox fritzschei*,* a small mudminnow-like fish from the Eocene brown coals of south-western Germany. From the Oligocene to the Miocene

* But see pages 30–31. *F.B.*

there is an assemblage of fragmentary fossils attributed to this group and called *Esox papyraceus*, *E. otto*, *E. destructus*, *E. waltschanus*, *E. robustus* and *E. lepidotus*. The last, *E. lepidotus*, from the upper Miocene of southern Germany, is well represented by complete fossils of an obvious pike-like fish with only minor difference from living *E. lucius*.

The fossil collection of the British Museum of Natural History contains several representatives of Pleistocene fossils of *E. lucius* from the freshwater beds of West Runton, Norfolk. The bones of these Pleistocene English pike seem more massive than those of today but this may reflect the process of fossilization.

The presence of these Norfolk fossils is convincing evidence that pike were not introduced into the UK by man. They probably found their way over from the continental mass during a period of land connection or when intervening waters were fresher, at least on the surface. Pike are unable to stand salt water but do occur in the Baltic Sea, where the salinity is low, close to land, as a result of the outflow of fresh water.

In Britain and Europe the pike is the sole representative of the family Esocidae. In the USSR, two species occur, the pike and the Amur pike, *E. reicherti*. In North America there are five species of this group. In descending order of maximum size, these are: the muskellunge or maskinonge *E. masquinongy*, the pike, the chain pickerel *E. niger*, the redfin pickerel *E. americanus americanus*, and the grass pickerel *E. a. vermiculatus*. On the basis of the idea that proliferation of form takes place on the periphery of the area of distribution, the presence of these several forms in North America would indicate an origin for the group in central Europe. This is further borne out by the presence in Europe, but not in North America, of the extensive fossil series mentioned above.

Those members of the pike family can be divided into two groups, the pikes and the pickerels. The pikes are the larger species, including the muskellunge, the pike and the

Amur pike. The pickerels are the smaller species native only to North America and include the chain pickerel, the redfin pickerel and the grass pickerel. The pikes have one half or all of the cheek covered with scales but only the upper half of the operculum is scaled. In all the pickerels the whole of both the cheek and operculum is scaled. In the pikes the lower surface of the lower jaw has between five and nine pores on each side whereas in the pickerels there are only four. There are other differences such as pattern, snout shape, etc., but the two basic differences mentioned are more easily recognized.

The derivation and use of the word 'pickerel' for these diminutive pikes is interesting. English colonists in the New England states discovered in the streams of their new home the species we now know as the chain pickerel and the redfin pickerel. Mistaking these small fishes for the young of the pike, with which they were familiar at home, they called them pickerel, the diminutive of pike (cock–cockerel). This name problem is further complicated by the fact that in Canada, until recently, the walleye *Stizostedion vitreum*, an important sport-fish, but a member of the perch family, was also called the pickerel, or pike perch. Briefly I will attempt to describe those species which do not occur in Britain.

Muskellunge *Esox masquinongy*

This is the largest member of the family, as individuals were taken in the past which weighed in excess of 100 lb. Now only rarely are specimens in excess of 50 lb taken by anglers. The present angling record is 69 lb 15 oz. This 'musky' or 'lunge' was $64\frac{1}{2}$ in. long (total length) and $31\frac{3}{4}$ in. in girth. It was caught on 22 September 1957, by Arthur Lawton, in the New York waters of the St Lawrence River.

Growth is rapid in early years, but rate of increase in length decreases with age. Beyond ten years of age, length increases slowly but weight continues to increase. The figures below are ranges for the whole muskellunge area in North America.

Age	Total length (in.)	Weight (lb)
1	10–14	½–2
2	13–22	1½–4
3	21–27	4–6
4	24–29	2½–8½
5	28–31	4½–9
6	29–39	6–10½
7	32–48	7–11
8	34–50	9–20
9	34–54	19–25
10	34–57	21–30
15	34–60	29–50

This species, like the other pikes, grows very rapidly and when 2–3 in. in length is capable of seizing and eating minnows of almost its own length. They grow to 4–6 in. by ten weeks after hatching. The muskellunge is slow to mature, however, and can take as long as five years before it is able to spawn for the first time. At this time females are 25–32 in. in length, males slightly smaller and weight will be 5–8 lb. Because of this they are one of the few sportfish still covered by a minimum-size regulation. They are long-lived fish for temperate fresh waters. I have determined up to twenty-one years, from scale growth, of a 37 lb fish. Beyond this age, scale growth is so slow that the scale method of age determination becomes unreliable.

Prime centres of muskellunge angling are: the St Lawrence River from Kingston to Montreal; the Trent River–Kawartha Lakes system in Ontario; the Niagara and St Clair rivers; north-western Wisconsin, eastern Minnesota and the south-west corner of Ontario; and Chautauqua Lake, New York, and other sections of the Ohio River drainage in New York, Pennsylvania and Ohio.

There is a tendency for fish in each of these areas to exhibit different colour patterns. Thus, at one time, the muskellunge in these areas were referred to as separate species. Several of these populations, St Lawrence–Great Lakes–Kawartha, Ohio River drainage,

A large muskellunge from the Kenora area of Ontario (By courtesy of Dr E. J. Crossman, Royal Ontario Museum)

Wisconsin–Minnesota–West Ontario, have been separated for some time, but the differences which exist presently in the populations are attributable to environmental influences.

The muskellunge is a fish of lakes and large meandering streams. They are almost always found in heavy cover of stumps, or aquatic vegetation, especially various pondweeds (*Potamogeton* spp), often referred to as lunge weed or musky weed, water lilies (*Nymphaea* and *Nuphar*) and pickerel weed (*Pontederia*).

From the time they are large enough, fish become almost the sole food of this species. Large muskellunge, like large pike, have been known at times to eat bullfrogs, mice, muskrats and small waterfowl. They will probably seize any type of animal except turtles, of an appropriate size, that they encounter in or on the water.

There appears to be in nature a direct

Art Lawton with the seventh largest rod-caught musky of all time – a 65 lb 13 oz fish which he took from the St Lawrence River in October 1959 (By courtesy of Larry Ramsell)

relationship between size of muskellunge and size of fish eaten. For this reason lures, such as spoons, spinner and bucktail, or plugs used for this species are often up to 10 or 12 in. in length. Usually muskellunge are taken by trailing artificial lures or live baitfish at shallow to moderate depths and at moderate speed. During early fall (September to 15 October), the end of the open season, they can be taken by casting along weed-beds. This is probably due to re-entry of shallow water when it starts to cool. The strike is sudden and hard, and leaves the angler in no doubt as to what fish he has. Unlike pike, the muskellunge fights at the surface and often may leap out of the water as many as a dozen times, and take thirty to forty-five minutes to boat even with a heavy rod and 18–28 lb BS line.

Muskellunge are extremely wary, and such strong fighters that they are easily lost after being hooked. These factors, combined with the low density, result in the expenditure, on the average, of 100 angler-hours for each legal-size muskellunge, and of course far more for specimen-size fish.

I once met a man in the Kawartha Lakes who had come from the United States every year for six years and fished with one of the best guides. He had landed and released many under-size muskellunge and had lost many larger ones, but had never boated a sizeable fish. This particular year he allowed his wife, for the first time, to accompany him as an angler in the boat. Within an hour of setting out, his wife captured a 32 lb muskellunge and he broke his fishing rod and apparently never returned to fish from that area again. I have seen many broken reels, broken rods, lacerated hands and tired but elated anglers after the fury of the battle with a large muskellunge.

Studies have shown that a stronger relationship exists between size of muskellunge and size of prey consumed than in pike. Since this is so, the muskellunge probably needs a greater area to find large enough prey-fish even though smaller prey, such as minnows, are in abundance. It must be kept in mind that the various species of minnows (other than the carp, which occur within the distribution of the muskellunge), while often in vast numbers, have a potential maximum size which rarely exceeds 6–8 in. This is distinctly different from many cyprinids in the UK which often grow to a size suitable as prey for a large pike. A muskellunge attacks an individual fish rather than taking a number of smaller ones from a school. In addition to this, studies have shown the muskellunge to be a less efficient food converter than the pike. Hatchery men know that this begins early, for young muskies when they first begin to prey on fish often kill two for every one they eat. If a minnow or small sucker is struck but struggles free badly injured, it is rarely struck again. Since they must range more widely in order to encounter an adequate number of prey of the appropriate size, and since they apparently benefit less per unit of food consumed, maintenance and growth requirements are higher. Hence an adequate habitat will probably carry fewer muskellunge than it might pike. The population size is also held down by the fact that it takes a female three to five years to reach the time of first spawning. As a result, each individual faces a greater risk of mortality prior to contributing to the replacement of the stock.

In certain lakes in Kawartha chain of Ontario, heavy weed cover and an abundance of adequate food make muskellunge a difficult quarry for the angler. The angler is prone then to say that the muskies have been depleted. Setting live-trapping nets in the lake generally proves this to be untrue.

It is not untrue to say that muskellunge no longer occur in the numbers they did in the past. In 1961 anglers in Chautauqua Lake, New York, the centre of the 'Ohio muskellunge', caught 5573 sizeable muskies averaging 10·9 lb or approximately 60,000 lb. Chautauqua Lake is 13,500 acres. Therefore about 2·4 acres are required to yield one legal musky and the harvest was about 4·6 lb of lunge per acre. Figures for Wisconsin in 1957 were 5·6 acres for one lunge.

Until 1898, muskellunge were part of the commercial catch in inland waters in Ontario.

In 1892, Ontario recorded a catch of 651,406 lb which sold for the high price of 6 cents or 1s./lb. Before the turn of the century, vast numbers of adults were taken off the spawning grounds each year. These were speared at night by torchlight.

Muskellunge are not interesting to eat when in excess of 15 lb but very good when smaller, if skinned rather than scaled, and especially if fried or poached with butter.

The pike *Esox lucius*

The pike itself is included in this discussion of related forms only to emphasize some of the differences in this species in North America as compared with Britain.

The official common name in North America is Northern pike, established by the Joint Names Committee of the American Fisheries Society and the American Society of Ichthyologists and Herpetologists (see *Am. Fish. Soc. Spec. Pub'n.* No. 2, 1960, 'A list of common and scientific names of fishes from the United States and Canada'). This group is being petitioned to change the name to the pike in keeping with the Eurasian usage.

At one time the pike in North America was thought to be distinct from that in Eurasia and was called *E. estor*. It has for some time now been considered to be a single species with a circumpolar distribution. In any species with such an extensive distribution there will be differences, especially between individuals at the two extremes. For the pike the two extremes are eastern North America and Britain if, as is believed, the pike entered North America via a Bering Sea land bridge.

A study of the world-wide variability in this species will not only pinpoint true differences between individuals on opposite sides of the Atlantic, but differences in North America. Present populations of pike in North America probably are of two post-glacial origins. Those in the southern and eastern part of the range probably result from immigrants from the ice-free area in the Mississippi Valley. Populations in the north and north-west may represent stocks which repopulated the area, after glaciation, from the Mississippi or from another area, in Alaska, which remained ice-free and a refugium for freshwater fishes.

Certainly, there are differences in body proportions. The pike in Britain and Europe appear much stouter for length than those in North America, and consequently the head and snout seem shorter and broader. Maximum size potential and growth rate in Britain are said to exceed that in North America but I am not certain that this is so if we discount the unauthenticated ones in the literature. Average (middle of north to south distribution) age–length–weight relationship in North America is as follows:

Age	Total length (in.)	Weight
1	8	2 oz
2	16	1 lb
3	23	3 lb
5	32	9 lb
8	40	16 lb
12	48	28 lb
15	52	34 lb

The present North American angling record is 46 lb 2 oz, $52\frac{1}{2}$ in. long, 25 in. girth caught by Peter Dubuc in Sacandaga Reservoir, New York state, on 15 September 1940.

The pike is not highly prized as a game fish in North America. Interest in it is on the increase, especially in northern Canada where its size constitutes an attraction to tourist anglers. It is possible that this lack of interest impedes the discovery of larger specimen fish. The largest record for North American pike was one reported to be 49 lb taken in Lake Tschotagama in Quebec in 1890. Fish of 32 to 38 lb are the top weights taken in any one recent year. The pike's fighting qualities are considered, in North America, not as good as other species on a weight basis. It generally fights deep rather than on the surface, unlike the muskellunge, and tires very quickly. Many people, who rather than skin them scale them, and neglect to scrape the pigment and the heavy mucus out of the skin claim that they taste 'muddy' and will not eat them. Personally I think pike, especially less than 10 lb, fried, boiled or steamed is delicious.

In North America the pike is found in almost all weedy warm-water habitats from the level of a line through Pennsylvania to Nebraska northwards, east of the Rocky Mountains, to Alaska. They are absent from the Canadian maritime provinces. The natural distribution has been greatly extended to the south and west by liberations.

At one time the distributions of the pike and the muskellunge were probably separate. Wherever the pike invades an area holding muskellunge, naturally or as a result of man's activities, the pike generally takes over. It is better able to compete for space and food. Where the two species spawn on the same grounds the pike spawn earlier and the young are large enough to prey on lunge when they hatch.

Where the two do overlap they hybridize. The hybrid is often referred to as a tiger musky as the sides have prominent dark stripes. The body is shorter and stouter than a muskellunge and the hybrid is said to be stronger and a better fighter than the pike.

In various places in North America there occurs a colour mutant of the pike, called the silver pike. This mutant is a silver-blue colour, lacks the characteristic spots, and shows a considerable ability to live after treatment which no pike would survive. There are supposed cases of silver pike having been angled, stunned, left on the deck of the boat for as long as two hours, but revived when put back in water.

As a freshwater sport-fish in North America the pike falls under the control of about twenty-seven separate political units with their varying game laws. In Canada, four provinces have closed seasons during spawning period, there is no size limit and bag limits vary from six to ten pike per day. The extent of protection reflects the local attitude to the pike as a sport-fish.

Yield of pike to the angler varies drastically over North America with figures given from 8·2 to 24·4 lb per acre. In a suitable habitat, pike may represent 20 to 50 per cent of the total weight of fish harvested. Similarly, angling success varies considerably; but, on the average, a good habitat will yield an angler two fish per hour.

In some Canadian provinces and parts of the United States the pike is a commercial species as well as a sport-fish. The total catch in Canada in 1966 was 7·86 million lb with a market value of $1.05 million. Comparable figures for the United States were 141,000 lb and $15,000.

It is interesting that there is nowhere near the wealth of folklore associated with the pike or muskellunge when compared with that in Britain and Europe.

Amur pike *E. reicherti*

This species occurs only in the watershed of the Amur River of the USSR. There it replaces the pike which occurs in the river basins to the north, east and west. This replacement in a whole watershed is similar to the distribution of muskellunge within the range of the pike in North America.

The back is dark green to olive in colour, the sides are silvery to golden and marked with brown to black spots about the size of the pupil of the eye. This coloration resembles the muskellunge of the Great Lakes, in that the pattern consists of dark spots on a light ground coat, whereas the pike has light spots on a dark background. In most other morphological characteristics the Amur pike is similar to the pike. It has fully scaled cheeks and the upper half of the operculum is scaled. The muskellunge has scales on only the upper half of both the cheek and the operculum.

This fish is said to be adapted to the open water of rivers and lakes, and lacks the definite association with vegetation so characteristic of *E. lucius* and the North American forms. The Amur pike differs from the pike also in a short but more definite migratory habit. The spawners move out of the main river into lakes and canals as soon as they are ice-free in April. The spent adults return almost immediately to the main channel of the river. The young leave the canals and lakes in September to November and move into the current of the main river. All fish are apparently active feeders all winter while dwelling in the river current.

Its potential maximum length is approximately 45 in. and its maximum weight 22 lb. Average length is 22 in. and average weight about 2½ lb.

The Amur pike, like the pike and the muskellunge, grows quickly, becoming a predator on other fishes in its first summer and eating little other than fish thereafter (various minnows and pond smelt predominantly). Growth rate is as follows:

Age	Total length (in.)	Age	Total length (in.)
1	8·7	5	23·3
2	13·0	6	26·4
3	17·1	7	29·3
4	20·3	8	30·9

Spawning time, locality and post-spawning distribution of newly hatched young are very similar to those of *E. lucius*.

The literature seen by me contains no definite statement of the Amur pike as a sport-fish but it would surprise me if it was not. It *is*, however, one of the most important commercial species of the Amur River fishery.

Until recently the only information, in English, available on this species was from short translations of Russian works, primarily Nikolsky's *Fishes of the U.S.S.R.* In May of 1968, I had the opportunity to see living animals. Eleven Amur pike, probably the first seen alive outside the USSR, were shipped to me for my research on this family of fishes, through the kindness of the Academy of Sciences of the USSR. They are most handsome fish and for their size I would suggest the strongest of all the pikes. In their leaps, 15 in.

fish were able to lift off their storage-tank lids, which were weighted with about 5 lb. I would suggest from this that they would make an exciting quarry for an angler and that they would fight on and above the water surface as muskellunge do.

We now shift to the second group in the family, the pickerels. These are the smaller forms, native only to North America, which have completely scaled cheeks and opercula and only four pores on the undersurface of the lower jaw.

The chain pickerel *E. niger*

This, the largest of the pickerels, is found from Nova Scotia south on the Atlantic slope, east of the Appalachian Mountains, to Florida, then westward along the Gulf Coast to Texas and north in the Mississippi system to southern Missouri and the Tennesee River in Alabama.

The present angling record is a 9 lb 6 oz fish, 31 in. long and 14 in. in girth, taken 17 February 1961 at Homerville, Georgia, by Baxley McQuaig Jnr.

Growth in Massachusetts is reflected by the following age–length–weight relationship:

Age	Total length (in.)	Weight
1	8·1	1·7 oz
2	10·7	4·4 oz
3	13·0	8·2 oz
4	15·6	14·5 oz
5	17·4	1·4 lb
6	20·2	1·5 lb
7	22·9	3·25 lb

Chain pickerel have been recorded as old as nine years but it is not often they exceed three or four years of age.

As in the larger species, food habits change with the growth of the pickerel. For the young, *Daphnia* and other Crustacea are most important. As the pickerel's size increases, fish become an increasingly large part of the diet. However, even for adult pickerel, aquatic insects and/or crayfish constitute upwards of 10 per cent of the diet.

This species hybridizes readily with the redfin pickerel, and many so-called record redfin pickerel probably are chain pickerel × redfin pickerel hybrids.

All of the species of *Esox* are primarily spring spawners. For the three members of the pickerel subgroup there is evidence of fall spawning as well. No such evidence has yet been published for the three species in the pike group.

Parallel to this is the fact that the members of the pike group are, in North America, considered primary freshwater species. There is no published evidence that either form penetrates salt or brackish water as the pike do in the Baltic Sea. I know of no such evidence for the Amur pike either. In the pickerel group there is published evidence that the chain pickerel and the redfin enter brackish water and it has been suggested salt water as well. In both cases it is my belief that this is in the spring when areas, which in August will be very brackish, are almost fresh as a result of heavy freshwater runoff.

The chain pickerel is a sport-fish and although not highly prized, it is sought after by anglers most frequently in winter or when seasons for more valued species are not open. It provides adequate sport when fished for with light spinning tackle and small lures. It is very acceptable as a food fish. Only this pickerel is a significant lake dweller where its habitat is similar to that of the pike. The other two pickerel live in streams and small weedy ponds.

The redfin pickerel *E. americanus americanus*

This is the more eastern and somewhat larger of a pair of subspecies which occur on opposite sides of the Appalachian Mountains.

The redfin occurs from the St Lawrence-Richelieu-Hudson rivers system from Quebec south along the Atlantic coastal plain to

Georgia. An intergrade form between the two subspecies lives in Gulf Coast streams from Florida to Mississippi. This intergrade form can, most simply, be referred to as redfin pickerel also.

Redfin pickerel live in sluggish streams, backwater areas of faster streams and lakes, ponds, acid water sloughs and drainage ditches. In these habitats they are always associated with heavy vegetation. This species, as are the others, is basically a piscivorous predator when adult. However, crayfish and immature aquatic insects, particularly dragon-flies, are a significant part of the diet of adults.

Growth of this species is particularly rapid in the south. In Georgia they are said to reach 1 lb at the end of one year. The maximum size would appear to be 10–13 in. and maximum age five–seven years. Pickerel of 14 and 19 in. have been reported but these were probably hybrids. Maximum weight will rarely exceed 12 oz. Length–weight relationship in the middle of its range is as follows:

Age	Fork length (in.)	Age	Fork length (in.)
1	4·3	4	8·5
2	5·5	5	9·5
3	6·8	6	11·2

This species is only rarely actively sought after, and then only by enthusiasts of extremely light tackle, when other sport-fish are unavailable. When taken incidental to other species they are sometimes kept. It is edible but not highly prized as a food-fish. No records are maintained for this species as a sport-fish.

Grass pickerel *E. a. vermiculatus*

This is the more westerly and somewhat smaller of the pair. It occurs from the lower Great Lakes – St Lawrence drainage south through the Mississippi River drainage to Louisiana and westward to south-central Texas.

Its habitat is much like that of the redfin, except that the streams are very small, most often muddy and neutral to basic. The preponderance of fish in the diet of adults and the significant contribution of crayfish and immature aquatic insects is characteristic of this form also. Rare specimens may grow to 14 in. but the usual maximum is 12 in., and the maximum age is probably seven years. As in other species initial growth is rapid. Age–length relationship in the north is as follows:

Age	Fork length (in.)	Age	Fork length (in.)
1	4·0	5	8·0
2	5·2	6	9·2
3	6·5	7	10·3
4	7·3		

No angling records are maintained for this species and I know of no locality where they are actively sought after or even retained if caught incidentally. Their habitat does not usually attract an angler. Consequently they are poorly known and usually mistaken for the young of the pike. This confusion is carried even to the extent that *E. lucius*, 9 or 10 in. long are, in North America, usually called grass pike.

3 Cooper's Masterpieces

An instance of the very fine work done by 'Coopers' is shown in the photograph. This case of fish – an exhibition in the art of taxidermy of freshwater fish – was illustrated and described in the *Angler's News* of 26 January 1918.

The pike, a 28-pounder, was caught on the Hampshire Avon in the very deep May Bush Hole formed at the confluence of Crickmeed stream and the main river. The lifelike representation of a feeding pike and its intended victims – in this instance a shoal of dace – is artistically represented.

As a final note of interest to my readers and as a tribute to this best-ever firm of fish taxidermists, Messrs John Cooper & Son, together with its most skilful servant W. B. Griggs, I have added a note by the illustrious editor of the *Fishing Gazette*, R. B. Marston.

The 28-pounder in its 'glass palace'. A case 5 ft by 2 ft was needed to show the pike's fine proportions

He describes the catching of a pike, on 21 May 1912, that had attempted to swallow the trout that he was playing on rod and line while may fly-fishing on the River Frome in Dorset.

The pike, as you will see, was duly landed. It was set up by Coopers with the trout still in the pike's mouth and the May Fly still in the trout's mouth.

This case of fish, a delightful example of the taxidermist's art, belongs to Patricia Walker (*née* Marston), grand-daughter of R. B. Marston and wife of Richard Walker.

Sure enough, close to the bank on the side I was fishing on, I saw a good rise, and soon had a light wing, honey dun hackle, Rouen G.O.M. falling on the stream near where I saw the rise. Two or three times the fly came down with no notice taken, then I got it within a foot of the bank and the fish had it. I had luckily pulled in the slack with my left hand as the fly came down, and he was well hooked, and I hoped I had got at least a 3-pounder. The stream is not wide, but deep and swift at this point, and as the fish came down I thought to myself this is no 3-

R. B. Marston's cased pike shows the pike together with the trout that it had tried to swallow

pounder – I have got hold of the Jubilee trout! Then the fish went into a tuft of bulrushes which here and there stand out of the stream. I could feel it boring in, resting a bit and then boring through, and by great good luck it came out, and the line as well. Then, to my surprise, I saw half of my trout, with the May Fly sticking in his mouth, was sticking out of the mouth of a pike. I thought to myself, 'Here's a game' – no wonder I thought it was at least an 8 lb trout – when I saw his ugly jaw round my trout. That pike hung on for fifty yards down the strong swirling stream, making short, vicious lunges every now and then. Of course, I thought every moment that the gut would break, or the fly come out of the trout's mouth, or the trout out of the pike's mouth. It was only a No. 2 'Hercules' cast, which is none too stout for May Fly work. Luckily I had taken off the last strand before putting the fly on. Half-way through the fight the pike saw me and tried to spit the pound trout out – he had luckily taken it tail first and swallowed more than half of it. I thought, 'If I can nurse you, my friend, I may get you as well,' so I coaxed him round into a quiet bay where some

sleepers had been put in to keep the stream from washing the bank away. I had only a folding collapsible landing-net hanging from my coat pocket by a spring catch, and I thought there was small chance of getting him into it. With the net in my left hand, I gradually drew the pike near enough, and put the hoop of the net over his nose; he gave a mighty splash with his tail and fairly pushed himself in as far as the net would let him! – and 'in half a tick' as 'Dragnet' says, he was kicking on the grass. He weighed over 12 lb – and no wonder I thought I had hooked the Jubilee trout! As I was playing him I kept thinking what was the best thing to do. Once I thought I would give him line and let him swallow the fish until the hook was in him also; but that would never do, as the fine gut would be cut by his teeth directly. So I decided that to play him out was the game. Soon afterwards, Mr Leonard Sturdy put me on to a rising trout – a 2-pounder – which I hooked, and, after a good fight, got near enough to use the net, but it was collapsed in a double sense. I had not noticed it, but the weight of the pike had bent the knuckle joint, so it would not catch, and the hinged lock of the steel hoop had come undone. Fortunately, the keeper had seen us and came up with another net.

Few humans have seen a fifty pound pike but as eyes scan this page their number is added to directly. The pike's weight is 55 lb 15¾ oz. It was caught on roach livebait by the Czechoslovakian Jiři Blaha from Lipno Reservoir (By courtesy of Jan Eggers and the *Rybárstvi* angling magazine, Prague)

Select bibliography

The following have provided me with a great deal of information. Sometimes extracts from the originals have been reproduced in order to illustrate certain vital points. I now acknowledge with grateful thanks both authors and publishers who have been kind enough to give me permission to reproduce these extracts.

Books

'A Treatyse of Fysshynge wyth an Angle' by DAME JULIANA BERNERS from the *Book of St. Albans* first printed in 1496

The Art of Angling by THOMAS BARKER printed by R. H. in 1651

The Compleat Angler by IZAAK WALTON first published in 1653

Northern Memoirs by RICHARD FRANCK written in 1658 published in 1694

The Experienc'd Angler by COLONEL R. VENABLES printed in 1662 (reprinted 1927)

Rural Sports by THE REV. W. B. DANIEL published by the Philanthropic Society in 1801

Thornton's Sporting Tour by COLONEL T. THORNTON published by Vernor & Hood in 1804

British Fishes by W. YARRELL published by John Van Voorst in 1836

By Lake and River by FRANCIS FRANCIS published by *The Field* in 1874

Sporting Sketches by FRANCIS FRANCIS and A. W. COOPER published by *The Field* in 1878

A Book on Angling by FRANCIS FRANCIS published by Longmans, Green & Co. in 1880

Bibliotheca Piscatoria by T. WESTWOOD and T. SATCHELL published by W. Satchell & Co. in 1880

The Book of the All Round Angler by JOHN BICKERDYKE published by L. Upcott Gill in 1888

Angling for Pike by JOHN BICKERDYKE 19th Edition published by Thorsons Publishers Ltd in 1959. (Taken from *The Book of the All Round Angler* first published in 1888)

Fishing by H. CHOLMONDELEY-PENNELL published by Longmans, Green & Co. in 1889

Walton & the Earlier Fishing Writers by R. B. MARSTON published by Elliot Stock in 1894

Pike and Perch by ALFRED JARDINE published by Routledge in 1896

Pike and Perch by WILLIAM SENIOR published by Longman & Co. in 1900

An Angler's Hours by H. T. SHERINGHAM published by Macmillan & Co. Ltd in 1905

My Fishing Days and Fishing Ways by J. W. MARTIN published by W. Brendon & Son in 1906

Days Among the Pike and Perch by J. W. MARTIN published by J. W. Martin in 1907

British Freshwater Fishes by C. TATE REGAN published by Methuen in 1911

Angling in British Art by W. SHAW SPARROW published by John Lane The Bodley Head Ltd in 1923

The Pike Fisher by EDWARD F. SPENCE published by A. & C. Black in 1928

Coarse Fish by E. MARSHALL-HARDY published by Herbert Jenkins in 1943

Hampton on Pike Fishing by J. F. HAMPTON published by Chambers in 1947

Angling from many Angles by 'SILVER DOCTOR' published by Bournemouth Guardian Ltd

Pike Fishing by NORMAN L. WEATHERALL published by Witherby in 1961

The Way I Fish by DENNIS PYE published by *Angling Times* in 1964

Papers

BUSS, K. AND MILLER, J. (1967). *Interspecific hybridization of Esocids*: Hatching success, pattern development, and fertility of some F1 hybrids. *United States Department of the Interior Fish and Wildlife Service*

BUSS, K. (1961). *The Northern Pike*. Pennsylvania Fish Commission. Benner Spring Fish Research Station Special Purpose Report

CROSSMAN, E. J. and BUSS, K. (1965). Hybridization in the Family Esocidae. *J. Fish. Res. BD. Cananda. 22(5)*

FROST, W. E. and KIPLING, C. (1959). The determination of the age and growth of pike (*Esox lucius L.*) from scales and opercular bones. *J. Cons. int. Explor. Mer. 24, 314–341*

FROST, W. E. and KIPLING, C. (1961). Some observations on the growth of the pike, *Esox lucius*, in Windermere. *Verh. int. Verein. theor. angew. Limnol. 14. 776–781*

FROST, W. E. and KIPLING, C. (1967) A Study of reproduction, early life, weight–length relationship and growth of pike, *Esox lucius*, in Lake Windermere. *J. Anim. Ecol. 36, 651–693*

JOHNSON, L. (1966). Consumption of food by the resident population of pike, *Esox lucius*, in Lake Windermere. *J. Fish. Res. Bd Can. 23, 1523–1535*

JOHNSON, L. (1966). Experimental determination of food consumption of pike, *Esox lucius*, for growth and maintenance. *J. Fish. Res. Bd Can. 23, 1495–1505*

SWIFT, D. R. (1965). Effect of temperature on mortality and rate of development of the eggs of the pike (*Esox lucius L.*) and the perch (*Perca fluviatilis L.*). *Nature, Lond. 206, 528*

SORENSON, L., BUSS, K. and BRADFORD, A. D. (1966). The artificial propagation of esocid fishes in Pennsylvania. *Prog. Fish Cult.*

Index

287